Library Database Management

Library Database Management

K. P. Singh

RANDOM

RANDOM PUBLICATIONS

NEW DELHI (INDIA)

Library Database Management

ISBN 978-93-5111-245-7

Published in 2014 in India by

Reprint 2020

RANDOM PUBLICATIONS
4376-A/4B, Gali Murari Lal, Ansari Road
New Delhi-110 002
Phone : +91-11-43580356, +91-11-23289044
e-mail: randomexports@gmail.com, sales@randompublications.com, info@randompublications.com

Type Setting by : Keystoneprintads, Delhi-110051
Printed at : Mehra Printers, Delhi-110 092

Preface

Database Management Systems (DBMS) are important. They underpin all the activities of a library management system by providing the basic storage and retrieval technology. The library application software sends data to and receives data from the DBMS which, if it is working properly, is hardly noticed at all. Yet great claims are made for different types of database and their particular offerings. You should at least be able to understand the basics to understand what you might be getting - or missing when you choose a Library Management System (LMS).

Early library systems developed their own systems for storing and retrieving records. Geac's GLIS, IME's TinLib, BLCMP's Circo all developed a methods of storing bibliographic records that were peculiar to themselves. By the early eighties, commercial products began to appear that offered advantages to application developers. Library software began to become more than just a fetch and display operation - the complexity of the business rules in all modules of library management software meant that off-loading the efficient storage and retrieval of records to a specialist piece of software became very cost effective.

Suppliers began to use the new relational database management systems (RDBMS) like Oracle and Ingres (CLSI). Other suppliers used PICK for products such as Dynix, ADVANCE and Bookshelf. Still others retained their own proprietary databases for example Adlib. It is important to note that a system can be relational in concept without necessarily employing a commercial Relational DBMS - both Libertas and Tinlib prove this (amongst others). By the mid-nineties virtually all systems use commercially maintained database software of some sort. The questions are - does it matter to the library which system is being used? What constraints and advantages are offered by the different systems? And where is the future taking database technology? How should you satisfy yourselves that the database technology will meet your needs.

Database management systems have evolved fairly slowly over the last 30 years. The first commercial programming languages had file handling systems that took the responsibility from the programmer for maintaining file structures and indexes - e.g. ISAM (Indexed Sequential Access Method). A DBMS can be viewed as a more sophisticated and flexible form of file management together with a flexible tool for data extraction and often other "high level" tools. Without being too fussy about the niceties of DBMS, and ignoring those that do not figure much in library systems, these are the main types - in a rough chronological/sophistication order of their development. Note that these divisions are not completely mutually exclusive - some DBMS can be considered to fall into more than one camp - others into none.

I thank all members of my team who have helped in the preparation of the book. My special thanks go to "Random Publications" who have published the book.

– *K. P. Singh*

Contents

1

Managing the Library and Archive Environment

INTRODUCTION

One of the most important aspects of adult learning. It explains that libraries in adult education set-ups have an important role to play in facilitating access to information for learning, education and training. They also play important role in supporting research programmes of adult education set-ups as well as their outreach programmes designed to educate and inform adult user groups on social, economic and educational issues, and problems. Another role of libraries is to raise awareness about economic opportunities available in the marketplace.

Like any other library in academic set-up or research institutions, adult education libraries have also to be planned, organised and managed using standard management principles and standard library procedures and techniques for access and retrieval. These issues and provides PALDIN learners with very useful skills to perform their tasks better. Besides enabling physical access to collections, libraries have to be organised for rendering information services such as instructions in the use of library catalogue and reading materials, reference service, information dissemination, etc.

LIBRARY OBJECTIVES

Strategic planning and development of a library is guided mainly by the goals and objectives of the parent institution of which the library is a part.

In any given adult education set-up, you could frame library objectives along the following lines:

- Facilitate access to information for knowledge, education, and learning;
- Support research activities and programmes of the set-up by offering proactive information services;
- Support outreach programmes of the adult education set-up, designed to educate and inform adult user groups on social,

economic and educational issues, problems, and opportunities of interest them;

- Offer proactive services for effective use of all types of library materials;
- Store and preserve information of archival nature such as local traditions, customs, and locally generated process documentation reports, etc; and
- Use library as the platform for social, economic, and cultural development of the target communities.

HOW TO MANAGE A LIBRARY

Library management involves functions such as planning, organising, leading, and controlling. Planning is about systematically making decisions about the library goals. Organising is about assembling and coordinating human, financial, physical, informational, and other resources needed to achieve library goals. Leading is about functions that involve efforts on the part of the librarian to stimulate high performance by employees, and controlling about monitoring various library operations and services. These four management functions are highly integrated, but libraries that excel in organising material resources and in leading their human capital are known to give better performance. Keeping in view the fact that libraries in adult education set ups are, by design, small budget libraries, confined to one room space, and adult education staff manages them manually on part time basis, these four management functions would occur in varying degree. In such a typical set up, the functions of organising and controlling would receive greater attention compared to other two functions.

For managing a library you may take the following step-by-step approach:

- *Step 1:* Defining library policies for collection development
- *Step 2:* Defining library authority and library advisory committee
- *Step 3:* Define procedures for library organisation and administration
- *Step 4:* Defining library space, equipment and tools for library operations and services
- *Step 5*: Defining procedures for maintenance of library collections

STEP 1: LIBRARY POLICIES FOR COLLECTION DEVELOPMENT

Step 1 includes the following task:

- *Define the Objectives of your Library:* State clearly the purpose of its existence;
- *Define your User Community and their Information Needs:* This requires complete knowledge and understanding about library stakeholders. This may include adult education teams, extension workers and adult education professionals, local community members and those

who provide funds for the library. Their information needs can be assessed through library surveys, personal interviews, and informal discussions with all stakeholders;

- *Define Library Policy for Building Collections:* The policy states the guiding principles and procedures under which collection development activities, including the selection, maintenance, and weeding of print, electronic, and media library materials will occur. This would also mean specifying subject areas of interest to library stakeholders, their languages preferences, and formats of published and unpublished material. Non-print material could include films, slides, transparencies, photographs, maps posters, charts, etc. The policy must also define the limits in terms of collection size, keeping in view the users strength in a given subject, space available within the library premises, and annual budget earmarked for the purpose. The policy may also specify the subject areas in which the library is going build its archival collection, if any. Such a policy statement on the part of the library ensures continuity and consistency in selection and revision of materials for the library collections;
- *Define what Different Collections are Required to be Developed and Sustained Keeping in View Users' Information Needs:* The possible options include books collection, reports collection, pamphlet collection, multimedia collection, and reference collection (comprising dictionaries, yearbooks, directories, who's who almanacs, general and subject encyclopaedias), etc. The library may decide on developing some of these collections keeping in view the users' information needs.
- *Define your Book Selection Policy:* State the distribution of library budget by subject and by collection. The policy may also state guidelines for acquiring multiple copies of books, guidelines for accepting books from donors, and guidelines for weeding out material.

STEP 2: LIBBRARY AUTHORITY AND LIBRARY ADVISORY COMMITTEE

Libraries in adult education setups are, by design, small budget libraries, confined to one room space, and managed manually on part time basis by adult education staff. The person incharge of the library should be the library authority, responsible for organisation and management of the library. He/she should play a dominant role in decision making, should enjoy the authority to communicate freely with groups across the organisation, and enjoy financial and administrative powers for managing library operations and services smoothly. The financial and administrative limits of the library authority should correspond to staff of equivalent status in the organisational hierarchy. The library authority should be reporting to the top management in the organisation. There is a need to set up a Library Advisory Committee, which would perform the role of advising the library on its growth and development. It will also act as interface between the library management and the top management in the organisation and between the users groups, for ensuring smooth functioning of the library operations and services without compromising on policies set out for library development. The Committee should comprise members mainly drawn from the organisation, and representing various user groups on the Committee.

Its terms of reference could be worked out on the following lines:

- To formulate policy for developing library resources for reading, reference and projects;
- To develop a general programme of library services to suit the interests and requirements of different categories of users;
- To frame, review and approve library rules;
- To recommend suitable budgetary provisions for the library and resource centre;
- To make recommendations for proper functioning of library as knowledge centre.

STEP 3: PROCEDURES FOR LIBRARY ORGANISATION AND ADMINISTRATION

In any larger set up, library organisation tasks involve assembling, forming logical units of works, defining hierarchical structures, identifying staffing requirements, assigning tasks and responsibilities, coordinating human, financial, physical, informational, and other resources needed to achieve library goals. Administration is another activity required to be undertaken for performance and achieving library goals. It is defined as the process of getting things done through men and materials within the organisational framework.

Library organisation and library administration are closely related to each other. The distinction between the two is very subtle. Organisation comes before administration. The latter starts when the organisation ends. One lays down theoretical principles, whilst the other puts those principles into practice. In the adult education set up, wherein libraries by design are small and are going to be managed on part time basis by adult education staff, not much needs to be done in so far as library organisation is concerned.

In such flat hierarchical structures, the staff has no option but to perform multitasking operations such as administration, technical functions, service support, and library maintenance. For effective performance, it is advisable for the library to opt for outsourcing of library maintenance operations such as stack maintenance, catalogue card maintenance, photocopy services, library up keep, stock verification, gate security, etc. It may also consider outsourcing classification and cataloguing operations if circumstances so warrant.

The libraries in adult education set ups need to undertake planning activities such as strategic planning (*i.e.* identifying library goals, objectives, methods, resources needed to carry out methods, responsibilities and dates for completion of tasks), budget planning (for document collections, library equipments, library furniture, library stationery, media library equipments, if planning for a multi-media library), and library promotion planning. These are not perennial activities and are required to be undertaken once in year.

The extent of budget planning activities would depend upon the size of adult education programmes, network linkages, and staff deployed within the organisation, etc. For building a library from the scratch, it must begin with a small annual budget of ₹100,000/-during the first three years. In the subsequent years, budget requirements may be reviewed and decided based on collection already built and actual requirements. It is a good practice to undertake budget planning exercise in consultation with the Library Advisory Committee for developing collections, library equipments, library furniture, media equipments, etc. It is also a good practice to formulate library plans for promoting and popularizing library services.

STEP 4: LIBRARY SPACE, EQUIPMENT AND TOOLS FOR LIBRARY OPERATIONS AND SERVICES

Bureau of Indian Standards provides that a library should have a stack room, a Librarian's room and a Reading Room having seating capacity of 40 to 120 chairs. The stack room should be big enough to accommodate between 6,000 and 10,000 books. The library-in-charge would need to plan actual library size and seating capacity of 'reading room' keeping in view the optimum number of members in an adult education setup, the variety of library services it is planning to offer, and the members of the adult community who would be coming to visit the library for social interactions. The library equipments and tools like furniture, fittings and accessories should of standard pattern and design, so that users feel comfortable in using them.

The following is the list of essential furniture and fittings for an adult education set up:

- Reading tables
- Chairs for pupils
- Librarian's table
- Circulation or charging desk and chair
- Librarian's shelf list trays
- Card catalogue trays
- Card catalogue cabinet
- Bulletin board and notice board
- Book supporters
- New arrivals display case
- Dictionary stands

- Periodicals display stand
- Newspaper display stand
- Storage cabinet for work room
- Filing cabinets
- Atlas stand
- Wall clock

Besides, the library may acquire radio and television set, tape recorder/ player, VCR and VCP, slide and film projector, overhead projectors, computers with internet connection, Xerox machine, etc.

STEP 5: PROCEDURES FOR MAINTENANCE OF LIBRARY COLLECTIONS

You will find that the following procedures help in maintenance of library collections.

Preservation of Library Material

Proper care of library collections is necessary with a view to prolong its life. This requires preserving and protecting books against decay and deterioration. As preventive measures, dusting and cleaning of books and shelves must be carried out on regular basis. Books must be exposed to adequate air and sunlight for a short time in case the library room does not get sufficient sunlight. Avoid keeping books is in damp places. Pest control treatment may be got done on periodic basis. Books and other reading material may be got bound from time to time. Besides, book supporters may be used to keep books upright on the shelves. Reference books such as dictionaries, encyclopedias, directories and picture books are costly and heavy in weight. They must be handled with care.

Organising Reading Materials on Shelves and Their Rectification

Normally, books and other reading display of new books and other reading material received in the library, preparing stack room guides, and shelving volumes returned after use, etc. Library may also perform stock verification on periodical basis, with a view to weed out books, as per its policy, and writing off books, etc.

2

Selection and Purchasing of Library Resources

INTRODUCTION

S.R. Ranganathan's five laws of librarianship:

- Books are for use
- Every book its reader
- Every reader his book
- Save the reader's time
- The library is a growing organism

These laws provide the ideas that decide the principles of effective selection.

Such principles may be summarized as follows:

- The selection process is related to other professional activities and is dependent on them both for policy decisions and practical procedures. Selection is part of the overall collection development process and must be viewed in this perspective;
- One should update professional competence by regular reading in the literature concerning the principles and practices of collection building, selection, publishing, reviewing and acquisitions;
- One must have an intimate knowledge of the library's purpose, its collections and its user groups. These are the key factors in effective, responsible selection of library materials;
- A good selector will develop over time a sound under-standing of how the publishing industry and the book trade operate; this includes how library materials of all types are generated, distributed and sold;
- One should become familiar with the publishing policies, advertising media, publicity outlets, names of senior editors and general reliability of those publishers whose lists are most directly relevant to the library's collection building requirements;
- One should become fully familiar with the key reviewing media

and should read reviews regularly in order to keep abreast of critical opinion on books and other library materials;

- One should become fully familiar with trade and national bibliographies, and should understand their strengths and weaknesses with regard to the library's collection-building requirements;
- One should always make independent but well-informed judgement about what materials are to be selected for a library, as the competent professional is in the best position to determine the right materials for the specific collection and its users.

THE SELECTION ENVIRONMENT

Selection of library materials occurs within a set of common factors:

- It is done on the basis of existing collection require-ments and user needs and wants with regard to subjects, formats and level of content;
- It proceeds within a carefully determined budget, with funds may be allocated to specific areas or other categories to the library;
- It involves a structured approach to the identification and evaluation of potentially suitable library materials.

Within this set of factors there are many permutations, depending largely on the specific variables which apply to the different types of medical libraries:

- In medical libraries within an academic setting, disciplines are being studied at specific levels, from basic undergraduate to advanced research, and both disciplines and levels can be determined accurately from the parent organisation's clearly defined teaching activities. There is generally substantial documentation upon which selectors can draw for information about user interests and needs. Academic libraries use a broader and more detailed range of selection tools, such as trade publications, national bibliographies, reviewing journals, scholarly journal, indexing services.
- Moreover, selection is not restricted to professional librarians, as academic staff are expected to have significant input in the process, particularly if the funds are allocated by departments and schools. This situation is challenged by professionals.
- In non-academic medical libraries, in which collections range from small collection in a single room to large collections in a multi-branch library. In such libraries the subject focus is relatively narrow and emphasizes currency. Here, a high proportion of the collection is devoted to serials. Such libraries are also characterized by the following features:
  - It is most likely for there to be a single professional in charge of the library operation, or at least for collection development

not to be the responsibility of professional appointed for this specific purpose.

- Selection relies heavily on information from publishers and suppliers, and on indexing and abstracting services.
- Reliance on intimate requirement, because libraries normally build up user profiles, particularly when they offer special dissemination services.

SELECTION PROCEDURES STATEMENT

Selection criteria, as a component of collection develop-ment policy. This part does not repeat the information given there, but rather elaborates and complements it. It is looked at as an administration device designed to facilitate implemen-tation of decisions about materials based on collection development policy guidelines. All administrative matters requiring consistency over time, require procedures formalized in a written statement.

The following reasons for advocating the adoption of a formal selection procedures statement, and many of these echo the rationale for having a written collection development policy:

- It sets standards for procedures to be followed;
- It reduces the likehood of bias and personal influence;
- It provides continuity despite staff changes;
- It serves as an orientation device for new staff;
- It provides guidelines for complaint handling;
- It assists in weeding.

SELECTION RESPONSIBILITIES

This addresses two questions:

- Who shall do the selecting?
- How shall the procedure be organised?

The answer to the first question is a combination of library staff and users. Within the library it may be done by:

- The chief librarian;
- Division or department heads engaged specially for this task (collection development librarian, acquisitions librarian);
- Subject or area specialists; or
- Other professional staff as part of their general duties (re-ference librarians, technical services librarians).

Whichever applies, it should be stated clearly in the written document. Outside the library, selection should involve input from users from all types, and these should be specified clearly: administrators, parent organisation staff, students, teaching staff, general public, etc. To facilitate and encourage participation of these groups, a request form is provided.

This form should have space for all essential information needed to identify an item: author, title, number of volumes or pages, place of publication, publisher, date of publication, series and price, as well as the name of requester.

This form is usually an attachment to statement. Copies should be made readily available and accessible to selectors both within and without the library.

HOW SELECTION IS ORGANISED

It should indicate clearly and precisely who has responsibility for what and who is responsible to whom. If a selection committee is used: who chairs the committee, and who appoints the members? How often does the committee meet? What are its terms of reference? If selection is the responsibility of individuals outside the library: How is this responsibility allocated and monitored? What resource does the librarian have if his external selectors fail to perform adequately? If selection is done jointly by external and internal selectors, what are the lines of demarcation? Who selects reference materials, serials, decides on multiple copies, etc.? All such questions should be addressed in the statement so that there is no doubt about responsibility and so that the newest member of staff has a clear grasp of procedures.

GENERAL GUIDELINES FOR SELECTION

This part turns to what to select. It presents only general guidelines derived from and based on the collection development policy. It lists here general selection sources, together with categories of more specific types of sources (publishers' catalogues, scholarly journals, indexing services, etc.). These listings help ensure that the named sources are used by selectors, and remind selectors of the other types of sources that they ought to be using.

Some libraries may actually name specific sources within each type, but this cannot be done in libraries selecting across a broad range of subjects and types of materials.

This part may list languages in which materials are selected, or other limitations which apply across the range of materials. In other words, all selection criteria derived from, or at least compatible with, the collection development policy should be stated here. This will enable all selectors to operate within the same set of guidelines.

HANDLING OF GIFTS AND DONATIONS

Basically, a donated item has to be taken into the collection according to the same criteria applied to purchased item. Therefore, the statement says this and indicates that gifts are received on the understanding that they may be disposed of in a manner deemed appropriate by the librarian. The statement also indicates acceptable conditions of gifts.

CRITERIA FOR WEEDING

The library may well have included a part on weeding in its collection development policy; if so, this needs to be taken into account at this stage. Weeding, often termed 'deselection' in USA and 'relegation' in the UK, involves a number of decisions that should be outlined in the selection procedures statement, involving criteria for weeding, scope of weeding procedures, frequency and purpose, together with a general allocation of staff responsibilities, so that there is no confusion about who is responsible for what and when.

HANDLING OF COMPLAINTS

Complaints about and censorship of library materials have been controversial issues for many years. although this case is less likely to occur in medical libraries than in other types of libraries such as public and school libraries, but it could happen. This part contains a statement of complaint-handling procedures and a standard form to be completed by potential censors. The written statement should be made available, together with a copy of the collection development policy, at the first hint that an item in the collection is being challenged.

The complaint-handling form should be completed only if a formal complaint is lodged. The exact procedure, who is to be involved and the documentation to be utilized must all be stated clearly in this part. The entire statement should be readily accessible not only to selectors, but also to all users, as this often alleviates the need for complaints to go beyond an informal discussion.

SERIALS AND BOOK SELECTION

SERIALS SELECTION

From the eighteenth century, the journal has been an important mechanism for communicating scientific findings, advances in techniques, and changes in accepted practice in medicine and other health professions. Journals continue to constitute the core of health sciences library collections. But biomedical journals now face price increases, dwindling number of personal and institutional subscribers and the threat that print publications will be overshadowed by electronic forms of scientific communication. They also face various changes in the title, the publishers, emerging or splitting, editorship, supercession, ceasing, format or size, numbering, or frequency.

Responsibility for Selection

Because a decision to subscribe to a journal is often a long-term one, with a financial commitment over several years, selection is rarely left to a single person, although the final decision is often so.

Selection Committee

This is the practice in academic medical libraries and in large hospital libraries, as suggestions or requests are brought to the committee for review. Criteria for evaluation are agreed upon and an evaluation form is used to collect data for decision-making and to document decisions. The information should be recorded in a consistent manner on a standard form to allow comparisons. The information may include the following: Title, publisher, frequency, starting date, cost, coverage of contents by standard indexing and abstracting services and online databases, published rankings or reviews, interlibrary loan data, information about purchase requests, information about other titles in the subject field, evidence of peer review of articles, assessment by faculty or hospital staff, availability in other affiliated library, relevance to the parent organisation's programmes. The frequency to committee meeting may vary from monthly to semiannually.

External Reviewers

These may be faculty or other health professional staff without forming any group. A form similar to the one used for selection committee may be used, preferrably with a sample issue of the journal. The library may use departmental representatives for this purpose. The librarian has to set a plan for follow-up.

Selection Criteria

Although selection criteria previously dealt with apply to all types of library materials, there are some unique characteristics of the journal format that need to be considered:

- *Quality*: Although no single measure will be sufficient to judge quality, there are several factors to be taken into account:
  - *Publisher*: Who is he? How reputable is he as a scientific publisher? Is the publisher a professional society or association? Is the membership of such society or association international? National? Regional?
  - *Editors*: Are they recognized? What is their institutional affiliation? are they themselves writers as well? Does the editorial board include prominent names?
  - Editorial review.
  - *Authors*: Are they members of the editorial board? What is there affiliation?
  - Content.
    a. *Research Journals*: Research journals should publish articles that follow the accepted format for describing scientific research.

   b. *Clinical Journals*: These may be evaluated by practitioners for selection.
   c. *Review Journals*: These require more selectivity than the previous types because they do not report new information, and reviews on similar topics may cover much of the same ground.

- Writing and Style:
  - *Writing Style*: Articles should be readable. The writing should be grammatically correct, well organised and clear.
  - *Abstracts*: These should be informative.
  - *References*: These should be pertinent, thorough and up-to-date. Citations should be complete and accurate.
- *Accessibility of Content*: The inclusion of the journal in indexing services may be a criterion for selection. Inclusion in a selective database may also be used for this purpose.
- *Bibliometric Indicators*: Bibliometrics, or statistical bibliography, analyses literature by numerically examining the publications of a discipline. Data can be used to identify journals with the greatest number of articles on a subject or that cover greatest percentage of the literature. But bibliomteric data must be used cautiously as a selection tool, as articles may be cited for multiple reasons and not necessarily to indicate useful research or clinical content.
- *Physical Quality*: It is to be noted here that not all countries have equal access to high-quality paper and printing.
  - *Illustrations*: Clarity and definition in reproduction of radiographs, photographs and other images. Use of colour may be important in some fields.
  - *Paper and Binding*: This may not be a factor to be considered as a factor for selection, although using acid-free paper is relevant for material preservation.
- *User Needs*: Patient care and current research needs are driving forces for selection. One indicator of need is the number of requests made to obtain copies of articles through interlibrary loan or document delivery services. The departmental representatives for selection may be a source for identifying department needs.
- Local Availability.
  - Whether the title is available in another library of the parent organisation.
  - Duplication is becoming less likely except for heavily used items.
  - Availability through a network to which the library subscribes.
  - Reliance on remote collections or document delivery services.
- *Cost:* The judgement on the benefit for cost may be difficult, and subject experts should be called upon for advice.

Electronic Journals

Electronic journals may be categorized either by availability of electronic and print parallels or by mode of access.

The first will result in:

- Electronic journals that have an electronic version only, such as Online journal of current clinical trials.
- Electronic journals that are versions of print journals, such as New England journal of medicine.

The second will result in:

- Electronic journals that are available through a commercial vendor.
- Electronic journals that are locally accessible through CD-ROM, floppy disk or other electronic format loaded on a library workstation or parent organisation's network.

The issues that electronic journals pose for libraries are not substantially different than those posed by print journals. Information on availability of electronic journals may be obtained from the Association of Research Libraries (ARL) in both print and electronic format.

Selection Sources

There are several sources or information about journals:

- *Advertising and Announcements*: Advertisements may be sent directly by publishers, or are published in library or medical journals. Vendors also alert libraries in various ways: through lists, order forms, and online information systems. Publishers' catalogues may also be used.
- *Sample Issues*: These are sent by the publisher as sample or trial issues, which often may be requested and sometimes purchased.
- *Core Lists:* Lists of key journals, sometimes together with some other library materials are compiled. The following are examples:
- *User Recommendations:* The library can encourage users to suggest new titles using request form available in the library, whether manually or electronically.
- *Interlibrary Loan Requests*: Repeated requests from users to obtain articles from a journal should prompt the library to consider a subscription.
- *Reviews:* There are scientific journals that publish reviews of new titles. Among these journals are Nature and Serials review.
- *Indexes*: Lists of journals indexed for major indexing services are used to make a judgement on titles already identified. Announcement of titles added can alert selectors to them. Examples of these lists are:
  - List of journals indexed in Index Medicus. New titles are announced in *NLM technical bulletin*.

- Serial sources for the BIOSIS Previews Database.
- Chemical Abstracts Service Source Index.

- *Other Sources*: There are general sources that cover a wide range of subjects. Among these are the following:
  - Ulrich's international periodicals directory. Bowker.
  - Standard periodical directory. Oxbridge.
  - New serial titles. OCLC.
  - Faxon's librarians' guide to serials.
  - EBSCO's librarians' handbook.
  - Computer databases such as OCLC, RLIN, SERLINE (an NLM database)
  - Serials review. Ann Arbor: Pierian. Quarterly

It has to be noted here that all such sources are also available in machine-readable form.

BOOK SELECTION

Books assist in the dissemination of information by providing a convenient means of access to recorded knowledge. It is true that a medical book is out-of-date when it is published, but this does not invalidate its use as a digest of available knowledge in a physically handy form.

The main categories of books are:

- *Quick Reference Books:* Dictionaries, directories, pharmacopoeias, data book. These are essential items in every collection. Now many of these books are also available in CD-ROM format.
- *Standard Works of Reference*: These provide access to knowledge in depth in subject at an advanced level. They are usually too detailed to serve as textbook guides to their subjects.
- *Postgraduate Textbooks:* The need to specialize is paramount and the number of courses leading to future qualifications is numerous in medicine. This ensures a good market of textbooks at the postgraduate level. They are among the most heavily used materials in the medical library.
- *Texts for Basic Study:* There is virtually no topic in the undergraduate level which is not suitably covered by this type of material.
- *Monographs*: A monograph consists of a treatise on a single subject, and it is always an advanced level work. They may also appear in series.
- *Theses and Dissertations:* Most of the smaller medical libraries do not hold this type of material and larger one will onlyhold those originating in their own parent organisations. If required, it is usual to have them collected by a central body such as national or depository libraries.
- *Pamphlets and other Ephemera:* Pamphlets are short topical and written

with a particular object in view. They may quickly lose their currency. They may be ordered and treatedas books. Many useful pamphlets are available free particularly from pharmaceutical companies.

- *Reports:* A report is a work written by a task force or particular group specially commissioned to study a particular issue or problem. They may be difficult to trace. Reports may also emanate from important bodies in the profession. Research reports in, for example, the pharmaceutical industry may be confidential. Another example of reports is the annual report of a research or teaching institution. Government departments generate a great deal of report literature, of which many are on social and medical subjects.
- *Conference Proceedings:* The quality of this type varies from carefully edited account of important meetings to mere photolithography of the authors' typescripts with little editing and no index.

Responsibilities

- Responsibilities for book selection should be formally agreed upon, and the flow of information and decisions clearly delineated. If most of the selection is distributed among several persons, a manual describing both the responsibilities and the process is useful. This manual promotes consistency and thoroughness in carrying out the functions
- In small libraries, there is little confusion regarding who has what responsibility. But in large libraries the situation is different as procedures need to document how selection tools are handled:
  - Who sees advertising materials, how they are divided, for instance by subject, how they are marked for follow up
  - If books reviews are used, the routing process should be established
  - Method of transmitting ordering information from the selector to the acquisitions unit
  - If interlibrary loan requests are to be reviewed, there must be a mechanism for receiving the information.
- The link between selection activity and the budget allocations must be established, whether the individual selectors have any fund management responsibilities or not.

Sources for Book Selection

Selection tools for book selection should be both alerting and evaluative to be convenient for selection. They may be in the form of bibliographies, review or advertising materials, and may be in print and/or electronic formats. Other sources are relevant for selection.

The various sources may be summarized as follows:

- *Publishers' Flyers and Catalogues*: Libraries usually receive a lot of announcements from the publishers about the availability of new books. Moreover, many publishers produce various types of catalogues for their publications, sometimes including previously published editions which are still in print. It is necessary for the library to be on the mailing list of the publishers in the disciplines that concern the library. Visiting their web sites is now enabled as well.
- *Vendors' Flyers and Catalogues*: Many vendors do the same thing as publishers. Make sure that you are regularly informed of their offerings. Some provide altering service, in print or electronically, of new titles.
- *Recommendations from Users*: This should be encouraged. Request forms must be readily accessible. Remember that they themselves receive flyers and catalogues from publishers and sometimes complimentary copies of new titles.
- *Interlibrary Loan Requests:* Although particularly appropriate for journal selection, they may be also relevant for selecting books that are not brand new.
- *Bibliographies and Library Catalogues:* Bibliographies are of several categories as there are national biblio-graphies, subject bibliographies both total and selective, author bibliographies, bibliographies of bibliographies, etc. Some of these bibliographies include health sciences while there is one devoted to medicine which is Medical books in print of Bowker.

Another tool that is considered here is what is usually called core lists:

- *British Council*: Core list of library materials: medicine.
- *EMRO*: List of basic sources in English for a medical faculty library. 8th ed. 1999.
- *Royal College of General Practitioners*: Books for general practice and primary health care. London, 1992. Regularly revised.
- *Royal College of Psychiatrists:* Lists of books suitable for a psychiatric library 1988-1993. London, 1993. Re-gularly revised and updated.
- *Royal College of Psychiatrists:* Key books for a psychiatric library. London. Regularly revised and updated.

Moreover, the most comprehensive catalogue of health sciences books is CATLINE. This is NLM's online catalogue. NLM Locator, which includes CATLINE, AVLINE for audiovisuals, and SERLINE for information on journal titles, is now available on the Internet.

- *Book Reviews*: There are two types of book reviews:
  - Those published in professional and scientific journals. Examples of such journals are:

a. *JAMA:* Journal of American Medical Association
b. Lancet
c. British medical journal
d. British journal of hospital medicine
e. Nursing times
f. Journal of advanced nursing
g. New England journal of medicine
h. Bulletin of the Medical Library Association

There are journals not limited to health sciences such as Nature, and Science, and Library journal:

- Those that are fully devoted as journal to reviews. Some of these reviews cover medicine among the disciplines that they serve. Among them, are the following:
  a. *New Technical Books*: New York Public Library (10/year).
  b. *Technical Book Review Index:* JAAD Publications (monthly).
  c. *Science Books and Films*: American Association for the Advancement of science (5/year).
  d. *The Bookseller:* Whitaker (weekly).
  e. *Contemporary Psychology*: A journal of reviews. American Psychological Association (monthly).
  f. *Directory of Published Proceedings*: Series SEMT-Science, Engineering, Medicine and Technology. InterDok (10/year)
  g. *Choice:* Association of College and Research Libraries (11/year).
  h. *British Book News*: The British Council (monthly).
  i. *American Book Publishing Record*: Bowker (monthly).
  j. *Cumulative Book Index*: H.W. Wilson (11/year).

The outstanding example of book reviews is the new publication of Doody Publishing set up in 1993.

This publication is entitled Doody's journal: health sciences book reviewing, issued bimonthly and evaluates about 250 titles in each issue. It can be accessed on Internet.

A British version is under discussion:

- *Approval Plan*: Although approval plans are concerned with acquisition. The selection function of the approval plan is summarized as follows:
  - The library supplies the vendor with a detailed profile of its requirements in specific fields, together with any budgetary limits, and the publishers to be considered;
  - The supplier selects and regularly supplies the materials as specified in the profile;
  - The library monitors the materials supplied and have the right to return any item received;

  - If the percentage of returns is high then the library should review the plan and take required action, which may include changing the supplier.
  - The approval plan does not fit with small medical libraries.

SELECTION IN SPECIAL SETTINGS

Electronic Resources

Selection decisions of electronic resources parallel those of print materials in many ways, but they are treated separately, because their unique characteristics introduce additional factors to collection decision-making and because these formats can affect information delivery, budgeting, equipment, and staffing. Electronic resources play an essential role in every health sciences library. But they are usually expensive, and thus may consume a great portion of a library's budget. So a greater degree of care should be taken in making decisions regarding what the library will provide to its users.

As knowledge-based computer programmes in clinical medicine and other health care disciplines are improved and gain wider acceptance, they appear more commonly as library resources, especially if they can be accessed remotely from offices and clinical care sites. Selection of computer software by students, hospital staff, faculty, clinicians, or researchers should be guided by the library's collection development policy. The policy should address the criteria by which these resources are selected. Scope, depth and audience will define the boundaries.

There are several types of software that may be acquired by health sciences libraries:

- Bibliographic
- *Full Text*: Books and journals
- Numeric or factual databases
- Clinical assist programmes for diagnosis or treatment decisions
- Educational software
- Applications software, such as word processing, analytical or statistical packages, file management, telecommunications, authoring software, graphics software (note here that such software is general pur-pose not resources)
- Administrative functions or staff support
- Criteria of Resources for Selection
  - *Scope*: The resource must fit the subject scope of the library.
  - *Depth*: The intensity of collecting in a discipline will dictate how many resources the library will acquire, or the degree of specialization needed.
  - *Audience*: The selection should answer the question whose needs should the library intend to serve with the software? Different

clientele will require different resources. Computer-based resources for student use should usually be selected with advice and recommendation from faculty or potential users.

- Selection Principles:
  - The resource should fit the mission of the library, and the scope and depth defined in the collection development policy, it should meet users' needs;
  - Specific criteria should address the content, the user interface retrieval software, the format, and the hardware and software required by the resource;
  - Careful investigation and evaluation of the cost-effective-ness of different formats should precede any decisions. An information policy both for the library and for the parent organisation will help guide these decisions.
- Selection Criteria:
  - Content:

    a. Quality of the material presented.

    i. Authoritiveness of content

    ii. Expertise of the authors

    iii. Reputation of the producer

    iv. Comprehensiveness of the information

    v. Quality of the images, if important

    b. *Currency*: Regular updates should be provided.

    c. *Content Usefulness*: Such as:

    i. Interactive capabilities of testing

    ii. Simultaneously hear and see as required

    iii. Combine text and images, sound and movement

    iv. Highly accurate and up-to-date knowledge

    v. Able to show relationships and probabilities, and suggest possibilities

    d. Relationship to Print Publications.

    i. Whether additional material is added

    ii. Convenience of access, amount of demand, need for permanent presentation

    iii. Are updates offered electronically through networks?
  - User Interface:

    a. Ease of use.

    b. Software functions.

    i. The search engine or other control functions should be powerful enough to support the resource;

    ii. Response time should be snappy;

    iii. Use of Boolean operators, adjacency feature, saving searches or search strategies are enabled.

c. Printing and Downloading Capabilities.
d. Duplication of Print Publications. When the software duplicates to a large extent a print publication, the library must determine whether the electronic version offers additional features, such as easier search, use hypertext, reformat information, manipulation or animation of illustrative material, extraction and manipulation.
e. Compatibility with Other Resources.
f. Documentation and Guides.

— *Format*: The library has several formats to choose from:

a. In print
b. On stand-alone CD-ROM
c. On CD-ROM on a LAN
d. By tapes mounted on local institutional network
e. By various routes to a remote utility through a gateway

The following factors should be considered in making this choice:

a. *Users*: Consider the likely users; if they are very few, the cost and support may not be justified.
b. *Expected Use*: The number and frequency of use.
c. *Accessibility*: Convenient access.
d. *Content*: Whether formats differ in comprehen-siveness or specialized contents. Compare the interface and performance characteristics. Updating.
e. Costs.
f. *Equipment*: Compatibility with local systems.
g. Legal Issues:
   i. Licensing
   ii. Restrictions to making backup copies, downloading, and printing
   iii. Possibility of sharing

— Hardware, Software, and Space Requirements.

a. Space:
   i. The facilities should be conducive to the types of use that will be made of them.
   ii. Whether the workstation has to be an open area.
   iii. Whether the resources can be used effectively in the available setting.
b. Workstation Configuration.
   i. Networking is to be provided.
   ii. Adequate number of workstations to ensure effective use of the resources.
   iii. Avoid workstations dedicated to single resource,

except for those that will be heavily used, such as MEDLINE, or the library's catalogue.

c. Compatibility.

i. Is the resource compatible with existing equipment?

ii. Is the memory sufficient and the machine fast enough for the type of content, such as images?

iii. Does the new software conflict with any other resources on the same equipment?

d. Additional Software.

i. Does the resource require specific software such as operating system or database loader?

ii. Audio and video require additional component.

iii. Is the existing hardware adequate to accommodate the required software?

Reference Collections

The policy for reference collection should relate to the general collection development policy, whether it forms part of it or written separately. All selection criteria applied to books in general apply here as well. It remains to cover here the types of materials that form the reference collection and the selection sources of reference items.

Types of Materials

Reference collections are used to locate the following:

- *Directory Information*: Brief factual information about people, institutions, organisations, programmes.
- *Data:* Compilations of such information as statistical data, biological facts, chemical compositions, drug descriptions.
- *Definitions:* Collections of medical terminology, foreign language, specialized nomenclature.
- *Descriptions:* Short or encylcopaedic summaries of diseases, procedures, biological processes, historical events.
- *Bibliographic Information:* References or abstracts by subject, author, citation, historical period, or source.

To enable this, the following types of materials have to be provided:

- *Bibliographies:* Examples include the various core lists and other sources for selection of books, journals and electronic resources mentioned previously.
- *Business or Corporate Information about Health Care Industry:* Examples: The medical and health information directory; the Patersons guides series; Research centres directory; World of learning; Encyclopedia of associations; the Medical and healthcare marketplace guide; the Foundations directory; Directory of medical and health care libraries in the United Kingdom and Republic of Ireland.

- *Dictionaries: Examples*: Dorlands illustrated medical dictionary; Stedman's medical dictionary; the International dictionary of medicine and biology; Taber encyclopedic dictionary; Segen's dictionary of modern medicine; the encyclopedia and dictionary of medicine, nursing and allied health; Jablonski's dictionary of syndromes and eponymic diseases; Mangalini's directory of syndromes; Encyclopedia of human biology; Sloane's medical abbreviations and eponyms; the Acronyms, initialisms and abbreviations dictionary; Mosby's medical, nursing and allied health dictionary.
- *Directories and Biographical Sources:* Examples are the various medical directories published in many countries of the world, such as the UK Medical directory.
- *Drug and Chemical Information:* Examples are the various pharmacopoeias published in many countries.
- *Funding Sources:* Some are listed under the second type mentioned.
- *Handbooks and Manuals:* This also includes style manuals. Examples: Merck index; CRC handbook of chemistry and physics.
- *Health Legislation, Regulations and Standards:* These are published and documented in various countries.
- *Indexes and Abstracts*: Many are available in both print and electronic formats. Examples include:
  - Index Medicus (Medline);
  - Science citation index (SCISEARCH);
  - Current contents;
  - Excerpta medica (EMBASE);
  - Cumulative index to nursing and allied health (CINAHL);
  - Hospital literature index (Health Planning and Administration);
  - Biological abstracts (BIOSIS Previews);
  - Chemical abstracts (CA Search);
  - Psychological abstracts (Psych-INFO);
  - CANCERLIT;
  - PDQ;
  - TOXLIT.
- *Statistical Compilations:* Many countries and health associations publish statistics on different aspects of health. WHO publishes World health statistics annual.
- *Tests*: Examples include: Mental measurements yearbook; stromborg's Instruments for clinical nursing research.
- Yearbooks and annual reviews.
- *General Works:* Most reference collections include a small number

of general reference works such as an encyclopaedia, dictionary, almanac, directories of local organisations, an atlas.

- *Textbook Collections:* If the library does not maintain a reserve collection. A representative collection of textbooks in the reference collection may provide convenient access to students who need information for assignments or patient care questions.
- *Electronic Resources:* There is an increasing number of electronic reference sources covering the range of print sources, including bibliographic and fulltext databases, handbooks, encyclopaedias, directories, and textbooks. The data is stored on CD-ROM, floppy disks, hard drives and mainframe or minicomputers. Some are duplicates or enhancements of printed sources or mainframe sources, such as CD-ROM versions of MEDLINE, others incorporate several publications or resources. Another electronic resource is the OPAC (Online Public Access Catalogue) were one or more workstations are dedicated for them.
- *Ephemeral Materials*: Collection of pamphlets, information sheets, brochures, and even reprints or bibliographies are maintained as adjuncts to reference collections. This collection may also include press clippings. A policy for selection criteria and guidelines for weeding and retention should be developed and followed.

Audiovisual Collections

Audiovisual materials comprise an important segment of many health sciences libraries. But they usually have requirements (such as space, equipment and funding) that make them different from collections of other materials. Collection development for audiovisuals is different from those for other materials in the following aspects:

- Selection of audiovisuals is more user-driven than that for other formats;
- Previewing is required in the selection process, whether this takes place in the library or at the supplier's place.

Audiovisuals supports all aspects of educational programmes in both academic settings and hospitals (whether for staff or patients).

Selection Criteria

In addition to the general criteria of selection previously discussed, the following additional criteria may be considered:

- *Audience:* The library's interest in the audience which may be professional, academics, or general public including patients and patient families, should be documented in the collection development policy and taken into account in the selection process.
- *Equipment Availability*: The following questions have to be answered:

Does the library already own the proper equipment so that users can view or listen to the programme? Are users likely to have access to compatible equipment at home or in their departments? Can the item be used on patient to other broadcast networks?

- *Appropriateness of Format*: Is the format in which the material is presented the most useful one to convey the information? Slides *vs.* videotapes, audiovisual *vs.* print, motion *vs.* still images, audiotape *vs.* printed description.
- *Origin of Format:* does the audiovisual conform to national standards: slides may differ in size.
- *Rental or Permanent Acquisition*: Can the need be satisfied through rental? Is there sufficient recurring demand to justify a purchase? Is it possible to borrow particular items from other library or institution?
- *Restriction on Use:* Are there special guidelines which must be followed regarding the use of the title, such as prohibition on group showings? If it is difficult to monitor and enforce such restrictions, it may not be advisable to procure the item.
- *Cost*: Is the item worth the investment?

Grey Literature

Grey literature is defined as the " literature which is not readily available through normal bookselling channels, and therefore difficult to identify and obtain". Examples of grey literature include reports, technical notes and specifications, conference proceedings and preprints, translations, official publications, supplementary publications and data, trade literature. It has to be noted that not all materials in all these categories are grey.

Grey materials are characterized by the following:

- Poor availability
- Poor bibliographic information and control
- Non-professional layout and format
- Low print run

Types of Grey Literature in Health Sciences

- Government Information.
  - The grey titles issued by government departments. These may outnumber the other normal publications in some countries.
  - The health agency documents, including circulars.
  - Documents produced by national statutory and nonstatutory bodies, academic units and voluntary sector.
  - *Health Authority Literature*: This includes:
    - *a.* Minutes and agenda papers
    - *b.* Annual reports

c. Public health reports
d. Strategic plans
e. Working party plans
f. Statistical series and bulletins
g. Medical audit plans
h. Policy documents
i. Research and surveys
j. Health needs assessment surveys
k. Public opinion surveys
l. Financial statements

- Documents of other relevant authorities, such as the ministries of interior, housing, transport, labour, sports and even police service.
- Grey literature of health service providers in both public and private sectors. This literature also includes research activities and statistics.

Sources for Selection

There are services concerning grey literature in various fields. They are normally with national covering although some may be international.

The following are examples:

- *Government Reports Announcements and Index. Virginia*: NTIS. This publication has three major headings related to health sciences in its subject categories:
  - Biomedical technology and human factor engineering
  - Health planning and health services research
  - Medicine and biology
- Scientific and Technical Aerospace Report (STAR). NASA. This has the following parts concerning health sciences:
  - Life sciences
  - Aerospace medicine
  - Behavioural sciences
  - Man/system technology and life support
  - Space biology
- Energy research abstract (ERA). US Department of Energy. It has:
  - Biomedical sciences, basic studies
  - Biomedical sciences, applied studies
  - Health and safety
- British reports, translations and theses. Boston. Spa: The British Library Document Supply Centre. It has: 06 biological and medical sciences.
- System for information on grey literature in Europe (SIGLE). The

European Association of Grey Literature Exploitation (EAGLE). It is a bibliographic database holding contributions from 9 European countries.

- For librarians seeking German language grey literature in medical and health care, there are two publications:
  - FTN (Forschungsberichte aus Technik und Nat-urwissencha ften). Weinheim: VCH Verlag. This is a bibliography of projects sponsored by the German Federal Ministry for Research and Technology.
  - Bibliography of medicine. Munich: K.G. Saur. This is a bibliography of German-language publications outside the book trade, and includes literature from Switzerland and Austria.
- PASCAL Bibliographies internationales. Paris INIST. This is an international bibliography with French emphasis covering science and medicine.
- Ethnic minorities health. Bradford: Bradford Community Quarterly bulletin covering conference proceeding, theses and much useful grey literature.
- The Cumulative index to nursing and allied health literature (CINAHL). It is useful for dissertations, standards and conference proceedings.
- *Health Service Abstracts. Oldham:* Department of Health Leaflets Unit. Monthly. It includes books, book chapters, NHS executive publications, reports and periodical references.
- *The European Union Biomedical and Health Research. Brussels:* European Commission. 3/year. It concentrates on national research into medical and health problems in Europe.
- Health Care Literature Information Network (HECLINET). Berlin: Institut für Krankenhausbau, Dokumentation Krankenhauswesen. Bimonthly. It covers the entire range of European literature, both grey and white, on hospitals and health care. It includes conference reports, theses and company publications.
- Conference papers index. Louisville, NY: Data Courier. Monthly. It covers published and unpublished papers.
- WHODOC. Geneva: WHO. Bimonthly. It lists all WHO publications, including periodicals, technical and policy documents, as well as documents emanating from WHO funded programmes.

Other disciplines, such as food and environment, are covered in international databases.

They include:

- *AGRIS. Rome*: Food and Agriculture Organisation (FAO). It has a print version, AGRINDEX.
- CAB abstracts. London: Commonwealth Agricultural Bureau.

- AGRICOLA. US National Agricultural Library. It has a printed version: bibliography of agriculture.
- International register of potentially toxic chemicals (IRPTC). Nairobi: United Nations Environment Programme (UNEP).
- Environmental Chemical Data and Information Network (ECDIN). European Communities at Ispra (Italy) Establishment. This is a factual database.

Consumer Health Collections

During the 1980s and 1990s, increasing attention has been given to the provision of information on health care issues to patients, relatives, carers and wider public. The information provided is called "Consumer Health Information (CHI)'. Deve-lopment of consumer health information is now a necessity dictated by law in some countries.

It has significant benefits:

- It leads to more truly informed consent
- It leads to increased patient's understanding and satisfaction
- It leads to increased compliance with treatment
- It leads to quicker and less stressful recovery from illness and surgery.

The increased availability of health information for lay people has also been influenced by the WHO declaration of " Health for All by the year 2000 " which says:

- "Health for all will be achieved by people themselves. A well informed, well motivated and actively participating community is a key element for attainment of the common goal".

Consumer health collections exist to serve library users seeking authoritative information, in clearly understood language, about normal anatomy and physiology, diseases, conditions, treatments and other health care topics. Besides the general public users of these collections include medical school students seeking materials to help explain health and disease concepts to patients and their relatives.

Others include primary care physicians, nurses and faculty members. It may be part of the reference collection, or on its own. But it is not always the responsibility of the medical library to contain consumer health collections. In some cases it is the responsibility of the parent organisation's public relations unit, while in other cases the responsibility rests with a variety of statutory and voluntary agencies, as it is rather common for the ministries of health and other health authorities to provide this information. Yet in other cases, the responsibility rests with public libraries.

Selection Criteria

The general selection criteria previously mentioned apply here.

But further criteria may be given:

- *Presentation of Information*: This includes the writing style, easiness of use, presence of index and table of contents, illustration, presentation of alternatives and presence of citations and sources.
- *Audience*: The collection development policy should document the audience to be served, to be taken into account in the selection process.
- *Pathway to Additional Information:* The item should have bibliographies, reading list, referral sources and resource organisations.
- Qualifications of the Author and Publisher.
- Currency.

Rare Book, History of Medicine and Archives Collections

Rare book, history of medicine and archives collections, are not found in all health sciences libraries. The difference between collection development in general, and that of rare books derives from the nature of the books themselves. Thus policies governing it are frequently singled out for special consideration in overall collection development policy statements. A distinction is often made between rare book collections and history of medicine collections, under the assumption that the latter are generally comprised of secondary works, the materials are collected in the same manner as other books for the medical library collections, and they are kept in open stacks with the rest of the library's collection.

Rare books are primary research materials, require more proper storage and security controls than the general stack collection, and may also be used as showplace for the parent organisation. The archives collection of the parent organisation is different and is not common in medical libraries as it may be under the responsibility of another department of the parent organisation.

If it exists, it may include: official correspondence, minutes, books of account, publications of the parent organisation, books by and about staff and students including alumni publications, theses from the parent organisation or its staff, records of parent organisation's clubs, associations, and societies catalogue, newsletters, personal papers of the more eminent members of the staff, and photographs. It may also contain records from other local health-related organisations, such as affiliated hospitals.

Selection Criteria

Additional to generic criteria, there are further ones that need to be considered:

- *Presence of other Editions of the Same Work*: In addition to availability of other editions or printings, there may be need for specific edition with special features. Some large libraries may require that all editions of a work be acquired for comparison.

- *Availability of a Facsimile Edition*: Facsimile editions may be useful as reading copies.
- *Physical Condition*: The physical condition may be the reason for selection as the item may be different from modern works. Items that need restoration are not usually acquired.
- *Cost:* This must be appropriate.
- *Research Value of the Artifact over Content:* This concerns signed or annotated copies, special bindings and illustrations. Works of particular publishers may be of interest.
- *Provenance*: Previous owners of the copy. Whether the copy is a stolen copy.
- *The Subject in Context*: This means that the copy may show whether the discipline changed over time.
- *Format:* Formats other than books may figure prominently in rare book and history of medicine collections.
- For archives there must be a policy for retention and disposal of the materials rather than a selection policy.

3

Digital Libraries in India: A Review

INTRODUCTION

Digital library to be an electronic collection of real or virtual resources, which may also be available elsewhere. Digital library is not identical to a website or a portal. However, while portals, specialized websites and search engines cover a wide range of subject areas, digital libraries are more narrowly focused around one or a specific group of disciplines. Digital libraries, moreover, attach contents pacific and highly descriptive metadata such as, descriptors or keywords to describe each item in the collection. Therefore, searches in a digital library can produce more useful results, save time and effort in searching, and in the best of cases browsers may directly access the text or multimedia content for which they executed their search. These include minimizing storage space and cutting down costs of library maintenance and resource distribution.

A digital library is also not merely an automated conventional library, where the resources are electronically catalogued and are available only for browsing purposes. Although conventional libraries do preserve socio-cultural ambiences within their spaces, a digital library can provide more equitable and widely distributed access at lower costs. Moreover, it may be most appropriate means of organizing intellectual artifacts that cannot be represented or distributed in printed formats, such as audio/video multimedia content.

At present, digital library initiatives in India make use of Dublin Core for web-based publications, Encoded Archival Description (EAD) for archiving and Visual Resources Association (VRA) for visual data. Consortia such as the INFLIBNET and INDEST are involved in developing Indian metadata standards and software applications as part of the Open Archives Initiative Protocol for Metadata Harvesting (OAI_PMH). This would be used to automatically extract metadata information from digital libraries and enhance interoperability between systems. This would also enable users to access all information repositories of participating institutions of the OAI. eprints@iisc, the eprint archive of Indian Institute of Science, is probably the first OAI compliant institutional repository initiative in India. In India, at present, Information Library Network (INFLIBNET), a consortium incubated under the rubric of UGC, is actively involved in Library Automation and The National Informatics Center (NIC) of India has also developed digital library software – DelSis – that is used by the Developing Library Network (DelNet), which is also an effort to network libraries and for resource sharing. DelNet aims to provide access to content in Indian Languages and in Urdu using this software.

Some of the other initiatives that will also contribute to this effort in the future include the Vidyanidhi Library of Theses and Dissertations and the Digital Library of India. The important visions that came out from the President of India, Dr. A.P.J. Abdul Kalama's inaugural speech at the International Digital Library Conference. There were strong optimistic feelings about the potential of digital libraries in their ability to springboard India towards an information economy.

REVIEW OF LITERATURE

Ranjita, Khaidem & Sophiarani, Soubam (2008) discuss the development of any society is directly dependent upon the extent of adoption of a changing environment. Nowadays, library becomes the center point of resource based learning. Digital library is essentially a fully automated information system with all resources in digital form. It not only facilitates the library functions but also saves the precious time, strength and energy of the users. The library professional should increase their skills to provide good access in Information and Communication Technologies. The present paper highlights the definition and historical development of digital library. It also discusses some of the initiatives of digital library in India.

Sinha,Manoj Kumar & etal (2006) emphasized the emergence of Internet has added a new dimension to information technology which gave birth to the new concepts of Digital Libraries (DLs), Knowledge Management (KM), and archiving of indigenous culture and heritage materials. The Digital Libraries have emerged as a crucial component of global information infrastructure, adopting the latest Information and Communication Technology (ICT) to promote an organisational structure that encourages communication and resource sharing between the academician and scholars across the nations.

The present paper gives an overview of the latest developments, which have been taken place in the areas of digital library and an attempt is also made to give a brief account of Indian initiatives for establishing digital libraries and also effort taken by university/ institutional libraries to transform themselves from the traditional libraries to computerised and ultimately digital or hybrid libraries. In addition to that some initiatives taken by North Eastern States for the digitisation of manuscripts and rare materials, preservation of digital content etc have also been described in brief. Bhuyan,Sewali (2007) discussed the time for comparisons and conflicts between print media and electronic media appear to be over as the world prepare itself for the next era in the digital society. The need of modern information society has changed the library from traditional type to digital one.

This paper discusses problems challenged and issues involved in design and development of worlds standard digital library focused on India Context. The paper explains the concept and architecture of a digital library. Digital libraries can immediately adopt innovations in technology providing users with improvements in electronic and audio book technology as well as presenting new form of communication. This Paper also discusses the Metadata concept as it is developed in the field of library and information science. If is an effective way of information management. It briefly touches upon concept of Metadata repository. It also discusses how Indian University Libraries can develop a digital library for electronic theses and Dissertation (ETD). Finally, it highlights the initiative taken by various Indian Organization towards the development of Digital Library.

Chandra Guru B.P.Mahesh, & etal (2009) stated the 21st Century knowledge management is increasingly becoming a crucial tool. It has already been successfully implemented in academic libraries in India and elsewhere. INFLIBNET, NICNET, INDONET, ERNET, CALIBNET, DELNET, ADINET, MALIBNET, etc. have emerged as the prominent academic libraries in India. Academic libraries are the treasure house of knowledge which cater to the needs of scholars, scientists, technocrats, researchers, students and others who are in the mainstream of higher education. The vision and mission of academic libraries are changing in India.

The vast literature gleaned from IFLA, ACRL and allied publications on academic libraries aptly reveal the changing roles and responsibilities of information professionals in the modern society. Academic libraries are positioning themselves to be the torch bearers and path makers of educational advancement by way of integrating knowledge systems and resources. The academic libraries have to be managed on the basis of constant introspection at the individual level and scientific evaluation at the institutional level in this age of knowledge management.

Walton,Graham (2009) clarifies the reasons for the prominence of uncertainty are identified from the broad management literature. The impact uncertainty has on the organisation, and the individual and strategic direction is also discussed using the literature. This provides the context to establish how uncertainty, has historically been faced, by libraries. The same approach is applied when the application of scenario planning in managing uncertainty is established. Scenario planning is investigated at the wider level and then the focus moves to its relevance for libraries. Uncertainty is a strategic concern for many organisations (both proffer and not for profit), which poses specific challenges for managers. It is caused by technological developments and changes in markets with other contributions from environmental, fiscal and political factors. Scenario planning is a proactive way to manage the impact of uncertainty. By using scenarios it is possible to identify key factors that will have serious implications in the future. Taking actions and informed decisions based upon the scenarios, future risks can be avoided and possible opportunities anticipated. Effective scenarios can be produced by going through an agreed group process.

Kavitha. R (2009) describes various trends in collection development in digital environment.The changes that have occurred in acquisition, retrieval and storage of information due to technological developments have been discussed. Limitations, restrictions and problems being faced by librarians and readers due to the same have also been discussed. The way these developments have affected the academic environment and changed the role of librarian has also been portrayed

Kumbargoudar,Praveenkumar (2006) stated that due to the information revolution, Digital Libraries are developing all over the world to collect, store and communicate the information through electronic media. Compared to the different developed countries, there is slow development of digital libraries in India. This is so because of many social, political and economical factors. These factors include Growing Population, Illiteracy, Low standard of living, less importance to telecommunication facilities, shortage in supply of Energy Sources, lower number of computer and Internet users. To improve the use of Information Technology applications, the Government of India and different state government already initiated certain policies and projects. The paper also discussed the policies and projects of Central and different State Governments to increase the use of Information Technology applications in administrate on.

Fullerton,Karen (1999) disused the recent initiatives in digital library research have suggested new models for the creation and organization of digital information and its dissemination to virtual communities. PEN-DOR (the Pennsylvania Education Network Digital Object Repository) is a digital library designed to provide access to the collective experience of teachers, students and administrators in public schools in building lesson plans and using curriculum materials. Using the WWW as a platform, PEN-DOR incorporates current research in digital libraries to provide K-12 educators with access to multimedia resources and tools to create new lesson plans and presentations, and to modify existing ones. Design problems addressed by the project include the design of distributed, object-oriented database architecture, the description and cataloguing of multimedia objects, and issues related to usability and training for a geographically scattered user community. Two critical aspects of the organization of this digital library are the development of a method for the persistent identification of resources, and the design of a record structure based on recent developments in metadata. Resource identification has been achieved by adopting a system-wide approach with an upgrade path to the emerging URN standards. In designing a record structure, the PEN-DOR project has elected to use the GEM (Gateway to Educational Materials) metadata standard developed as part of the GEM union catalogue project. Content for the database is solicited from project partners, government agencies and educational resources Web sites, as well as from participating teachers. Once incorporated in the repository, materials can be organized in frameworks that form the basis for lessons, tutorials and presentations. As frameworks are developed, used, critiqued and modified, they will form a community memory of past experience. Supported by the state's Link-to-Learn programme, the system will function as a resource for educators throughout Pennsylvania.

OBJECTIVES OF THE STUDY

Libraries are the repositories of the wisdom of ages stored in the form of recorded information for use of present and future generations. This paper describes development of digital library in digital environment; the basic components for establishing Digital Library System and the establishment of a digital library network in a country. The present study will be conducted with the following objectives:

- To study the development of digital library;
- To discuss the management of infrastructure for digital libraries.
- To analysis the management of Indian libraries and rights in digital environment.

DISCUSSION OF THE PAPER

Development of Digital Library

The Digital Libraries are electronic libraries where the information is acquired, stored and retrieved in digital form. Digital Libraries are the group-interlinked workstations connected to the high-speed networks. In the context of digital imaging, librarians face greater challenges in capturing, storing, formatting, retrieval and reproduction of non-textual materials. In digital libraries the e-resources are mounted on the servers located at remote places and the member libraries using user login and password on yearly subscription basis may access the information.

The digital collection resources may be e-journals, bibliographic and full text databases, e-books, e-prints etc called e-resources that may be shown in the digital collection and catalogue of the member libraries for a particular period of time. The member libraries can access the resources simultaneously at a time or at different time. Therefore many libraries may use the digital collection available at one site at the same time without any problems over the Internet through Dial Up, DSL, Lease Line or VSAT Connectivity. So the digital libraries are libraries without wall and it is also known as virtual library in broader sense. Library collection in digital form can be shared, exchanged and accessed by the members of the library and information network libraries as per their agreements or requirement. An important feature of the Digital object is that it can be stored, processed, and played back using a computer system, computer network and Internet. It allows us to search for any keywords of phrase or subject descriptor in the entire collection. It also occupies less space; require less manpower to run and manage the digital library, therefore it is very much cost effective. In India, Indian Institute of Science, Bangalore has established a digital library. It used IBM Digital Library Software.

MANAGEMENT OF INFRASTRUCTURE FOR DIGITAL LIBRARY

For establishing Digital Library various hardware and software are needs to be integrated for the development and deployment of digital libraries to access huge collection of digital information in network environment. The basic components for establishing Digital Library System are as follows: The Hardware, which comprises of followings: Digital Computer powered by Pentium IV with high capacity hard disk for Server and Clients in the LAN, Web Servers and FTP Server etc; Desktop Workstations –PCs; Capture Devices such as Scanners, Cameras Cards etc. Cartridge Tape or Disk for backup; High Power UPS (10 or 20 KV) Printers (Laser and Ink jet printers (latest model), Consoles and Test Computers; Secondary Storage or Output Devices comprising of CD-ROM Disk (R and RW), DVD, CD-Tower, Flatbed Scanners and Optical Character Recognizer (OCR), Data Compression Device; High Speed Local Area Network (LAN, WAN), Internet Connectivity ether through Dial-up Connectivity or V-SAT, or through Lease Line or Radio Modem etc. The Software's are such as Software: comprises of Operating software; Optical Character Recognition (OCR) Software; Scanning Software; Adobe Acrobat Reader; CD-Read/ Write Software; Digital Library Software ie DSpace, Greenstone, Fedora. E-Print etc.

Windows-NT Networking Software, SQL Server Software, Database Management Software; Web Designing Software like Java, Front Page, XML etc. RDMBS (Relational Database) Supporting the variety of Digital Databases like ORACLE, PosgreSQL, My SQL etc; Full Text Search Engines to index and provide access to digital resources. For establishing Digital Libraries some operational software is required. For this purpose, a number of digital library software is available which aim to offer complete digital library solutions. Generally the emphasis is being given to use open source software package, which can offer the solution to construct customized applications for handling and providing access to digital collection available over the Internet of in

Digital Library Archives connected to Web. Besides this some supporting software is also required. Followings are some digital Library Software available, which can be used in developing digital library: Dspace is available at http://www.dspace.org: DSpace is a digital library system to capture, store, index, preserve, and redistribute the intellectual output of a university's research faculty in digital formats developed jointly by MIT Libraries and Hewlett-Packard (HP), DSpace is available to research institutions world-wide as an open source system that can be customized and extended. Green Stone Digital Library Software: It is Open Source Software available from http:// greenstone.org under the term of the GNU General Public License. GNU E-Prints Archiving Software (Version 2.2.2): The software is available from http:/ / www.eprints.org Ganesha Digital Library Software: GDL can be downloaded free of cost at http://gdl.itb.ac.id/ download/ Libraonix Digital Library System: The Libronix DLS is available from the site http://www.logos.com/ products.

MANAGEMENT OF INDIAN LIBRARIES IN DIGITAL ERA

India is rich in various kinds of traditional knowledge that is documented in various forms and is available in museums, archives and some libraries. With digital library technology and tools, it is possible not only to archive these for posterity but also to replicate and disseminate such information with ease. For establishing digital libraries in the university/ institutional libraries, some basic information infrastructure in terms of hardware, software, electronic resources, Internet connectivity, specialized equipments like digital camera, scanners, sheet feeders, barcode printers etc. are required. 142 University Libraries in India has developed minimum information infrastructure from the Non-Recurring and Recurring grants received from the INFLIBNET Centre (an IUC of UGC) during IX Plan Period.

These libraries have developed in-house bibliographical databases of books, serials, theses, reports, and projects and converted the various manual operations into computerized modules using library application software SOUL or some other commercially available software. Under UGC-INFONET: E-journals Consortium Projects of UGC, which are coordinated by the INFLIBNET Centre, are accessing the facility of full –text on-line e-journals, various full text and bibliographical databases over Internet, which are connected by the Broad Band VSAT, Leased Line, SCPC VSAT through ERNET.

Now these libraries are hybrid library and partially trying to convert themselves into digital libraries by building the collection of digital library resources either by subscribing or by digitization of their own resources and hosting them on web. In India, at present, Information Library Network (INFLIBNET), a consortium incubated under the rubric of UGC, is actively involved in Library Automation, Database Creation, Software Development, Human Resources Development, Information Services and Networking. They have developed a software SOUL based on relational database management language, which is used for cataloguing, archiving as well as enabling online public access of resources. The Indian Institute of Science in Bangalore is closely involved with the INFLIBNET for developing and standardizing protocols of information management for digital library as well as information repository initiatives.

The National Informatics Center (NIC) of India has also developed digital library software – DelSis – that is used by the Developing Library Network (DelNet), which is also an effort to network libraries and for resource sharing. DelNet aims to provide access to content in Indian Languages and in Urdu using this software some of examples are Efforts at The Energy and Resources Institute (TERI) to create an integrated digital library. The concept of the hybrid digital library and the steps involved in its creation are also discussed. The hybrid digital library is a digital library that holds the metadata for accessing resources available in cyberspace and in the organization's library. Deb also discusses the physical digital library for born-digital documents in TERI and explains the TERI integrated digital library that provides a single window to provide access to born-digital resources as well as digitized documents.

Vidyanidhi, the Indian Digital Library of Electronic. Vidyanidhi is a direct consequence of government policy initiatives and is intended to demonstrate the utility of digital library technologies in maintaining and enhancing access to and visibility of Indian academic research. A conceptual model of Networked Digital Libraries (NDL) for IIMs (Indian Institutes of Management). Yet another consortium approach to digital libraries, in this case primarily of licensed e-resources, is the INDEST consortium. INDEST (Indian National Digital Library of Engineering Science and Technology) includes licensed e-resources acquired and shared on the principles of the other widespread U.S. e-resources consortia like GALILEO (Georgia Library Learning Online), OhioLINK, VIVA (The Virtual Library of Virginia) and SUNYConnect.

INDEST also envisages including in its collection CD-ROMs, DVDs, portal sites, content creation by scanning/digitalization. Another case study describes the building of digital resources at the Indian National Science Academy (INSA), New Delhi. The growing acceptance of digital media has resulted in libraries buying and providing access to Internet resources, acquiring CD-ROM-based data sets and providing services for standalone or networked CD-ROMs environments and digitizing documents.

It further goes on to explain these three facilities at the INSA library. Digital library services in the Indian Statistical Institute (ISI), Bangalore. According to the author, to create true digital libraries, not just digital collections, will require librarians to work closely together to create open, distributed, publicly accessible resources, as well as to establish a collaborative structure to coordinate and guide implementation. Interestingly, the digital library at ISI seems to be digital collections of consortia- based e-resources, OPAC and CD-ROM databases.

MANAGEMENT OF DIGITAL RIGHTS IN INDIA

Given the vulnerability of materials accessible over the public access networks like the Internet, issues of IPR of material over the digital domain has become a serious concern. Digital Rights Management involves ways in which the digital library operators manage issues of IPR, those of ownership of material made available on the digital library, how one controls access to as well as dissemination of copyrighted material. Several methods of managing digital rights do exist nowadays from which one could choose to adopt the more convenient one for their purposes.

Examples include, (i) charging a fee for the use of material as part of a copyright fee if that is mandatory, (ii) act as a middleman for other libraries so as not to get involved in these issues and to let the source organization deal with its IPR. For example, the TIFR online catalog provides access to the ACM Digital Library, Springer-Verlag list of publications and IEEE subscriptions. The NIT Calicut Digital Library – Nalanda also acts as an intermediary in providing access to standard international publications and journals (iii) holding restricted access to resources using user authentification method for those paid/registered users.

This can be enabled using magnetic swipe cards, biometric methods or simple online security software that pops a username/password dialog box (iv) withholding original material and sending photocopies to the addresses. Of course, this works only at a local level and also for only an automated library that provides access to its catalog online and allows requests for materials to be sent. (v) Using logos, logotypes as watermarks to protect source ownership of the materials.

CONCLUSION

Digital libraries are characterized by equitable access, reduced barrier of distance, timeliness, shared resources and content delivery. They can provide access to a large quantity of collections of primary and secondary documents. They can also support publicity and integration of new information. Besides this digital libraries offer greater opportunities for users to deposit and use information.

The digital library can also help and organize printed works in to a universal library and thus provide access to it from anywhere in the world. There is limitation of digital library in archiving and preserving of digital resources. Unlike paper media electronic media become obsolete and degraded at faster rate. Therefore long time preservation strategy is formulated to preserve digital resources for future use.

4

Distributed Data Processing (DDP)

A distributed database is a database in which portions of the database are stored on multiple computers within a network. Users have access to the portion of the database at their location so that they can access the data relevant to their tasks without interfering with the work of others.

A centralised distributed database management system (DDBMS) manages the database as if it were all stored on the same computer. The DDBMS synchronises all the data periodically and, in cases where multiple users must access the same data, ensures that updates and deletes performed on the data at one location will be automatically reflected in the data stored elsewhere.

DISTRIBUTED DATA PROCESSING (DDP)

Arrangement of networked computers in which data processing capabilities are spread across the network. In DDP, specific jobs are performed by specialised computers which may be far removed from the user and/or from other such computers. This arrangement is in contrast to 'centralised' computing in which several client computers share the same server (usually a mini or mainframe computer) or a cluster of servers. DDP provides greater scalability, but also requires more network administration resources.

BASIC BUSINESS DATA PROCESSING PRINCIPLES

The basic principles associated with business data processing relate to privacy protection. Data processing governs how a business handles consumer, client and other personal information obtained to comply with both stated and implied ethical and legal requirements. Currently, the processing of information occurs mostly on computer systems.

Limiting the Quantity and Purpose

Two of the most basic principles of data processing include making sure that the information collected pertains to a specific purpose and making sure that the business uses the collected data strictly for that purpose. This means that a business should not retain excess information on file needlessly.

Additionally, the business should not use any retained data for any reason outside the scope of the reasons the business originally collected the data. Further, a business should not keep data for any length of time beyond the data's useful purpose.

Complying with Laws

A business should also make sure that its data processing standards and practices comply with established privacy laws. This usually means staying up to date with any legislation changes relating to data processing and making sure the data itself remains up to date.

Allowing data to expire can unintentionally lead to a business creating a data history for its customers. Current laws also require businesses to make sure that all practices comply with the rights of each individual whose data the company obtains.

Transferring Data

Data processing must also consider the transfer of data. Business partnerships and mergers often result in the transfer of data. In many cases, the average consumer may not have any knowledge of this data transfer. If a company transfers data, the business must ensure that these transfers occur legally and safely.

This becomes exponentially more important in cases where a business transfers data to another country, because this generally results in less control over the information.

Securing the Information

Data protection also requires a business to make sure that the data remains secure from outside parties. Not only do these basic principles apply to the employees and decision-makers within an organisation, but to potential data miners outside of the organisation. The business has an obligation and responsibility to make sure that the information does not get into the wrong hands. As a result, businesses widely implement security systems to safeguard data.

EXPLAIN THE AUDIT PROCEDURES IN AN ELECTRONIC DATA PROCESSING AUDIT

Organisations have the challenge of dealing with employees' honesty and trustworthiness. Auditing is used to circumvent any question of integrity. An electronic data processing audit is an evaluation of the accuracy and proper function of an organisation's data processing. Organisations mainly audit the accounting department. Other areas like project management, quality management and energy conservation are also audited. Auditing ensures compliance and checks on fraud of the company's resources.

Get Electronic Data

To commence the auditing process, auditors must first retrieve the data stored in the computer. Documents such as sales receipts and supplies invoices are used to verify the data entered into the computer. This ensures that correct information was input into the computer.

Data Conversion

Organisations use different types of software to store their data. This data should be converted from the stored software to the auditing software. This is done using special software programmes known as package and utility programmes. This ensures that there is no inconsistency when auditing data stored in different software.

Compliance Test

Auditors need to verify that procedures followed when entering data into the data processing system are being applied as prescribed. These procedures act as the underlying evidence of whether the accounting data is correctly fed into the processing system. Obtaining this evidence involves reviewing the accounting journals, ledgers and worksheets. Compliance tests, which are tests used to verify the correct functioning of internal controls, are then carried out to indicate whether such internal controls are working properly. This provides the auditor with the overall picture of the truthfulness of data entered in the processing system.

Substantive Test

Auditors obtain evidence to verify the completeness, validity and accuracy of a client's records. This evidence is an important factor in determining the auditor's opinion on the records. Substantive tests in a merchandising firm would include examining inventory at the end of the period to verify that the levels of such inventory are as indicated in the records. An auditor can also request that suppliers confirm in writing the details of the debts owed by a firm at the end of the trading period.

Reporting

The main aim of an audit is to report to the client. A report should be written and signed after completing the audit examination; it also should include the auditor's opinion and the basis for it. The date of the report should also be included, along with recommendations for improvements of the entity's reporting system. Finally, reports should be objective, clear, concise and timely.

DISTRIBUTED DATABASE

A Distributed Database (BDD) is a collection of data distributed in different nodes of a network of computers. Each web site is independent, you can run local applications and at least one global application, which requires access to data located in various places, using a communication subsystem. For the design of BDDs have defined two main strategies: The Top-Down Approach and Bottom-Up. In the Top-Down approach begins designing the global schema, then sees the fragmentation of the database and the location of the fragments at the sites. Running is completed at each site, the physical design of the data. On the other hand, the Bottom-Up approach is based on schema integration and a global schema created from the existing BD.

Systems Distributed Database naturally represent more geographically decentralised structure of an organisation, increase data availability, reduce communication traffic and defensible, moreover, by the lowering of costs in equipment and communications infrastructure computer networks. The design of Distributed Database design phases has centralised and also has two new problems that characterise the data distribution process, and include determining: how to split the database to locate components in different sites, how much data should be replicated and how they should be located replicated fragments.

There are several definitions of what a distributed system but there are differences between them, for our purposes it is sufficient to say that a distributed system is a collection of independent computers interconnected displayed to users of the system as a single computer.

ADVANTAGES AND DISADVANTAGES OF DISTRIBUTED SYSTEMS

Advantages

- Access to data is faster because the data is located closest to where they are used.
- The processing is fast because a number of nodes involved in processing a workload
- New nodes can be added quickly and easily.
- The probability that a fault in one node affects the system is low and there is autonomy and independence among the nodes.
- Local control of data with which it interacts.
- Increased fault tolerance.

Disadvantages

- It is more difficult to control and manipulation of data
- Is complex ensuring the integrity of the information in the presence of unpredictable failures of both hardware and software. Integrity refers to the consistency, validity and accuracy of the information.
- Concurrency control and recovery mechanisms are much more complex than in a centralised system because the data can be replicated.

The distribution of the database required to determine the fragmentation and localisation. Fragmentation is the process of dividing a relation into smaller fragments called. The main reasons for the fragmentation is the increase in the level of competition and performance of the system. There are two alternatives for data fragmentation: horizontal fragmentation (FH) and vertical fragmentation (VF). The combination of the above results in a hybrid fragmentation. It is important to follow three rules, which ensure that the BD has no semantic changes during fragmentation: completeness, reconstruction and disjuntura.

MANAGEMENT SYSTEM DISTRIBUTED DATABASE

A management system of distributed databases (SGBDD) is a management system that manages databases distributed DB.

Additional Features of a SGBDD

- Access to remote sites and transmit queries and data across multiple sites through a communication network.
- Stores the scheme of distribution and replication of data in the system catalogue.
- Establish implementation strategies of consultation and the transactions that access data in more than one site.
- Decide on which copies of replicated data access.
- Maintain consistency of replicated data copies.
- Perform recovery from failures.

The BDD can be:

- *Homogeneous*: All sites have the same DBMS, are aware of the existence of other sites and cooperate in processing applications. Local sites maintain the same schema and DBMS.
- *Heterogeneous*: Each site can have a different DBMSs and different schemas. Maybe some other sites do not know. It may only offer limited facilities for cooperation in transaction processing.

Solve Fundamental Problems in Distributed Databases

- Design of distributed databases
- Query processing and optimisation
- Transaction management and concurrency control.

Design Stages

The differentiator between the design stage of a centralised database and distributed database is the "Design of distribution" that consists of two activities:

- *Fragmentation*: Decide "and" split the database and "that" parts.
- *Assignment*: Decide "where" each party are located, and whether we will have data replication.

Issues to Consider in Designing a Distributed BD

- *Fragmentation*: A relationship can be divided into a number of sub-relations, called fragments, which are then distributed
- *Assignment*: Each fragment must be stored in a site based on an optimal distribution.
- *Replication*: The SGBDD can keep a copy of a fragment in different sites.

FRAGMENTATION

The fragmentation problem concerns the partitioning of information to distribute each part to different web sites.

Objectives of the Fragmentation

The purpose of fragmentation is to divide the relationship into a set of smaller relations such that some user applications only make use of a fragment. In this framework, an optimal fragmentation is one that produces a type of division that minimizes the execution time of applications using these fragments. The ideal drive fragmentation is not the table but a subdivision thereof.

This is because:

- Applications using views defined on multiple relationships, that is, formed from "pieces" of several tables. If we can view each of the subtables is defined on local (or failing that the most "close" as possible) to each application, we expect an increase in performance.
- If multiple views of different applications are defined on a table is not fragmented, we have:
- If the table is not replicated then there is traffic generation for remote access.
- If the table is replicated in all or some of the places where they live each of the applications then needless traffic generation caused by the need to update your copies.

Advantages

Decomposing a relation into fragments (distribution units):

- We allow concurrent processing of transactions and are not locking entire tables but subtables, so that two queries can access the same table to different fragments.
- We allow parallelisation of queries to be breaking them down into subqueries, each of which works with a different fragment thus increasing performance.

Disadvantages

- Performance degradation defined views on several fragments located in different places (you need to perform operations on those bits which is expensive)

- The semantic control is difficult and the performance degrades due to the verification of integrity constraints (foreign keys, uniques, etc.) search involving fragments from multiple sites.

Therefore division and location of the fragments is not trivial.

For a fragmentation of a relationship is correct must meet the following conditions:

- *Condition of completeness.* The decomposition of a relation R into fragments $R_1, R_2, \ldots, R_n$ is complete if and only if each data element in R is found in some of the fragments R_i
- *Status of Reconstruction.* If relation R is decomposition into fragments $R_1, R_2, \ldots, R_n$ then there should exist some relational operation V such that $R = V_{1 \leq i \leq n} R_i$
- *Condition of disjointed fragments.* If the relation R is decomposed into fragments $R_1, R_2, \ldots R_n$, and R_j is d_i figure, then, should not be in any other parts R_k ($k \neq J$).

Horizontal Fragmentation

Horizontal fragmentation of a relation R produces a series of fragments $R_1, R_2, \ldots, R_r$, each of which contains a subset of the tuples of R that satisfy certain properties (predicates).

Primary and Derived Horizontal Fragmentation

Primary Horizontal Fragmentation (PHF) of a relationship is obtained using predicates that are defined in the relationship. Derived Horizontal Fragmentation (DHF) on the other hand, is the partitioning of a relationship as a result of predicates that are defined in another relationship.

Vertical Fragmentation

The vertical fragmentation of a relation R produces a series of fragments $R_1, R_2, \ldots, R_r$ each of which contains a subset of the attributes of R and the primary key of R.

Vertical Fragmentation Complexity

Vertical fragmentation is more complicated than horizontal. In the vertical case, if a relationship has m non-primary key attributes, the number of possible fragments is equal to B (m), *i.e.* the m-th Bell number. For large values of m, B (m) (mm, for example, for m = 10, B (m) (115,000, for m = 15, B (m) (109, for m = 30, B (m) = 1023.

These values indicate that obtaining an optimal solution of vertical fragmentation is an impossible task, but we rely on the use of heuristics.

The Problem of Allocation of Fragments

Assume that a set of fragments $F = \{F_1, F_2, \ldots F_n\}$ and a network consisting of sites $S = \{S_1, S_2, \ldots, S_m\}$ in which a set $Q = \{q_1, q_2, \ldots, q_q\}$ query to be executed.

The assignment problem is to determine the distribution of "optimal" in S.F. *Optimality can be defined according to two measures:*

- Minimum cost. Consists of the cost of data communication, storage cost and processing cost (reads and updates to each fragment). The allocation problem is to find an allocation scheme or location that minimizes the combined cost function.

Performance: The allocation strategy is designed to maintain a performance metric. The two most commonly used metrics are response time and the "throughput" (number of jobs processed per unit time).

ALLOCATION OF FRAGMENTS

Assignment

Process by which you decide where you placed the fragments of the previous stage and if you make replicas of them. *Making sense of replicas:*

- *Reliability*: Increased security against data loss
- *Availability*: Increased fault tolerance with computers falls
- *Increased parallelism*: Increased efficiency in reading queries by enabling its decomposition into subqueries and parallelising them.

But has the drawbacks of writing queries, which involve the updating of all copies of the network.

In practice: reading vs. writing Weighing:

- More reads than writes: Replication is a good idea
- Plus scripts that read: Do not replicate.

Depending on the degree of replication, we distinguish between:

- BD fragmented, disjointed fragments, each node (no replicas)
- Fully replicated BD: It is a copy of all the BD in each node
- Partially replicated BD: Mix the above. Some fragments are replicated.

As is the fragmentation and replication techniques are combined in practice.

Replication of Fragments

The problem of replication of segments consists of determining allocation of fragments to be replicated in different sites despite the problems associated with the upgrade.

The 12 Rules of SGBDD

The fundamental principle of Distributed Database zero or rule states that: "From a user standpoint, a distributed system must be identical to a non-distributed". The zero rule leads to the remaining 12 rules. All the rules are not independent of each other or are of equal importance but are useful for understanding the distributed technology.

- *Local Autonomy*: The sites of a distributed system must be autonomous.

Local Autonomy implies:

- Local owner.
- Local government.
- Local responsibility.
- Local integration.
- Local representation.

- No dependence on a central site.

There should be a single site, since, it would involve:

- Bottleneck.
- Vulnerability.

- Continuous operation.
  - Add Items
  - Updated versions.
- Independence Location.

The user does not know where they are physically the data.

- Independence fragmentation. Desirable because it simplifies the user programmes and activities in the terminal.
- Independence reply. The creation and destruction of replicas should be made transparent to the user.

The replica provides:

Advantages:

- Increased Performance: the data is local.
- Increased availability: data is always accessible.

Disadvantages:

- You must propagate the updates.

- *Distributed Query Processing:*
  - The relational systems provide highly efficient query tools.
  - Several ways to transfer data
- *Distributed Transaction Management:*
  - Distributed Transaction: the transaction number of agents in various places.
  - Control of recovery: an atomic transaction. All agents advance or retreat together.
  - Concurrency Control: Locking by passing messages.
- *Independence from team:*
  - The DBMS will execute as whatever the team.
- *Independence from OS.*
  - The DBMS must be multi-operating without affecting the user.
- *Independence from the Network.*
  - The DBMS must support multiple networks without affecting the user.

DISTRIBUTED DATABASE SYSTEM (DDBMSS)

Recent years have witnessed an increasing trend in the implementation of distributed database management systems (DDBMSs) for more effective access to information. An important quality of these systems, consisting of n servers loosely connected via a communication network, is to adjust to changes in workloads. To service increases in demand, for example, additional servers may be added to the existing distributed system and new data allocations computed. Conventionally, this requires a system shutdown and an exhaustive data reallocation. Such static methods are not practical for most organisations for these methods result in high costs and in periods of data unavailability.

We present the incremental growth framework to address incremental expansion of distributed database systems. Data is reallocated using one of two data reallocation heuristics—Partial REALLOCATE or Full REALLOCATE. Both heuristics are greedy, hill-climbing algorithms that compute new data allocation based on the specified optimisation parameter of the objective cost function. Due to their linear complexity, both heuristics can be used to solve both small and large complex problems, based on organisational needs.

The REALLOCATE algorithms in conjunction with the SimDDBMS simulator can be used to answer many practical questions in distributed database systems. For example, in order to improve system response time, a database administrator (DBA) may use SimDDBMS for parametric evaluation. For example, the DBA may analyse the effect of upgrading CPU processing capability, increasing network transfer speed, or adding additional servers into the distributed database system. Furthermore, SimDDBMS may easily be modified to evaluate heterogeneous servers with different CPU processing capabilities. A DBA may also use SimDDBMS to determine the impact and cost-benefit analysis of adding some number,s [is greater than or equal to] 1, additional servers at one time.

BACKGROUND

Following the pioneering work in Porcar (1982), many researchers have studied the file or data allocation problem. Since, optimal search methods can only be used for small problems, heuristic methods are often used for solving large data allocation problems. Researchers have studied both the static data allocation problem, in which data allocations do not change over time, and the dynamic data allocation problem, which may be adaptive or non-adaptive.

Adaptive models are implemented when the system senses a substantial deviation in access activities; these models determine a one-time reallocation (for a relatively short period of time) in response to surges in demand. For example, the volume of reservations for a particular airline route may increase during a specific season.

Therefore, an airline reservation system may temporarily store additional copies of the files associated with the route at a local server. However, this is a short-term situation, which is resolved by introducing replicated file copies. Non-adaptive models are employed at the initial system design stage or upon system reorganisation; these models do not adjust to variations in system activities.

Most previous research on data allocation assumes a fixed number of servers in the distributed database system. Experiments and simulations are designed to test DDBMS factors such as the degree of data replication, workloads per server, and different levels and classes of queries and transactions. Simulation runs vary the number of servers to arbitrary values. However, these values are fixed per run and vary only between runs.

Incremental Growth Framework

The incremental growth framework is invoked when system performance, as computed using the objective cost function, is below the acceptable threshold (specified by the DBA). To return to an acceptable state, new servers are introduced incrementally, one at a time, into the distributed database system. With the introduction of each new server, a new data reallocation for the system is computed.

This process is iteratively executed until acceptable performance is achieved or the number of servers equals the number of relations in the distributed database system (the latter constraint can easily be relaxed in a distributed database system housing partitioned data). The incremental growth framework, which can easily be adapted for one-server or multiple-server systems, can be used by small, midsize, and large organisations, each having distributed database systems of varying size. In one-server systems, the initial data allocation locates all relations at the server. In multiple-server systems, the current data allocation is required as input into the framework. Additional input information required for the incremental growth framework includes: the database server or servers, including the local processing capacity; the network topology, including transmission capacity; the database relations, including relation sizes and selectivities; the query set; the optimisation parameter; and the acceptable threshold for the optimisation parameter.

ORACLE'S DISTRIBUTED DATABASE ARCHITECTURE

A *distributed database* is a set of databases stored on multiple computers that typically appears to applications as a single database. Consequently, an application can simultaneously access and modify the data in several databases in a network. Each Oracle database in the system is controlled by its local Oracle server but cooperates to maintain the consistency of the global distributed database.

CLIENTS AND SERVERS

A database *server* is the Oracle software managing a database, and a *client* is an application that requests information from a server. Each computer in a system is a *node*. A node in a distributed database system act as a client, a server, or both, depending on the situation. The computer that manages the HQ database is acting as a database server when a statement is issued against its local data, and is acting as a client when it issues a statement against remote data.

Direct and Indirect Connections

A client can connect directly or indirectly to a database server. The client application issues the first and third statements for each transaction, the client is connected directly to the intermediate HQ database and indirectly to the SALES database that contains the remote data.

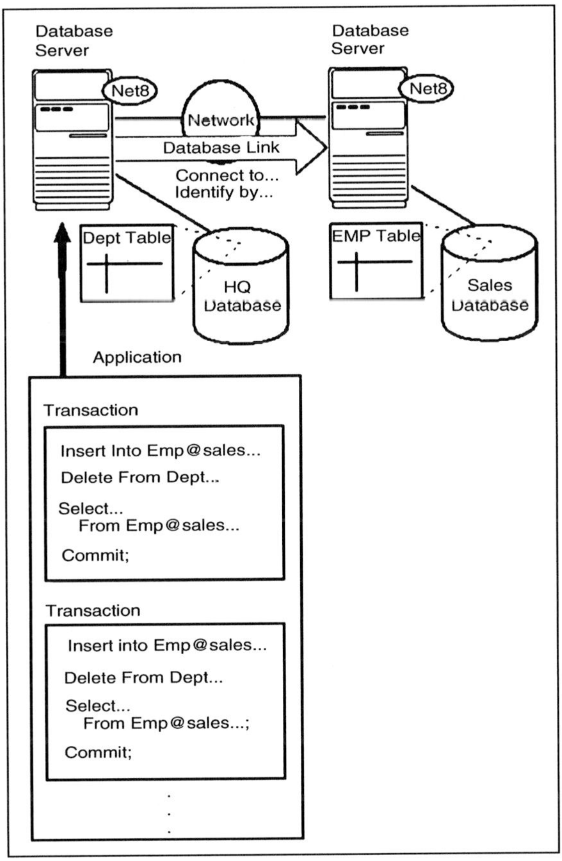

Fig. An Oracle Distributed Database System.

The Network

To link the individual databases of a distributed database system, a network is necessary. The explain more about network issues in an Oracle distributed database system.

Net8

All Oracle databases in a distributed database system use Oracle's networking software, Net8, to facilitate inter-database communication across a network. Just as Net8 connects clients and servers that operate on different computers of a network, it also allows database servers to communicate across networks to support remote and distributed transactions in a distributed database. Net8 makes transparent the connectivity that is necessary to transmit SQL requests and receive data for applications that use the system. Net8 takes SQL statements from a client and packages them for transmission to an Oracle server over a supported industry-standard communication protocol or programmatic interfaces. Net8 also takes replies from a server and packages them for transmission back to the appropriate client. Net8 performs all processing independent of an underlying network operating system.

Oracle Names

Optionally, an Oracle network can use Oracle Names to provide the system with a global directory service. When an Oracle network supports a distributed database system, you can use Oracle Names servers as a central repositories of information about each database in the system to ease the configuration of distributed database access.

DATABASES AND DATABASE LINKS

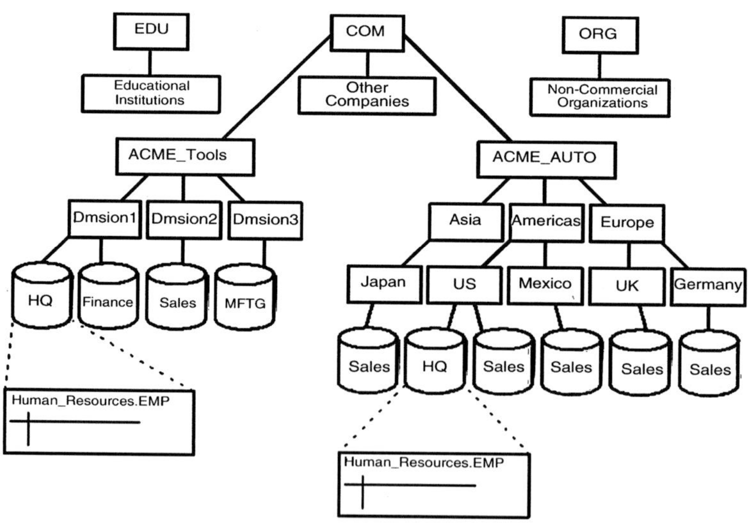

Fig. Network Directories and Global Database Names.

Each database in a distributed database is distinct from all other databases in the system and has its own *global database name*. Oracle forms a database's global database name by prefixing the database's network domain with the individual database's name. A representative hierarchical arrangement of databases throughout a network.

While several database's can have the same individual name, each database must have a unique global database name. For example, the network domains US.AMERICAS.ACME_ AUTO.COM and UK.EUROPE.ACME_ AUTO.COM each contain a SALES database.

```
SALES.US.AMERICAS.ACME_AUTO.COM
SALES.UK.EUROPE.ACME_AUTO.COM
```

Database Links

To facilitate application requests in a distributed database system, Oracle uses *database links*. A database link defines a one-way communication path from an Oracle database to another database. Database links are essentially transparent to the users of an Oracle distributed database system, because the name of a database link is the same as the global name of the database to which the link points. For example, the following SQL statement creates a database link in the local database that describes a path to the remote SALES.US.AMERICAS.ACME_AUTO.COM database.

```
CREATE DATABASE LINK sales.us.americas.acme_auto. com...;
```

After creating a database link, applications connected to the local database can access data in the remote SALES.US.AMERICAS.ACME_AUTO.COM database. The explains how applications can reference remote schema objects in a distributed database and includes examples of how SQL statements use database links.

Schema Object Name Resolution

To resolve application references to schema objects (a process called *name resolution*) Oracle forms object names using a hierarchical approach. For example, within a single database, Oracle guarantees that each schema has a unique name, and that within a schema, each object has a unique name. As a result, a schema object's name is always unique within the database. Furthermore, Oracle can easily resolve application references to an object's local name.

In a distributed database, a schema object such as a table is accessible to all applications in the system. Oracle simply extends the hierarchical naming model with global database names to effectively create *global object names* and resolve references to the schema objects in a distributed database system. For example, a query can reference a remote table by specifying its fully qualified name, including the database in which it resides.

```
SELECT * FROM scott.emp@sales.us.americas.acme _auto.com;
```

To complete the request, the local database server implicitly uses a database link that connects to the remote SALES database.

Connecting Between Oracle Server Versions

An Oracle distributed database system can incorporate Oracle databases of different versions. All supported releases of Oracle can participate in a distributed database system. However, the applications that work with the distributed database must understand the functionality that is available at each node in the system. For example, a distributed database application cannot expect an Oracle7 database to understand the object SQL extensions that are available with Oracle8*i*.

DISTRIBUTED DATABASES AND DISTRIBUTED PROCESSING

The terms "distributed database" and "distributed processing" are closely related, but have very distinct meanings.

Distributed Database	A distributed database is a set of databases stored on multiple computers that appears to applications as a single database.
Distributed Processing	Distributed processing occurs when an application system distributes its tasks among different computers in a network. For example, a database application typically distributes front-end presentation tasks to client PCs or NCs and allows a back-end database server to manage shared access to a database. Consequently, a distributed database application processing system is more commonly referred to as a "client-server" database application system.

Oracle distributed database systems employ a distributed processing architecture to function. For example, an Oracle server acts as a client when it requests data that another Oracle server manages.

Distributed Databases and Database Replication

The terms "distributed database" and "database replication" are also closely related, yet different. In a pure distributed database, the system manages a single copy of all data and supporting database objects. Distributed database applications typically use distributed transactions to access both local and remote data and modify the global database in real-time.

Replication is the process of copying and maintaining database objects in multiple databases that make up a distributed database system. While replication relies on distributed database technology to function, database replication can offer applications benefits that are not possible within a pure distributed database environment. Most commonly, replication is useful to improve the performance and protect the availability of applications because alternate data access options exist. For example, an application might normally access a local database rather than a remote server to minimize network traffic and achieve maximum performance. Furthermore, the application can continue to function if the local server experiences a failure, but other servers with replicated data remain accessible.

HETEROGENEOUS DISTRIBUTED DATABASES

In an Oracle *heterogeneous distributed database system* at least one of the database systems is a non-Oracle system. To the application, the heterogeneous distributed database system appears as a single, local, Oracle database; the local Oracle server will be able to hide the distribution and heterogeneity of the data. The Oracle server accesses the non-Oracle system using Oracle8*i* Heterogeneous Services and a non-Oracle system-specific Heterogeneous Services Agent.

HETEROGENEOUS SERVICES

Heterogeneous Services is an integrated component within the Oracle8*i* server and the enabling technology for Oracle's next generation of Open Gateway products. Heterogeneous Services provides the common architecture and administration mechanisms for future Oracle gateway products and other heterogeneous access facilities, while providing upwardly compatible functionality for users of earlier Oracle Open Gateway releases.

Heterogeneous Services Agents

For each non-Oracle system that you want to access, Heterogeneous Services requires an *agent* to access that particular non-Oracle system. The Heterogeneous Services agent communicates with the non-Oracle system, and with the Heterogeneous Services component in the Oracle server. On behalf of the Oracle server, the agent executes SQL, procedure, and transactional requests at the non-Oracle system. A version 8 Gateway is the Oracle product name for a Heterogeneous Services agent that accesses a non-Oracle system procedurally or using SQL. However, Heterogeneous Services agents will also become available as products other than Oracle Transparent Gateways or Oracle Procedural Gateways. Throughout this guide we will use the more generic term Heterogeneous Services agents. If you purchased an Oracle Open Gateway version 8, you can substitute "Oracle Gateway version 8" for Heterogeneous Services Agent.

Features

The features of the Heterogeneous Services include:

- *Distributed Transactions.* A transaction can span both Oracle and non-Oracle systems, while still guaranteeing, through Oracle's two phase commit mechanism, that changes are either all committed or all rolled back.
- *Transparent SQL access.* Integrate data from non-Oracle systems into

the Oracle environment as if the data is stored in one single, local database. SQL statements issued by the application are transparently transformed into SQL statement understood by the non-Oracle system.

- *Procedural Access.* Procedural systems, like messaging and queuing systems, are accessed from an Oracle8*i* server using PL/SQL remote procedure calls.
- *Data Dictionary translations.* To make the non-Oracle system appear as another Oracle server, SQL statements containing references to Oracle's data dictionary tables are transformed into SQL statements containing references to a non-Oracle system's data dictionary tables.
- *Pass-through SQL.* Optionally, application programmers can directly access a non-Oracle system from an Oracle application using the non-Oracle system's SQL dialect.
- *Accessing stored procedures.* Stored procedures in SQL-based non-Oracle systems are accessed as if they were PL/SQL remote procedures.
- *National Language Support.* Heterogeneous Services supports multi-byte character sets, and translate character sets between a non-Oracle system and the Oracle8*i* server.
- Multi-Threaded Agents. Multi-threaded agents take advantage of your operating system's thread in capabilities. Multi-threaded agents reduce the number of required processes by taking advantage of multi-threaded server capabilities.
- Agent Self-Registration. Agent self-registration automates the process of updating Heterogeneous Services configuration data on remote hosts, ensuring correct operation over heterogeneous database links.
- Management Interface. Provides a graphic representation of active Heterogeneous Services agents and of which user sessions are accessing those agents.

DEVELOPING DISTRIBUTED DATABASE APPLICATIONS

When you build applications on top of a distributed database system, there are several issues to consider. The explain how applications access data in a distributed database.

DISTRIBUTED QUERY OPTIMISATION

Distributed query optimisation is a default Oracle8*i* feature that reduces the amount of data transfer required between sites when you retrieve data from remote tables referenced in distributed SQL statements. Distributed query optimisation uses Oracle's cost-based optimiser to find or generate SQL expressions that extract only the necessary data from remote tables, process that data at a remote site, and send the results back to the local site for final processing. This reduces the amount of required data transfer, when compared to transferring all the table data to the local site for processing. Using cost-based optimiser hints, such as DRIVING_SITE, NO_MERGE, and INDEX hints, you can further control where Oracle processes the data and how it accesses the data.

REMOTE AND DISTRIBUTED SQL STATEMENTS

A *remote query* is a query that selects information from one or more remote tables, all of which reside at the same remote node. For example:

```
SELECT * FROM scott.dept@sales.us.americas.acme _auto.com;
```

A *remote update* is an update that modifies data in one or more tables, all of which are located at the same remote node.

For example:

```
UPDATE scott.dept@sales.us.americas.acme_auto.com
    SET loc = 'NEW YORK'
    WHERE deptno = 10;
```

A *distributed query* retrieves information from two or more nodes. For example:

```
SELECT ename, dname
    FROM scott.emp e, scott.dept@sales.us.americas.acme
    _auto.com d
    WHERE e.deptno = d.deptno;
```

A *distributed update* modifies data on two or more nodes. A distributed update is possible using a PL/SQL subprogram unit, such as a procedure or trigger, that includes two or more remote updates that access data on different nodes. For example:

```
BEGIN
    UPDATE scott.dept@sales.us.americas.acme_auto.com
      SET loc = 'NEW YORK'
      WHERE deptno = 10;
    UPDATE scott.emp
      SET deptno = 11
      WHERE deptno = 10;
END;
```

Statements in the programme are sent to the remote nodes, and the execution of it succeeds or fails as a unit.

Remote Procedure Calls (RPCs)

Developers can code PL/SQL packages and procedures to support applications that work with a distributed database. Applications can make local procedure calls to perform work at the local database and *remote procedure calls (RPCs)* to perform work at a remote database. When a programme calls a remote procedure, the local server passes all procedure parameters to the remote server in the call. For example:

```
BEGIN
emp_mgmt.del_emp@sales.us.americas.acme_auto.com(1257);
END;
```

When developing packages and procedures for distributed database systems, developers must code with an understanding of what programme units should do at remote locations, and how to return the results to a calling application.

Remote and Distributed Transactions

A *remote transaction* is a transaction that contains one or more remote statements, all of which reference the same remote node. For example:

```
UPDATE  scott.dept@sales.us.americas.acme_auto.com
    SET loc = 'NEW YORK'
    WHERE deptno = 10;
UPDATE  scott.emp@sales.us.americas.acme_auto.com
    SET deptno = 11
    WHERE deptno = 10;
COMMIT;
```

A *distributed transaction* is a transaction that includes one or more statements that, individually or as a group, update data on two or more distinct nodes of a distributed database. For example:

```
UPDATE  scott.dept@sales.us.americas.acme_auto.com
    SET loc = 'NEW YORK'
    WHERE deptno = 10;
UPDATE  scott.emp
    SET deptno = 11
    WHERE deptno = 10;
COMMIT;
```

Two-Phase Commit Mechanism

A DBMS must guarantee that all statements in a transaction, distributed or non-distributed, either commit or rollback as a unit, so that if the transaction is designed properly, the data in the logical database is always consistent. The effects of an ongoing transaction should be invisible to all other transactions at all nodes; this should be true for transactions that include any type of operation, including queries, updates, or remote procedure calls.

The general mechanisms of transaction control in a non-distributed database. In a distributed database, Oracle must coordinate transaction control with the same characteristics over a network and maintain data consistency, even if a network or system failure occurs.

Oracle's *two-phase commit* mechanism guarantees that *all* database servers participating in a distributed transaction either all commit or all roll back the statements in the transaction. A two-phase commit mechanism also protects implicit DML operations performed by integrity constraints, remote procedure calls, and triggers.

TRANSPARENCY IN A DISTRIBUTED DATABASE SYSTEM

With minimal effort, you can make the functionality of an Oracle distributed database system transparent to users that work with the system. The goal of transparency is to make a distributed database system appear as though it is a single Oracle database. Consequently, the system does not burden developers and users of the system with complexities that would otherwise make distributed database application development challenging and detract from user productivity. The explain more about transparency in a distributed database system.

Location Transparency

An Oracle distributed database system has features that allow application developers and administrators to hide the physical location of database objects from applications and users. *Location transparency* exists when a user can universally refer to a database object such as a table, regardless of the node to which an application connects.

Location transparency has several benefits, including:

- Access to remote data is simple, because database users do not need to know the physical location of database objects.
- Administrators can move database objects with no impact on end-users or existing database applications.

Most typically, administrators and developers use synonyms to establish location transparency for the tables and supporting objects in an application schema.

For example, the following statements create synonyms in a database for tables in another, remote database.

```
CREATE PUBLIC SYNONYM emp
  FOR scott.emp@sales.us.americas.acme_auto.com
CREATE PUBLIC SYNONYM dept
  FOR scott.dept@sales.us.americas.acme_auto.com
```

Now, rather than access the remote tables with a query such as:

```
SELECT ename, dname
  FROM scott.emp@sales.us.americas.acme_auto.com e,
       scott.dept@sales.us.americas.acme_auto.com d
  WHERE e.deptno = d.deptno;
```

an application can issue a much simpler query that does not have to account for the location of the remote tables.

```
SELECT ename, dname
  FROM emp e, dept d
  WHERE e.deptno = d.deptno;
```

In addition to synonyms, developers can also use views and stored procedures to establish location transparency for applications that work in a distributed database system.

Statement and Transaction Transparency

Oracle's distributed database architecture also provides query, update, and transaction transparency. For example, standard SQL commands such as SELECT, INSERT, UPDATE, and DELETE work just as they do in a non-distributed database environment. Additionally, applications control transactions using the standard SQL commands COMMIT, SAVEPOINT, and ROLLBACK—there is no requirement for complex programming or other special operations to provide distributed transaction control.

- The statements in a single transaction can reference any number of local or remote tables.
- Oracle guarantees that all nodes involved in a distributed transaction take the same action: they either all commit or all roll back the transaction.
- If a network or system failure occurs during the commit of a distributed transaction, the transaction is automatically and transparently resolved globally; that is, when the network or system is restored, the nodes either all commit or all roll back the transaction.

Internal Operations

Each committed transaction has an associated *system change number* (*SCN*) to uniquely identify the changes made by the statements within that transaction.

In a distributed database, the SCNs of communicating nodes are coordinated when:

- A connection is established using the path described by one or more database links.
- A distributed SQL statement is executed.
- A distributed transaction is committed.

Among other benefits, the coordination of SCNs among the nodes of a distributed database system allows global distributed read-consistency at both the statement and transaction level. If necessary, global distributed time-based recovery can also be completed.

Replication Transparency

Oracle also provide many features to transparently replicate data among the nodes of the system.

ADMINISTERING AN ORACLE DISTRIBUTED DATABASE SYSTEM

Just as there are unique issues to consider when developing applications for an Oracle distributed database system, there are special issues to understand for distributed database administration. The explain the some special topics for managing databases in an Oracle distributed database system.

Site Autonomy

Site autonomy means that each server participating in a distributed database is administered independently from all other databases, as though each database operates as a non-distributed database. Although several databases can work together, each database is a distinct, separate repository of data that you manage individually.

Some of the benefits of site autonomy in an Oracle distributed database include:

- Nodes of the system can mirror the logical organisation of companies or cooperating organisations that need to maintain an "arms length" relationship.
- Local database administrators control corresponding local data. Therefore, each database administrator's domain of responsibility is smaller and more manageable.
- Independent failures are less likely to disrupt other nodes of the distributed database. The global Oracle database is partially available as long as one database and the network are available; no single database failure need halt all global operations or be a performance bottleneck.
- Administrators can recovery from isolated system failures independent of other nodes in the system.
- A data dictionary exists for each local database—a global catalogue is not necessary to access local data.
- Nodes can upgrade software independently.

Although Oracle allows you to manage each database in a distributed database system independently, that is not to say that you should ignore the global requirements of the system. For example, additional user accounts might be necessary in each database are necessary to support the links that you create to facilitate server-to-server connections. The explain more about these particular topics and demonstrate the need for a global perspective of the entire distributed database environment when managing individual nodes in the system.

Distributed Database Security

Oracle supports all of the security features that are available with a non-distributed database environment for distributed database systems, including:

- Password or external service authentication for users and roles
- Login packet encryption for client-to-server and server-to-server connections.

The explain some additional topics to consider when configuring an Oracle distributed database system.

Supporting User Accounts and Roles

In a distributed database system, you must carefully plan the user accounts and roles that are necessary to support applications using the system.

- The user accounts necessary to establish server-to-server connections must be available in all databases of the distributed database system.
- The roles necessary to make available application privileges to distributed database application users must be present in all databases of the distributed database system.

Global Users and Roles

In a distributed environment, users typically require access to many network services.

When it's necessary to configure separate authentications for each user to access each network service, security administration can become unwieldy, especially for large systems. The use of a global authentication service is a common technique for simplifying security management for distributed environments.

In an Oracle client/server or distributed database environment, you have two options to support global authentication for users and roles:

- Oracle Security Server is a product that supports centralised authentication and distributed authentication in an Oracle network.
- When global database user and role authentication must work within the framework of a non-Oracle authentication service (for example, DCE), an Oracle distributed database environment can use Net8's Advanced Networking Option. The Net8 Advanced Networking Option is an optional product that bundles a number of features that you can use to enhance Net8 and the security of an Oracle distributed database system.

Data Encryption

The Net8 Advanced Networking Option also enables Net8 and related products to use network data encryption and checksumming so that data cannot be read or altered. It protects data from unauthorised viewing by using the RSA Data Security RC4 or the Data Encryption Standard (DES) encryption algorithm.

To ensure that data has not been modified, deleted, or replayed during transmission, the security services of the Advanced Networking Option can generate a cryptographically secure message digest and include it with each packet sent across the network.

TOOLS FOR ADMINISTERING ORACLE DISTRIBUTED DATABASES

The database administrator has several choices for tools to use when managing an Oracle distributed database system:

- Oracle Enterprise Manager
- third-party administration tools
- SNMP support.

Enterprise Manager

Enterprise Manager is Oracle's database administration tool. The graphical component of Enterprise Manager (Enterprise Manager/GUI) allows you to perform database administration tasks with the convenience of a graphical user interface (GUI).

The line mode component of Enterprise Manager provides a line-mode interface.

Enterprise Manager provides administrative functionality via an easy-to-use interface. You can use Enterprise Manager to:

- Perform traditional administrative tasks, such as database startup, shutdown, backup, and recovery. Rather than manually entering the SQL commands to perform these tasks, you can use Enterprise Manager's graphical interface to execute the commands quickly and conveniently by pointing and clicking with the mouse.
- Concurrently perform multiple tasks. Because you can open multiple windows simultaneously in Enterprise Manager, you can perform multiple administrative and non-administrative tasks concurrently.
- Administer multiple databases. You can use Enterprise Manager to administer a single database or to simultaneously administer multiple databases.
- Centralise database administration tasks. You can administer both local and remote databases running on any Oracle platform in any location worldwide. In addition, these Oracle platforms can be connected by any network protocol(s) supported by Net8.
- Dynamically execute SQL, PL/SQL, and Enterprise Manager commands. You can use Enterprise Manager to enter, edit, and execute statements. Enterprise Manager also maintains a history of statements executed.

Thus, you can re-execute statements without retyping them, a particularly useful feature if you need to execute lengthy statements repeatedly in a distributed database system.

- Perform administrative tasks using Enterprise Manager's line-mode interface when a graphical user interface is unavailable or undesirable.

Third-Party Administration Tools

Currently more than 60 companies produce more than 150 products that help manage Oracle databases and networks, providing a truly open environment.

SNMP Support

Besides its network administration capabilities, Oracle *Simple Network Management Protocol (SNMP)* support allows an Oracle server to be located and queried by any SNMP-based network management system.

SNMP is the accepted standard underlying many popular network management systems such as:

- HP's OpenView
- Digital's POLYCENTER Manager on NetView
- IBM's NetView/6000
- Novell's NetWare Management System
- SunSoft's SunNet Manager.

FACTORS AFFECTING THE DISTRIBUTION OF AN APPLICATION'S DATA

In a distributed database environment, you should coordinate with the database administrator to determine the best location for the data.

Some issues to consider are:

- Number of transactions posted from each location
- Amount of data (portion of table) used by each node
- Performance characteristics and reliability of the network
- Speed of various nodes, capacities of disks
- Importance of a node or link when it is unavailable
- Need for referential integrity among tables

CONTROLLING CONNECTIONS ESTABLISHED BY DATABASE LINKS

When a global object name is referenced in a SQL statement or remote procedure call, database links establish a connection to a session in the remote database on behalf of the local user. The remote connection and session are only created if the connection has not already been established previously for the local user session.

The connections and sessions established to remote databases persist for the duration of the local user's session, unless the application (or user) explicitly terminates them. Terminating remote connections established using database links is useful for disconnecting high cost connections (such as long distance phone connections) that are no longer required by the application. The application developer or user can close (terminate) a remote connection and session using the ALTER SESSION command with the CLOSE DATABASE LINK parameter. For example, assume you issue the following query:

```
SELECT * FROM emp@sales;
COMMIT;
```

The following statement terminates the session in the remote database pointed to by the SALES database link:

```
ALTER SESSION CLOSE DATABASE LINK sales;
```

To close a database link connection in your user session, you must have the ALTER SESSION system privilege.

REFERENTIAL INTEGRITY IN A DISTRIBUTED SYSTEM

Oracle does not permit declarative referential integrity constraints to be defined across nodes of a distributed system (that is, a declarative referential integrity constraint on one table cannot specify a foreign key that references a primary or unique key of a remote table). However, parent/child table relationships across nodes can be maintained using triggers.

For example, assume that the child table is in the SALES database and the parent table is in the HQ database. If the network connection between the two databases fails, some DML statements against the child table (those that insert rows into the child table or update a foreign key value in the child table) cannot proceed because the referential integrity triggers must have access to the parent table in the HQ database.

DISTRIBUTED QUERIES

A distributed query is decomposed by the local Oracle into a corresponding number of remote queries, which are sent to the remote nodes for execution. The remote nodes execute the queries and send the results back to the local node. The local node then performs any necessary post-processing and returns the results to the user or application.

If a portion of a distributed statement fails, for example, due to an integrity constraint violation, Oracle returns error number ORA-02055. Subsequent statements or procedure calls return error number ORA-02067 until a rollback or rollback to savepoint is issued.

You should design your application to check for any returned error messages that indicate that a portion of the distributed update has failed. If you detect a failure, you should rollback the entire transaction (or rollback to a savepoint) before allowing the application to proceed.

Tuning Distributed Queries

The most effective way of optimising your distributed queries is to access the remote database(s) as little as possible and to retrieve only the required data. Specifically, if you reference 5 remote tables from two different remote databases in a distributed query and have a complex filter (*e.g.*, WHERE r1.salary + r2.salary > 50000), you can improve the performance of the query by rewriting the query to access the remote databases once and to apply the filter at the remote site (causing less data to be transferred to the query execution site). Rewriting your query to access the remote database once is achieved by using collocated inline views.

With the above information in mind, the following terms need to be defined:

- *Collocated*: Two or more tables located in the same database.
- *Inline View*: A SELECT statement that is substituted for a table in a parent SELECT statement. The embedded SELECT statement (in bold) is an example of an inline view:

```
SELECT e.empno, e.ename, d.deptno, d.dname
    FROM (SELECT empno, ename from
      emp@orcl.world) e, dept d;
```

- Collocated Inline View: An inline view that selects data from multiple tables from a single database only (reduces the amount of times that the remote database is accessed, improving the performance of a distributed query).

Though you can write a distributed query in any fashion that you like, it is highly recommended that you form your distributed query using collocated inline views to increase the performance of your distributed query if possible.

Oracle's cost based optimisation can transparently rewrite many of your distributed queries to take advantage of the performance gains offered by collocated inline views.

Cost Based Optimisation

In addition to rewriting your queries with collocated inline views, the cost based optimisation method will optimise your distributed queries according to the gathered statistics of the referenced tables and the computations performed by the optimiser. For example, cost based optimisation will analyse the following query (notice that it analyses the query inside a CREATE TABLE statement):

```
CREATE TABLE AS (SELECT l.a, l.b, r1.c, r1.d, r1.e, r2.b,
r2.c
    FROM local l, remote1 r1, remote2 r2
        WHERE l.c = r.c AND r1.c = r2.c AND r.e > 300);
```

and rewrite it as:

```
CREATE TABLE AS (SELECT l.a, l.b, v.c, v.d, v.e
    FROM (SELECT r1.c, r1.d, r1.e, r2.b, r2.c FROM remote1
r1, remote2 r2
    WHERE r1.c = r2.c AND r1.e > 300) v, local l
WHERE l.c = r1.c);
```

The alias V is assigned to the inline view which can then be referenced as a table in the above SELECT statement. Creating a collocated inline view reduces the amount of queries performed at a remote site, thereby reducing costly network traffic.

Setup Cost Based Optimisation

After you have set up your system to use cost based optimisation to improve the performance of your distributed queries, the operation will be transparent to the user, that is the optimisation will occur automatically when the query is issued.

You need to complete the following tasks to set up your system to take advantage of Oracle's optimiser:

- Set Up Database Environment
- Analyse Tables (to generate table statistics).

Set Up Environment

To enable cost based optimisation, the OPTIMISER_MODE parameter must be set to CHOOSE or COST. This parameter can be persistently set by modifying the OPTIMZER_MODE parameter in the parameter file (INIT.ORA) or set on a session-level by issuing an ALTER SESSION command.

The *Oracle8i Tuning* manual for information on setting the OPTIMZER_MODE parameter in the parameter file (INIT.ORA) file.

Issue the following ALTER SESSION statement to set the OPTIMISER_MODE at the session level (this setting will be valid for the current session only):

```
ALTER SESSION OPTIMISER_MODE = CHOOSE;
```

or

```
ALTER SESSION OPTIMISER_MODE = COST;
```

Analyse Tables

In order for cost based optimisation to select the most efficient path for your query, you must provide accurate statistics for the tables involved in the distributed query.

The easiest way to generate statistics for a table is to execute the ANALYSE command. For example, if you reference the EMP and DEPT tables in your distributed query, you would execute the following to generate the necessary statistics:

```
ANALYSE TABLE emp COMPUTE STATISTICS;
ANALYSE TABLE dept COMPUTE STATISTICS;
```

Cost Based Optimisation Work

As illustrated in the introduction to "Tuning Distributed Queries", the optimiser's main task is to rewrite a distributed query to use collocated inline views.

This optimisation is performed in three steps:

- All Mergeable Views are Merged
- Optimiser Performs Collocated Query Block Test
- Optimiser Rewrites Query Using Collocated Inline Views.

After the query is rewritten, it is executed and the data set is returned to the user.

Cost Based Optimisation Restrictions

While cost based optimisation is performed transparently to the user, there are several distributed query scenarios that cost based optimisation is not able improve the performance upon. Specifically, if your distributed query contains any of the following, cost based optimisation will not be effective:

- Aggregates
- Subqueries
- Complex SQL.

EXTEND COST BASED OPTIMISATION WITH HINTS

Additionally, if you have special knowledge about the database environment (*i.e.,* statistics, load, network and CPU limitations, distributed queries, etc.), you can specify a hint to guide cost based optimisation. For the purposes of optimising distributed queries, you will provide hints based on your knowledge of the distributed query. Specifically, if you have written your own optimised query using collocated inline views that are based on your knowledge of the database environment, specify the NO_MERGE hint to prevent the optimiser from rewriting your query. This technique is especially helpful if your distributed query contains an aggregate, subquery, or complex SQL. Since, this type of distributed query cannot be rewritten by the optimiser, specifying NO_MERGE will cause the optimiser to skip the steps. The DRIVING_SITE hint allows you to define a site that is remote to you to act as the query execution site. This is especially helpful when the remote site contains the majority of the data and the query will perform better if executed from that remote site and the resultant data set returned to the local site.

NO_MERGE

The NO_MERGE hint prevents Oracle from merging an inline view into a potentially non-collocated SQL statement. This hint is embedded in your SELECT statement and can appear either at the beginning of the SELECT statement with the inline view as an argument or in the query block that defines the inline view.

With Argument

```
SELECT/*+NO_MERGE(v)*/t1.x, v.avg_y
    FROM t1, (SELECT x, AVG(y) AS avg_y FROM t2 GROUP BY
x) v,
    WHERE t1.x = v.x AND t1.y = 1;
```

In Query Block

```
SELECT t1.x, v.avg_y
    FROM t1, (SELECT/*+NO_MERGE*/x, AVG(y) AS avg_y FROM
t2 GROUP BY x) v,
    WHERE t1.x = v.x AND t1.y = 1;
```

DRIVING_SITE

The DRIVING_SITE hint allows you to specify the site where the query execution is performed. It is highly recommended that you let the cost based optimisation determine where the execution should be performed, but if you want to override the optimiser (either because your statistics are stale or performance on a particular machine has been severely degraded), you can specify the execution site with the DRIVING_SITE hint. A SELECT statement with a DRIVING_SITE hint might look like:

```
SELECT/*+DRIVING_SITE(dept)*/* FROM emp, dept@remote.com
    WHERE emp.deptno = dept.deptno;
```

Verifying Optimisation

An important aspect to tuning your distributed queries is to analyse the execution plan for a query. The feedback that you receive from your analysis is an important element to testing and verifying your database. This verification is increasingly important when you want to compare the execution plan for a distributed query that is optimised by cost based optimisation versus the execution plan for a distributed query that you manually optimise (using hints, defining collocated inline views, etc.).

Prepare Database

Before you can view the execution plan for you distributed query, you must prepare you database to store the execution plan. This preparation is easily performed by executing a script; complete the following to prepare your database to store an execution plan:

```
@utlxplan.sql
```

Generate Execution Plan

Once you have prepared your database to store the execution plan, you are ready to view the execution plan for a specified query. Instead of directly executing the SQL statement, you append the statement with the EXPLAIN PLAN FOR clause. For example, you might execute the following:

```
EXPLAIN PLAN FOR
    SELECT d.dname FROM dept d
      WHERE d.deptno IN
        (SELECT deptno FROM emp@orc2.world
            GROUP BY deptno
                HAVING COUNT (deptno) >3);
```

View Execution Plan

After you have executed the above SQL statement, the execution plan will be stored temporarily in the PLAN_TABLE that you created earlier. To view the results of the execution plan, execute the following script:

```
@utlxpls.sql
```

Executing the UTLXPLS.SQL file will display the execution plan for the SELECT statement that you specified.

HANDLING ERRORS IN REMOTE PROCEDURES

When a procedure is executed locally or at a remote location, four types of exceptions can occur:

- PL/SQL user-defined exceptions, which must be declared using the keyword EXCEPTION.
- PL/SQL predefined exceptions, such as NO_DATA_FOUND keyword.
- SQL errors, such as ORA-00900 and ORA-02015.
- Application exceptions, which are generated using the RAISE_APPLICATION_ERROR() procedure.

When using local procedures, all of these messages can be trapped by writing an exception handler, such as shown in the following example:

```
BEGIN
   ...
EXCEPTION
   WHEN ZERO_DIVIDE THEN
   /*...handle the exception */
END;
```

Notice that the WHEN clause requires an exception name. If the exception that is raised does not have a name, such as those generated with RAISE_APPLICATION_ERROR, one can be assigned using PRAGMA_EXCEPTION_INIT, as shown in the following example:

```
DECLARE
   null_salary EXCEPTION;
   PRAGMA EXCEPTION_INIT(null_salary, -20101);
BEGIN
   ...
   RAISE_APPLICATION_ERROR(-20101, 'salary is missing');
   ...
EXCEPTION
   WHEN null_salary THEN
   ...
END;
```

When calling a remote procedure, exceptions can be handled by an exception handler in the local procedure. The remote procedure must return an error number to the local, calling procedure, which then handles the exception as shown in the previous example. Note that PL/SQL user-defined exceptions always return ORA-06510 to the local procedure.

DISTRIBUTED DATABASE

A distributed database is a database in which storage devices are not all attached to a common processing unit such as the C.P.U. It may be stored in multiple computers located in the same physical location, or may be dispersed over a network of interconnected computers. Unlike parallel systems, in which the processors are tightly coupled and constitute a single database system, a distributed database system consists of loosely coupled sites that share no physical components. Collections of data (*e.g.*, in a database) can be distributed across multiple physical locations. A distributed database can reside on network servers on the Internet, on corporate intranets or extranets, or on other company networks. The replication and distribution of databases improves database performance at end-user worksites.

To ensure that the distributive databases are up to date and current, there are two processes: replication and duplication. Replication involves using specialised software that looks for changes in the distributive database. Once the changes have been identified, the replication process makes all the databases look the same. The replication process can be very complex and time consuming depending on the size and number of the distributive databases. This process can also require a lot of time and computer resources. Duplication on the other hand is not as complicated. It basically identifies one database as a master and then duplicates that database. The duplication process is normally done at a set time after hours. This is to ensure that each distributed location has the same data. In the duplication process, changes to the master database only are allowed. This is to ensure that local data will not be overwritten. Both of the processes can keep the data current in all distributive locations.

Besides distributed database replication and fragmentation, there are many other distributed database design technologies. For example, local autonomy, synchronous and asynchronous distributed database technologies. These technologies' implementation can and does depend on the needs of the business and the sensitivity/confidentiality of the data to be stored in the database, and hence, the price the business is willing to spend on ensuring data security, consistency and integrity.

ARCHITECTURE

A database user accesses the distributed database through:

- *Local Applications:* Applications which do not require data from other sites.
- *Global Applications:* Applications which do require data from other sites.

A distributed database does not share main memory or disks.

Important Considerations

Care with a distributed database must be taken to ensure the following:

- The distribution is transparent—users must be able to interact with the system as if it were one logical system. This applies to the system's performance, and methods of access among other things.

- Transactions are transparent—each transaction must maintain database integrity across multiple databases. Transactions must also be divided into sub-transactions, each sub-transaction affecting one database system.

There are mainly two approaches to store a relation r in a distributed database system:

- *Replication*: In replication, the system maintains several identical replicas of the same relation r in different sites.
  - Data is more available in this scheme.
  - Parallelism is increased when read request is served.
  - Increases overhead on update operations as each site containing the replica needed to be updated in order to maintain consistency.
- *Fragmentation*: The relation r is fragmented into several relations r_1, r_2, r_3....r_n in such a way that the actual relation could be reconstruc-ted from the fragments and then the fragments are scattered to different locations. There are basically two schemes of fragmenta-tion:
  - Horizontal fragmentation-splits the relation by assigning each tuple of r to one or more fragments.
  - Vertical fragmentation-splits the relation by decomposing the schema R of relation r.

Advantages

- Management of distributed data with different levels of transparency like fragmentation transparency, replication transparency, etc.
- Increase reliability and availability.
- Easier expansion.
- Reflects organisational structure—database fragments are located in the departments they relate to.
- Local autonomy or site autonomy—a department can control the data about them (as they are the ones familiar with it.)
- Protection of valuable data—if there were ever a catastrophic event such as a fire, all of the data would not be in one place, but distributed in multiple locations.
- Improved performance—data is located near the site of greatest demand, and the database systems themselves are parallelised, allowing load on the databases to be balanced among servers. (A high load on one module of the database won't affect other modules of the database in a distributed database.)
- Economics—it costs less to create a network of smaller computers with the power of a single large computer.

- Modularity—systems can be modified, added and removed from the distributed database without affecting other modules (systems).
- Reliable transactions - Due to replication of database.
- Hardware, Operating System, Network, Fragmentation, DBMS, Replication and Location Independence.
- Continuous operation.
- Distributed Query processing.
- Distributed Transaction management.

Single site failure does not affect performance of system. All transactions follow A.C.I.D. property: a-atomicity, the transaction takes place as whole or not at all; c-consistency, maps one consistent DB state to another; i-isolation, each transaction sees a consistent DB; d-durability, the results of a transaction must survive system failures. The Merge Replication Method used to consolidate the data between databases.

Disadvantages

- Complexity—extra work must be done by the DBAs to ensure that the distributed nature of the system is transparent. Extra work must also be done to maintain multiple disparate systems, instead of one big one. Extra database design work must also be done to account for the disconnected nature of the database—for example, joins become prohibitively expensive when performed across multiple systems.
- Economics—increased complexity and a more extensive infrastructure means extra labour costs.
- Security—remote database fragments must be secured, and they are not centralised so the remote sites must be secured as well. The infrastructure must also be secured (*e.g.*, by encrypting the network links between remote sites).
- Difficult to maintain integrity—but in a distributed database, enforcing integrity over a network may require too much of the network's resources to be feasible.,
- Inexperience—distributed databases are difficult to work with, and as a young field there is not much readily available experience on proper practice.
- Lack of standards—there are no tools or methodologies yet to help users convert a centralised DBMS into a distributed DBMS.
- Database design more complex—besides of the normal difficulties, the design of a distributed database has to consider fragmentation of data, allocation of fragments to specific sites and data replication.
- Additional software is required.
- Operating System should support distributed environment.
- Concurrency control: it is a major issue. It can be solved by locking and timestamping.

5

Relational Database Management System

INTRODUCTION TO RDBMS

RDBMS stands for Relational Database Management System. RDBMS is the basis for SQL, and for all modern database systems like MS SQL Server, IBM DB2, Oracle, MySQL, and Microsoft Access.

A Relational database management system (RDBMS) is a database management system (DBMS) that is based on the relational model as introduced by E.F. Codd.

RDBMS TABLE

The data in RDBMS is stored in database objects called tables. The table is a collection of related data entries and it consists of columns and rows.

Remember, a table is the most common and simplest form of data storage in a relational database. Following is the example of a CUSTOMERS table:

ID	Name	Age	Address	Salary
1	Ramesh	32	Ahmedabad	2000.00
2	Khilan	25	Delhi	1500.00
3	Kaushik	23	Kota	2000.00
4	Chaitali	25	Mumbai	6500.00
5	Hardik	27	Bhopal	8500.00
6	Komal	22	MP	4500.00
7	Muffy	24	Indore	10000.00

RDBMS Field

Every table is broken up into smaller entities called fields. The fields in the CUSTOMERS table consist of ID, NAME, AGE, ADDRESS and SALARY. A field is a column in a table that is designed to maintain specific information about every record in the table.

RDBMS Record, or Row

A record, also called a row of data, is each individual entry that exists in a table. For example there are 7 records in the above CUSTOMERS table. Following is a single row of data or record in the CUSTOMERS table:

1	Ramesh	32	Ahmedabad	2000.00

A record is a horizontal entity in a table.

RDBMS column

A column is a vertical entity in a table that contains all information associated with a specific field in a table.

For example, a column in the CUSTOMERS table is ADDRESS which represents location description and would consist of the following:

Address
Ahmedabad
Delhi
Kota
Mumbai
Bhopal
MP
Indore

RDBMS NULL Value

A NULL value in a table is a value in a field that appears to be blank which means A field with a NULL value is a field with no value. It is very important to understand that a NULL value is different than a zero value or a field that contains spaces. A field with a NULL value is one that has been left blank during record creation.

SQL Constraints

Constraints are the rules enforced on data columns on table. These are used to limit the type of data that can go into a table. This ensures the accuracy and reliability of the data in the database. Constraints could be column level or table level. Column level constraints are applied only to one column where as table level constraints are applied to the whole table.

Following are commonly used constraints available in SQL:

- *NOT NULL Constraint*: Ensures that a column cannot have NULL value.
- *DEFAULT Constraint*: Provides a default value for a column when none is specified.
- *UNIQUE Constraint*: Ensures that all values in a column are different.
- *PRIMARY Key*: Uniquely identified each rows/records in a database table.
- *FOREIGN Key*: Uniquely identified a rows/records in any another database table.

- *CHECK Constraint*: The CHECK constraint ensures that all values in a column satisfy certain conditions.
- *INDEX*: Use to create and retrieve data from the database very quickly.

Data Integrity

The following categories of the data integrity exist with each RDBMS:

- *Entity Integrity*: There are no duplicate rows in a table.
- *Domain Integrity*: Enforces valid entries for a given column by restricting the type, the format, or the range of values.
- *Referential integrity*: Rows cannot be deleted, which are used by other records.
- *User-Defined Integrity*: Enforces some specific business rules that do not fall into entity, domain, or referential integrity.

CONCEPTS OF RELATIONAL DATABASES

Database management systems (DBMSs) have evolved to overcome the limitations of file-based approach, and now it is an integral part of our day-to-day life. Database management systems have wide ranging applications in almost all areas, which include business, education, engineering, medicine, law, and modern computing environments. A database is a collection of interrelated data, and a DBMS is a set of programmes that are used to store, retrieve, and manipulate the data in the database. The main objective of a DBMS is to integrate organisational data into a centralised location and to provide secure shared access to data.

The integration of organisational data at a central location controls data redundancy and thereby ensures data consistency. An important benefit of DBMS is that it provides data independence. In traditional file-based approach, data and programmes that access the data are dependent on each other; thus, changing of one affects the other. In a DBMS, data independence is provided by its three-tier architecture.

The relational data model was first introduced by E.F. Codd of IBM Research in 1970. The relational model is based on the concept of mathematical relation, and it uses set theory and first-order predicate logic as its theoretical basis. In relational data model, the database is expressed as a collection of relations. A relation is physically represented as a table in which each row corresponds to an individual record, and each column corresponds to an individual attribute, where attributes can appear in any order within the table. In formal relational data model terminology, a row is called a tuple, a column header is called an attribute, and the table is called a relation. The degree of a relation is represented by the number of attributes it contains, while the cardinality of a relation is represented by the number of tuples it contains. For each attribute in the table there is a set of permitted values, known as the domain of the attribute. Domains may be distinct for each attribute or two or more attributes may be defined in the same domain. A named relation defined by a set of attributes and domain name pairs is called relational schema. Formally, a relation can be defined as follows:

A relation R defined over a set of n attributes A_1, A_2..., A_n with domains D_1, D_2..., D_n is a set of n tuples denoted by $<d_1, d_2..., d_n>$ such that $d_1 \varepsilon D_1$, $d_2 \varepsilon D_2$..., $d_n \in D_n$. Hence, the set $\{A_1{:}D_1, A_2{:}D_2..., A_n{:}D_n)$ represents the relational schema.

By definition, all tuples within a relation should be distinct. To maintain the uniqueness of tuples in a relation, the concept of different relational keys is introduced into the relational data model terminology. The key of a relation is the non-empty subset of its attributes that is used to identify each tuple uniquely in a relation. The attributes of a relation that make up the key are called prime attributes or key attributes. In contrast, the attributes of a relation that do not participate in key formation are called non-prime attributes or non-key attributes. The superset of a key is usually known as superkey. A superkey uniquely identifies each tuple within a relation, but a superkey may contain additional attributes. A candidate key is a superkey such that no proper subset of it is a superkey within the relation. Thus, a minimal superkey is called candidate key. In general, a relational schema can have more than one candidate key among which one is chosen as primary key during design time. The candidate keys that are not selected as primary key are called alternate keys.

The information stored in a table may vary over time, thereby producing many instances of the same relation. Thus, the term relation refers to a relation instance. The value of an attribute in a relation may be undefined. This special value of the attribute is generally expressed as null value.

INTEGRITY CONSTRAINTS

The term data integrity, which is expressed by a set of integrity rules or constraints, refers to the correctness of data. A constraint specifies a condition and a proposition that must be maintained as true. For instance, a domain constraint imposes a restriction on the set of values of an attribute, which indicates that the values must be projected only from the associated domain. In relational data model, there are two principal integrity constraints known respectively as entity integrity constraint and referential integrity constraint.

Entity integrity constraint specifies that each attribute of a primary key in a relation must be not null in a relational data model. This integrity rule ensures that no subset of the primary key is sufficient to provide uniqueness of tuples. To define referential integrity constraint it is necessary to define the foreign key first. A foreign key is an attribute or a set of attributes within one relation that matches the candidate key of some other relation (possibly the same relation). In relational databases, sometimes it requires to ensure that a value that appears in one relation for a given attribute (or a given set of attributes) also appears for a certain attribute (or a certain set of attributes) in another relation. This is known as referential integrity constraint, which is expressed in terms of foreign key. Referential integrity constraint specifies that if a foreign key exists in a relation either the foreign key value must match a candidate key value of some tuples in another relation (may be the same relation), or the foreign key value must be null. The relation that contains the foreign key is called referencing relation, and the relation that contains the candidate key is called referenced relation.

Database modifications may violate the referential integrity constraint.

The following anomalies can occur in a relational database owing to referential integrity constraint:

- *Repetition anomaly*: If a foreign key exists between two relations certain information may be repeated unnecessarily. This is known as repetition anomaly. Repetition anomaly results in wastage of storage space.
- *Insertion anomaly:* This anomaly may occur during the insertion of new records into the referencing relation. Therefore, to preserve referential integrity constraint, it must be ensured that the foreign key values of new records in the referencing relation are matched with the candidate key values in the referenced relation.
- *Update anomaly:* This anomaly may occur during updating of existing records in both referencing and referenced relations. Hence, before updating, it must be ensured that there is no violation of referential integrity constraint.
- *Deletion anomaly:* During deletion of existing records from referenced relation, this anomaly may occur. To maintain referential integrity, either all records from the referencing relation whose foreign key values match with candidate key values of deleted records should be deleted or foreign key values should be updated.

NORMALISATION

The process of normalisation was first developed by E.F. Codd in 1972. In relational databases, normalisation is a step-by-step process of replacing a given relation with a collection of successive relations to achieve simpler and better data representation. The main objective of normalisation is to eliminate different anomalies that may occur owing to referential integrity constraint and to identify a suitable set of relations in database design. In normalisation, a series of tests are performed to determine whether a relation satisfies the requirements of a given normal form or not. Initially, three normal forms were introduced, namely, 1NF (First normal form), 2NF (Second normal form) and 3NF (Third normal form). In 1974, a stronger version of 3NF called Boyce-Codd normal form (BCNF) was developed. All these normal forms are based on functional dependencies among the attributes in a relation. Later, higher normal forms such as 4NF (Fourth normal form) and 5NF (Fifth normal form) were introduced. 4NF is based on multi-valued dependencies, while 5NF is based on join dependencies.

The process of normalisation is a formal method in which a single relation is decomposed into a number of relations based on the primary key or candidate key and the functional dependencies among the attributes. The single relation for the entire database is called global relation or Universal relation. In normalisation process, two criteria are to be satisfied during decomposition. The first criterion is lossless decomposition, and the second is dependency-preserving decomposition. The first criterion ensures no loss of information during decomposition. If it is possible to reconstruct the original relation by joining decomposed relations, then it is called lossless decomposition. Decomposition is said to be dependency-preserving, if the union of the functional dependencies in decomposed relations is equivalent to the closure of the functional dependencies of the original relation.

Functional Dependencies

Functional dependencies are used to decompose relations in the normalisation process. Formally, a functional dependency can be defined as follows: In a relation R, an attribute or a set of attributes Y is said to be functionally dependent on another attribute or a set of attributes X, denoted by $X \rightarrow Y$, if each value of X is associated with exactly one value of Y. Thus, X functionally determines Y.

In a relation, non-prime attributes are functionally dependent on the key attribute. In relational data model, various types of functional dependencies may exist, which are listed in the following:

- *Full functional dependency:* In a relation R, a functional dependency of the form $X \rightarrow Y$ is said to be full, if the dependency no more sustains when any attribute is removed from X (left-hand side of the arrow of functional dependency).
- *Partial functional dependency:* In contrast with full functional dependency, in a relation R, a functional dependency of the form $X \rightarrow Y$ is said to be partial, if the dependency persists even when any attribute is removed from X.
- *Trivial functional dependency*: In a relation R, a functional dependency of the form $X \rightarrow Y$ is called trivial functional dependency, if Y is a subset of X (not necessarily a proper subset), that is, $Y \subseteq X$. For instance, $A \rightarrow A$ is a trivial functional dependency.
- *Non-trivial functional dependency*: In a relation R, a functional dependency of the form $X \rightarrow Y$ is said to be non-trivial, if Y is not a subset of X, that is, $Y \not\subset X$.
- Transitive functional dependency - Consider a relation R in which Y is functionally dependent on X, and Z is functionally dependent

on Y, that is, $X \rightarrow Y$ and $Y \rightarrow Z$. Then, Z is functionally dependent on X via rules of transitivity. In this case, the functional dependency $X \rightarrow Z$ is called transitive functional dependency.

- *Multi-valued dependency:* Consider a relation R in which X, Y and Z are three different attributes (or sets of attributes) such that $X \subset R$, $Y \subset R$ and $Z \subset R$. In this relation R, if for every value of X there exists a set of values for Y and Z, but the set of values for Y and Z are not dependent on each other, then Y and Z are multi-valued dependent on X. That is, $X \rightarrow Y$ and $X \rightarrow Z$. Multi-valued dependency is further classified into trivial and non-trivial categories. In a relation R, a multi-valued dependency of the form $X \rightarrow Y$ is said to be a trivial multi-valued dependency, if Y is a subset of X or $X \rightarrow Y = R$. On the other hand, a multi-valued dependency of the form $X \rightarrow Y$ is said to be a non-trivial multi-valued dependency if $Y \not\subset X$ and $X \cup Y \neq R$.

In this context, it is necessary to mention that every multi-valued dependency is also a functional dependency, but the reverse is not necessarily true.

RELATIONAL ALGEBRA

Relational algebra is a high-level procedural language that is derived from mathematical set theory. It consists of a set of operations that are used to produce a new relation from one or more existing relations in a database. Each operation takes one or more relations as input and produces a new relation as output, which can be used further as input to another operation. This allows expressions to be nested in the relational algebra, which is known as closure.

In 1972, Codd originally proposed eight operations of relational algebra, but several others have also been developed subsequently. The five fundamental operations of relational algebra are selection, projection, Cartesian product, union and set difference. The first two among these are unary operations and the last three are binary operations. In addition, there are three derived operations of relational algebra, namely, join, intersection and division, which can be represented in terms of the five fundamental operations.

Selection Operation

The selection operation operates on a single relation and selects those tuples from the relation that satisfies a given predicate. It is denoted by the symbol σ (sigma), and the predicate appears as a subscript of it. The predicate may be simple or complex.

Complex predicates can be represented by using the logical connectors Λ(AND), $\vee$ (OR) and $\neg$ (NOT). The comparison operators that are used in selection operation are $<$, $>$, $=$, $\neq$, $\leq$ and $\geq$.

Projection Operation

The projection operation works on a single relation and defines a new relation that contains a vertical subset of the attributes of the input relation. This operation extracts the values of specified attributes and eliminates duplicates. It is denoted by the symbol Π.

Union Operation

The union operation is a binary operation, and it is denoted by the symbol $\cup$. The union operation of two relations R and S selects all tuples that are in R, or in S, or in both, eliminating duplicate tuples. Hence, R and S must be union-compatible. Two relations are said to be union-compatible, if they have the same number of attributes and each pair of corresponding attributes have the same domain.

Set Difference Operation

The set difference operation of two relations R and S, denoted by R – S, defines a new relation that consists of the tuples that are in R but not in S. Hence, R and S must be union-compatible. It is to be noted that $R - S \neq S - R$. This operation allows deletion of tuples from a relation.

Cartesian Product Operation

The Cartesian product operation is a binary operation, and it is denoted by the symbol ×. The Cartesian product of two relations R and S, denoted by R × S, defines a new relation, which is the concatenation of each tuple of relation R with each tuple of relation S.

If the relation R has n attributes and the relation S has m attributes, then there should be (n + m) attributes in the resultant relation. It is possible that the two relations have attributes with the same name. In this case, to maintain the uniqueness within a relation, the attribute names are to be prefixed with the original relation names.

Intersection Operation

The intersection operation of two relations R and S, denoted by $R \cap S$, defines a new relation consisting of the set of tuples that are in both R and S. Hence, R and S must be union-compatible. In terms of the set difference operation, the intersection operation, $R \cup S$, can be represented as R – (R – S).

Join Operation

The join operation is derived from the Cartesian product operation of relational algebra. We can say join operation is a combination of the operations selection, projection and Cartesian product. There are various forms of join operation such as theta join, equi join, natural join, outer join and semijoin.

The outer join operation is further classified into full outer join, left outer join and right outer join.

- *Theta join* (ϑ): The most common join operation is theta join. The theta join operation of two relations R and S defines a relation that contains tuples satisfying a join predicate from the Cartesian product of R and S. The join predicate is defined as R.A1 ϑ S.B1, where ϑ may be one of the comparison operator $<$, $>$, $=$, $\neq$, $\leq$ and $\geq$. In terms of selection and Cartesian product operations, the theta join operation can be represented as follows:
  $R \infty_F S = \sigma \xi F (R \times S)$.
- *Equi join:* Equi join operation is a theta join operation where the comparison operator equality (=) is used in the join predicate.
- *Natural join:* The natural join operation is an equi join operation performed over all the attributes in two relations that have the same name. One occurrence of each common attribute is eliminated from the resultant relation.
- *Outer join:* Generally, a join operation selects tuples from two relations that satisfies the join predicate. In outer join operation, those tuples that do not satisfy the join predicate also appear in the resultant relation. The left outer join operation on two relations R and S selects unmatched tuples from the relation R along with the matched tuples from both the relations R and S that satisfy the join predicate. Missing values in the relation S are set to null. The right outer join operation on two relations R and S selects unmatched tuples from the relation S along with the matched tuples from both the relations R and S that satisfy the join predicate. In the case of right outer join, the missing values in the relation R are set to null. In the case of full outer join, unmatched tuples from both the relations R and S appear in the resultant relation along with the matched tuples.
- *Semijoin:* The semijoin operation on two relations R and S defines a new relation that contains the tuples of R that participate in the join of R with S. Hence, only the attributes of relation R are projected in the resultant relation. The advantage of semijoin operation is that it decreases the number of tuples that are required to be handled to form the join. The semijoin operation is very useful for performing join operations in distributed databases. The semijoin operation can be rewritten as follows using the projection and join operations of relational algebra:
  $R \triangleright_F S = \prod_A (R \infty_F S)$, where A is the set of all attributes for R.

Division Operation

Consider two relations R and S defined over the attribute sets A and B respectively such that $B \subseteq A$ and $C = A - B$. The division operation of the two relations R and S defines a relation over the attribute set C that consists of the set of tuples from R that matches the combination of every tuple in S. In terms of fundamental operations in relational algebra, the division operation can be represented as follows:

$$R \div S = \Pi_C(R) - \Pi_C((S \times \Pi_C(R)) - R).$$

RELATIONAL DATABASE

A relational database is a collection of data items organised as a set of formally described tables from which data can be accessed easily. A relational database is created using the relational model. The software used in a relational database is called a relational database management system (RDBMS). A relational database is the predominant choice in storing data, over other models like the hierarchical database model or the network model.

TERMINOLOGY

The term relational database was originally defined by and is attributed to Edgar Codd at IBM Almaden Research Centre in 1970.

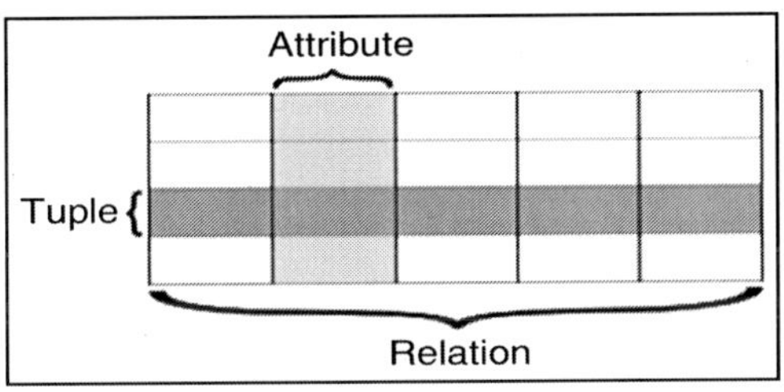

Fig. Relational Database Terminology.

Relational database theory uses a set of mathematical terms, which are roughly equivalent to SQL database terminology. The table below summarises some of the most important relational database terms and their SQL database equivalents.

Relational term	SQL equivalent
Relation, base relvar	Table
Derived relvar	View, query result, result set
Tuple	Row
Attribute	Column

Relations or Tables

A relation is defined as a set of tuples that have the same attributes. A tuple usually represents an object and information about that object. Objects are typically physical objects or concepts. A relation is usually described as a table, which is organised into rows and columns. All the data referenced by an attribute are in the same domain and conform to the same constraints. The relational model specifies that the tuples of a relation have no specific order and that the tuples, in turn, impose no order on the attributes. Applications access data by specifying queries, which use operations such as select to identify tuples, project to identify attributes, and join to combine relations. Relations can be modified using the insert, delete, and update operators. New tuples can supply explicit values or be derived from a query. Similarly, queries identify tuples for updating or deleting. It is necessary for each tuple of a relation to be uniquely identifiable by some combination (one or more) of its attribute values. This combination is referred to as the primary key.

Base and Derived Relations

In a relational database, all data are stored and accessed via relations. Relations that store data are called "base relations", and in implementations are called "tables". Other relations do not store data, but are computed by applying relational operations to other relations. These relations are sometimes called "derived relations". In implementations these are called "views" or "queries". Derived relations are convenient in that they act as a single relation, even though they may grab information from several relations. Also, derived relations can be used as an abstraction layer.

Domain

A domain describes the set of possible values for a given attribute, and can be considered a constraint on the value of the attribute. Mathematically, attaching a domain to an attribute means that any value for the attribute must be an element of the specified set. The character data value 'ABC', for instance, is not in the integer domain. The integer value 123, satisfies the domain constraint.

Constraints

Constraints make it possible to further restrict the domain of an attribute. For instance, a constraint can restrict a given integer attribute to values between 1 and 10. Constraints provide one method of implementing business rules in the database. SQL implements constraint functionality in the form of check constraints.

Constraints restrict the data that can be stored in relations. These are usually defined using expressions that result in a boolean value, indicating whether or not the data satisfies the constraint. Constraints can apply to single attributes, to a tuple (restricting combinations of attributes) or to an entire relation. Since, every attribute has an associated domain, there are constraints (domain constraints). The two principal rules for the relational model are known as entity integrity and referential integrity. ("'Referential integrity is the state in which all values of all foreign keys are valid. Referential integrity is based on entity integrity. Entity integrity requires that each entity have a unique key. For example, if every row in a table represents relationships for a unique entity, the table should have one column or a set of columns that provides a unique identifier for the rows of the table. This column (or set of columns) is called the parent key of the table. To ensure that the parent key does not contain duplicate values, a unique index must be defined on the column or columns that constitute the parent key. Defining the parent key is called entity integrity"'

Primary Keys

A primary key uniquely defines a relationship within a database. In order for an attribute to be a good primary key it must not repeat. While natural attributes are sometimes good primary keys, surrogate keys are often used instead. A surrogate key is an artificial attribute assigned to an object which uniquely identifies it (for instance, in a table of information about students at a school they might all be assigned a student ID in order to differentiate them). The surrogate key has no intrinsic (inherent) meaning, but rather is useful through its ability to uniquely identify a tuple. Another common occurrence, especially in regards to N:M cardinality is the composite key. A composite key is a key made up of two or more attributes within a table that (together) uniquely identify a record.

Foreign Key

A foreign key is a field in a relational table that matches the primary key column of another table. The foreign key can be used to cross-reference tables. Foreign keys need not have unique values in the referencing relation. Foreign keys effectively use the values of attributes in the referenced relation to restrict the domain of one or more attributes in the referencing relation. A foreign key could be described formally as: "For all tuples in the referencing relation projected over the referencing attributes, there must exist a tuple in the referenced relation projected over those same attributes such that the values in each of the referencing attributes match the corresponding values in the referenced attributes."

Stored Procedures

A stored procedure is executable code that is associated with, and generally stored in, the database. Stored procedures usually collect and customise common operations, like inserting a tuple into a relation, gathering statistical information about usage patterns, or encapsulating complex business logic and calculations.

Frequently they are used as an application programming interface (API) for security or simplicity. Implementations of stored procedures on SQL DBMSs often allow developers to take advantage of procedural extensions (often vendor-specific) to the standard declarative SQL syntax. Stored procedures are not part of the relational database model, but all commercial implementations include them.

Index

An index is one way of providing quicker access to data. Indices can be created on any combination of attributes on a relation. Queries that filter using those attributes can find matching tuples randomly using the index, without having to check each tuple in turn. This is analogous to using the index of a book to go directly to the page on which the information you are looking for is found *i.e.*, you do not have to read the entire book to find what you are looking for.

Relational databases typically supply multiple indexing techniques, each of which is optimal for some combination of data distribution, relation size, and typical access pattern. Indices are usually implemented via B+ trees, R-trees, and bitmaps. Indices are usually not considered part of the database, as they are considered an implementation detail, though indices are usually maintained by the same group that maintains the other parts of the database. It should be noted that use of efficient indexes on both primary and foreign keys can dramatically improve query performance. This is because B-tree indexes result in query times proportional to log(n) where N is the number of rows in a table and hash indexes result in constant time queries (no size dependency so long as the relevant part of the index fits into memory).

RELATIONAL OPERATIONS

Queries made against the relational database, and the derived relvars in the database are expressed in a relational calculus or a relational algebra. In his original relational algebra, Codd introduced eight relational operators in two groups of four operators each.

The first four operators were based on the traditional mathematical set operations:

- The union operator combines the tuples of two relations and removes all duplicate tuples from the result. The relational union operator is equivalent to the SQL UNION operator.
- The intersection operator produces the set of tuples that two relations share in common. Intersection is implemented in SQL in the form of the INTERSECT operator.
- The difference operator acts on two relations and produces the set of tuples from the first relation that do not exist in the second relation. Difference is implemented in SQL in the form of the EXCEPT or MINUS operator.
- The cartesian product of two relations is a join that is not restricted by any criteria, resulting in every tuple of the first relation being matched with every tuple of the second relation. The cartesian product is implemented in SQL as the CROSS JOIN join operator.

The remaining operators proposed by Codd involve special operations specific to relational databases:

- The selection, or restriction, operation retrieves tuples from a relation, limiting the results to only those that meet a specific criteria, *i.e.*, a subset in terms of set theory. The SQL equivalent of selection is the SELECT query statement with a WHERE clause.
- The projection operation extracts only the specified attributes from a tuple or set of tuples.
- The join operation defined for relational databases is often referred to as a natural join. In this type of join, two relations are connected by their common attributes. SQL's approximation of a natural join is the INNER JOIN join operator.
- The relational division operation is a slightly more complex operation, which involves essentially using the tuples of one relation (the dividend) to partition a second relation (the divisor). The relational division operator is effectively the opposite of the cartesian product operator (hence, the name).

Other operators have been introduced or proposed since, Codd's introduction of the original eight including relational comparison operators and extensions that offer support for nesting and hierarchical data, among others.

Normalisation

Normalisation was first proposed by Codd as an integral part of the relational model. It encompasses a set of procedures designed to eliminate nonsimple domains (non-atomic values) and the redundancy (duplication) of data, which in turn prevents data manipulation anomalies and loss of data integrity. The most common forms of normalisation applied to databases are called the normal forms. Normalisation trades reducing redundancy for increased information entropy. Normalisation is criticised because it increases complexity and processing overhead required to join multiple tables representing what are conceptually a single item.

RELATIONAL DATABASE MANAGEMENT SYSTEMS

Relational databases, as implemented in relational database management systems, have become a predominant choice for the storage of information in new databases used for financial records, manufacturing and logistical information, personnel data and much more. Relational databases have often replaced legacy hierarchical databases and network databases because they are easier to understand and use, even though they are much less efficient. As computer power has increased, the inefficiencies of relational databases, which made them impractical in earlier times, have been outweighed by their ease of use. However, relational databases have been challenged by Object

Databases, which were introduced in an attempt to address the object-relational impedance mismatch in relational database, and XML databases. The three leading commercial relational database vendors are Oracle, Microsoft, and IBM. The three leading open source implementations are MySQL, PostgreSQL, and SQLite. Amazon Relational Database Service is a database as a service offering MySQL and Oracle database engines.

MAJOR DATABASE USAGE REQUIREMENTS

The major purpose of a database is to provide the information system (in its broadest sense) that utilises it with the information the system needs according to its own requirements. A certain broad set of requirements refines this general goal.

These database requirements translate to requirements for the respective DBMS, to allow conveniently building a proper database for the given application. If this goal is met by a DBMS, then the designers and builders of the specific database can concentrate on the application's aspects, and not deal with building and maintaining the underlying DBMS. Also, since, a DBMS is complex and expensive to build and maintain, it is not economical to build such a new tool (DBMS) for every application. Rather it is desired to provide a flexible tool for handling databases for as many as possible given applications, *i.e.,* a general-purpose DBMS.

Functional Requirements

Certain general functional requirements need to be met in conjunction with a database. They describe what is needed to be defined in a database for any specific application.

Data Modelling and Data Definition Languages

The database needs to be based on a data model that is sufficiently rich to describe in the database all the needed respective application's aspects. A data definition language exists to describe the databases within the data model. Such language is typically data model specific.

Manipulating the Data

A database data model needs support by a sufficiently rich data manipulation language to allow all database manipulations and information generation (from the data) as needed by the respective application. Such language is typically data model specific.

Protecting the Data

The DB needs built-in security means to protect its content (and users) from dangers of unauthorised users (either humans or programmes). Protection is also provided from types of unintentional breach. Security types and levels should be defined by the database owners.

Describing Processes that use the Data

Manipulating database data often involves processes of several interdependent steps, at different times (*e.g.*, when different people's interactions are involved; *e.g.*, generating an insurance policy). Data manipulation languages are typically intended to describe what is needed in a single such step. Dealing with multiple steps typically requires writing quite complex programmes. Most applications are programmed using common programming languages and software development tools. However the area of process description has evolved in the frameworks of workflow and business processes with supporting languages and software packages which considerably simplify the tasks. Traditionally these frameworks have been out of the scope of common DBMSs, but utilisation of them has become commonplace, and often they are provided as add-on's to DBMSs.

Operational Requirements

Operational requirements are needed to be met by a database in order to effectively support an application when operational. Though it typically may be expected that operational requirements are automatically met by a DBMS, in fact it is not so in most of the cases: To be met substantial work of design and tuning is typically needed by database administrators. This is typically done by specific instructions/operations through special database user interfaces and tools, and thus may be viewed as secondary functional requirements (which are not less important than the primary).

Availability

A DB should maintain needed levels of availability, *i.e.*, the DB needs to be available in a way that a user's action does not need to wait beyond a certain time range before starting executing upon the DB. Availability also relates to failure and recovery from it: Upon failure and during recovery normal availability changes, and special measures are needed to satisfy availability requirements.

Performance

Users' actions upon the DB should be executed within needed time ranges.

Isolation between Users

When multiple users access the database concurrently the actions of a user should be uninterrupted and unaffected by actions of other users. These concurrent actions should maintain the DB's consistency (*i.e.*, keep the DB from corruption).

Recovery from Failure and Disaster

All computer systems, including DBMSs, are prone to failures for many reasons (both software and hardware related). Failures typically corrupt the DB, typically to the extent that it is impossible to repair it without special measures. The DBMS should provide automatic recovery from failure procedures that repair the DB and return it to a well defined state.

Backup and Restore

Sometimes it is desired to bring a database back to a previous state (for many reasons, *e.g.*, cases when the database is found corrupted due to a software error, or if it has been updated with erroneous data). To achieve this a backup operation is done occasionally or continuously, where each desired database state (*i.e.*, the values of its data and their embedding in database's data structures) is kept within dedicated backup files (many techniques exist to do this effectively). When this state is needed, *i.e.*, when it is decided by a database administrator to bring the database back to this state (*e.g.*, by specifying this state by a desired point in time when the database was in this state), these files are utilised to restore that state.

Data Independence

Data independence pertains to a database's life cycle. It strongly impacts the convenience and cost of maintaining an application and its database, and has been the major motivation for the emergence and success of the Relational model, as well as the convergence to a common database architecture. In general the term "data independence" means that changes in the database's structure do not require changes in its application's computer programmes, and that changes in the database at a certain architectural level do not affect the database's levels above. Data independence is achieved to a great extent in contemporary DBMS, but it is not completely attainable, and achieved at different degrees for different types of database structural changes.

RELATIONAL DATABASE CONCEPTS

An important part of every business is to keep records. We need to keep records of our customers, the employees of our company, the e-mails, etc. To keep all the data individually is quite difficult and hectic job, because whenever if we need the record of a particular customer or an employee we need to search manually. It takes lot of time and still not reliable. Here comes the concept of databases.

DATABASE ORGANISATION

A database is an organised collection of information. A simple example of a database are like your telephone directory, recipe book, etc.

A Relational model is the basis for any relational database management system (RDBMS). A relational model has mainly three components:

- A collection of objects or relations.

- Operators that act on the objects or relations.
- Data integrity methods.

To design a database we need three things:

- Table
- Rows
- Columns.

A table is one of the most important ingredient to design the database. It is also known as a relation, is a two dimensional structure used to hold related information. A database consists of one or more tables. A table contains rows: Rows is a collection of instance of one thing, such as the information of one employee. A table contains the columns: Columns contains all the information of a single type. Each column in a table is a category of information referred to as a field. One item of data, such as single phone number of a person is called as a Data Value.

ACID Properties

ACID properties are one of the important concept for databases. ACID stands for Atomicity, Consistency, Isolation, and Durability. These properties of a DBMS allow safe sharing of data. Without these properties the inaccuracy in the data will be huge. With the help of the ACID properties the accuracy can be maintained.

Normalisation

Normalisation is a design technique which helps the to design the relational databases. Normalisation is essentially a two step process that puts data into tabular form by removing redundant data from the relational tables. A basic goal of normalisation is to create a set of relational tables that are free of redundant data and the data should be consistent. Normalisation has been divided into following forms.

- *First Normal Form*: A relational table, by definition are in first normal form. All values of the columns are atomic. It means that it contains no repeating values.
- A relational table is in second normal form if it is in 1NF and every non- key column is fully dependent upon the primary key.
- A relational table is in third normal form (3NF) if it is already in 2NF and every non- key column is non transitively dependent upon its primary key. The advantage of having table in 3NF is that it eliminates redundant data which in turn saves space and reduces manipulation anomalies.

6

Fundamentals of Relational Database Design and System

Database design theory is a topic that many people avoid learning for lack of time. Many others attempt to learn it, but give up because of the dry, academic treatment it is usually given by most authors and teachers. But if creating databases is part of your job, then you're treading on thin ice if you don't have a good solid understanding of relational database design theory.

This chapter begins with an introduction to relational database design theory, including a discussion of keys, relationships, integrity rules, and the often-dreaded "Normal Forms."

THE RELATIONAL DATABASE MODEL

The relational database model was conceived by E.F. Codd in 1969, then a researcher at IBM. The model is based on branches of mathematics called set theory and predicate logic. The basic idea behind the relational model is that a database consists of a series of unordered tables (or relations) that can be manipulated using non-procedural operations that return tables. This model was in vast contrast to the more traditional database theories of the time that were much more complicated, less flexible and dependent on the physical storage methods of the data.

Note: It is commonly thought that the word relational in the relational model comes from the fact that you relate together tables in a relational database. Although this is a convenient way to think of the term, it's not accurate. Instead, the word relational has its roots in the terminology that Codd used to define the relational model. The table in Codd's writings was actually referred to as a relation (a related set of information). In fact, Codd (and other relational database theorists) use the terms relations, attributes and tuples where most of us use the more common terms tables, columns and rows, respectively (or the more physical-and thus less preferable for discussions of database design theory-files, fields and records).

The relational model can be applied to both databases and database management systems (DBMS) themselves. The relational fidelity of database programmes can be compared using Codd's 12 rules (since, Codd's seminal paper on the relational model, the number of rules has been expanded to 300) for determining how DBMS products conform to the relational model. When compared with other database management programmes, Microsoft Access fares quite well in terms of relational fidelity. Still, it has a long way to go before it meets all twelve rules completely.

Fortunately, you don't have to wait until Microsoft Access is perfect in a relational sense before you can benefit from the relational model. The relational model can also be applied to the design of databases, which is the subject of the remainder of this chapter.

RELATIONAL DATABASE DESIGN

When designing a database, you have to make decisions regarding how best to take some system in the real world and model it in a database. This consists of deciding which tables to create, what columns they will contain, as well as the relationships between the tables. While it would be nice if this process was totally intuitive and obvious, or even better automated, this is simply not the case. A well-designed database takes time and effort to conceive, build and refine.

The benefits of a database that has been designed according to the relational model are numerous.

Some of them are:

- Data entry, updates and deletions will be efficient.
- Data retrieval, summarisation and reporting will also be efficient.
- Since, the database follows a well-formulated model, it behaves predictably.
- Since, much of the information is stored in the database rather than in the application, the database is somewhat self-documenting.
- Changes to the database schema are easy to make.

The goal of this article is to explain the basic principles behind relational database design and demonstrate how to apply these principles when designing a database using Microsoft Access. This book is by no means comprehensive and certainly not definitive. Many books have been written on database design theory; in fact, many careers have been devoted to its study. Instead, this chapter is meant as an informal introduction to database design theory for the database developer.

Tables, Uniqueness and Keys

Tables in the relational model are used to represent "things" in the real world. Each table should represent only one thing. These things (or entities) can be real-world objects or events. For example, a real-world object might be a customer, an inventory item, or an invoice. Examples of events include patient visits, orders, and telephone calls. Tables are made up of rows and columns. The relational model dictates that each row in a table be unique. If you allow duplicate rows in a table, then there's no way to uniquely address a given row via programming. This creates all sorts of ambiguities and problems that are best avoided. You guarantee uniqueness for a table by designating a primary key-a column that contains unique values for a table. Each table can have only one primary key, even though several columns or combination of columns may contain unique values. All columns (or combination of columns) in a table with unique values are referred to as candidate keys, from which the primary key must be drawn. All other candidate key columns are referred to as alternate keys. Keys can be simple or composite. A simple key is a key made up of one column, whereas a composite key is made up of two or more columns.

The decision as to which candidate key is the primary one rests in your hands-there's no absolute rule as to which candidate key is best. Fabian Pascal, in his book SQL and Relational Basics, notes that the decision should be based upon the principles of minimality (choose the fewest columns necessary), stability (choose a key that seldom changes), and simplicity/familiarity (choose a key that is both simple and familiar to users). Let's illustrate with an example. Say that a company has a table of customers called tblCustomer, which looks like the table shown in Figure below.

Table: tblCustomer

CustomerId	LastName	FirstName	Address	City	State	ZipCode	Phone#
1	Jones	Paul	1313 Mockingbird Lane	Seattle	WA	98117	2068886902
2	Nelson	Greg	45-39 173rd St	Redmond	WA	98119	2069809099
3	Madison	Ken	2345 16th NE	Kent	WA	98109	2067837890
4	Jones	Geoff	1313 Mockingbird Lane	Seattle	WA	98117	2068886902

Record: 1 of 4

Fig. The best Choice for Primary Key for tblCustomer would be CustomerId.

Candidate keys for tblCustomer might include CustomerId, (LastName + FirstName), Phone#, (Address, City, State), and (Address + ZipCode). Following Pascal's guidelines, you would rule out the last three candidates because addresses and phone numbers can change fairly frequently. The choice among CustomerId and the name composite key is less obvious and would involve tradeoffs. How likely would a customer's name change (*e.g.*, marriages cause names to change)? Will misspelling of names be common? How likely will two customers have the same first and last names? How familiar will CustomerId be to users? There's no right answer, but most developers favour numeric primary keys because names do sometimes change and because searches and sorts of numeric columns are more efficient than of text columns in Microsoft Access (and most other databases). Counter columns in Microsoft Access make good primary keys, especially when you're having trouble coming up with good candidate keys, and no existing arbitrary identification number is already in place. Don't use a counter column if you'll sometimes need to renumber the values-you won't be able to-or if you require an alphanumeric code-Microsoft Access supports only long integer counter values. Also, counter columns only make sense for tables on the one side of a one-to-many relationship.

Note: In many situations, it is best to use some sort of arbitrary static whole number (*e.g.*, employee ID, order ID, a counter column, etc.) as a primary key rather than a descriptive text column. This avoids the problem of misspellings and name changes. Also, don't use real numbers as primary keys since, they are inexact.

Foreign Keys and Domains

Although primary keys are a function of individual tables, if you created databases that consisted of only independent and unrelated tables, you'd have little need for them. Primary keys become essential, however, when you start to create relationships that join together multiple tables in a database. A foreign key is a column in a table used to reference a primary key in another table.

Continuing the example presented in the last section, let's say that you choose CustomerId as the primary key for tblCustomer. Now define a second table, tblOrder, as shown in Figure below.

Table: tblOrder

OrderId	CustomerId	OrderDate
1	1	5/1/94
2	3	5/9/94
3	1	7/4/94
4	2	8/1/94
5	1	8/2/94
6	2	8/2/94

Record: 4 of 6

Fig. CustomerId is a Foreign Key in tblOrder which can be used to Reference a Customer Stored in the tblCustomer Table.

CustomerId is considered a foreign key in tblOrder since, it can be used to refer to given customer (*i.e.*, a row in the tblCustomer table).

It is important that both foreign keys and the primary keys that are used to reference share a common meaning and draw their values from the same domain. Domains are simply pools of values from which columns are drawn. For example, CustomerId is of the domain of valid customer ID #'s, which in this case might be Long Integers ranging between 1 and 50,000. Similarly, a column named Sex might be based on a one-letter domain equalling 'M' or 'F'. Domains can be thought of as user-defined column types whose definition implies certain rules that the columns must follow and certain operations that you can perform on those columns. Microsoft Access supports domains only partially. For example, Microsoft Access will not let you create a relationship between two tables using columns that do not share the same datatype (*e.g.*, text, number, date/time, etc.). On the other hand, Microsoft Access will not prevent you from joining the Integer column EmployeeAge from one table to the Integer column YearsWorked from a second table, even though these two columns are obviously from different domains.

RELATIONSHIPS

You define foreign keys in a database to model relationships in the real world. Relationships between real-world entities can be quite complex, involving numerous entities each having multiple relationships with each other. For example, a family has multiple relationships between multiple people-all at the same time. In a relational database such as Microsoft Access, however, you consider only relationships between pairs of tables. These tables can be related in one of three different ways: one-to-one, one-to-many or many-to-many.

One-to-One Relationships

Two tables are related in a one-to-one (1-1) relationship if, for every row in the first table, there is at most one row in the second table. True one-to-one relationships seldom occur in the real world. This type of relationship is often created to get around some limitation of the database management software rather than to model a real-world situation. In Microsoft Access, one-to-one relationships may be necessary in a database when you have to split a table into two or more tables because of security or performance concerns or because of the limit of 255 columns per table.

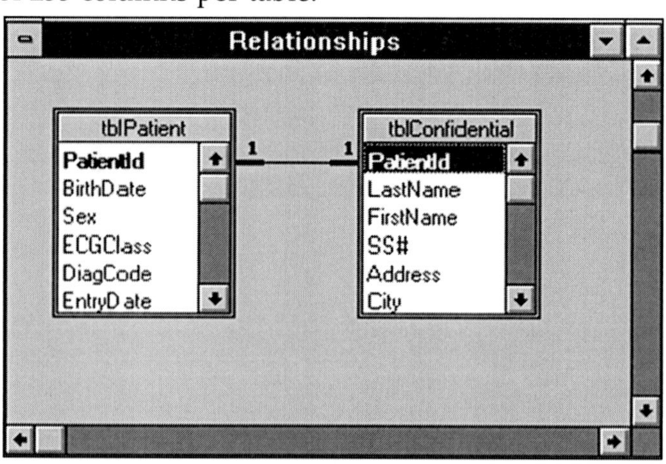

Fig. The Tables tblPatient and tblConfidential are Related in a One-to-one Relationship. The Primary Key of both Tables is PatientId.

For example, you might keep most patient information in tblPatient, but put especially sensitive information (*e.g.*, patient name, social security number and address) in tblConfidential. Access to the information in tblConfidential could be more restricted than for tblPatient. As a second example, perhaps you need to transfer only a portion of a large table to some other application on a regular basis. You can split the table into the transferred and the non-transferred pieces, and join them in a one-to-one relationship. Tables that are related in a one-to-one relationship should always have the same primary key, which will serve as the join column.

One-to-Many Relationships

Two tables are related in a one-to-many (1-M) relationship if for every row in the first table, there can be zero, one, or many rows in the second table, but for every row in the second table there is exactly one row in the first table. For example, each order for a pizza delivery business can have multiple items. Therefore, tblOrder is related to tblOrderDetails in a one-to-many relationship. The one-to-many relationship is also referred to as a parent-child or master-detail relationship. One-to-many relationships are the most commonly modelled relationship.

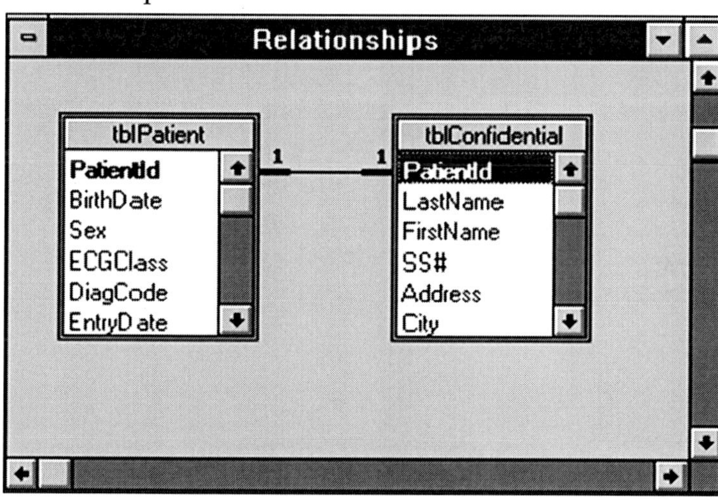

Fig. There can be Many Detail Lines for each Order in the Pizza Delivery Business, so tblOrder and tblOrderDetails are Related in a one-to-Many Relationship.

One-to-many relationships are also used to link base tables to information stored in lookup tables. For example, tblPatient might have a short one-letter DischargeDiagnosis code, which can be linked to a lookup table, tlkpDiagCode, to get more complete Diagnosis descriptions (stored in DiagnosisName). In this case, tlkpDiagCode is related to tblPatient in a one-to-many relationship (*i.e.*, one row in the lookup table can be used in zero or more rows in the patient table).

Many-to-Many Relationships

Two tables are related in a many-to-many (M-M) relationship when for every row in the first table, there can be many rows in the second table, and for every row in the second table, there can be many rows in the first table. Many-to-many relationships can't be directly modelled in relational database programmes, including Microsoft Access. These types of relationships must be broken into multiple one-to-many relationships. For example, a patient may be covered by multiple insurance plans and a given insurance company covers multiple patients.

Thus, the tblPatient table in a medical database would be related to the tblInsurer table in a many-to-many relationship. In order to model the relationship between these two tables, you would create a third, linking table, perhaps called tblPtInsurancePgm that would contain a row for each insurance programme under which a patient was covered. Then, the many-to-many relationship between tblPatient and tblInsurer could be broken into two one-to-many relationships (tblPatient would be related to tblPtInsurancePgm and tblInsurer would be related to tblPtInsurancePgm in one-to-many relationships).

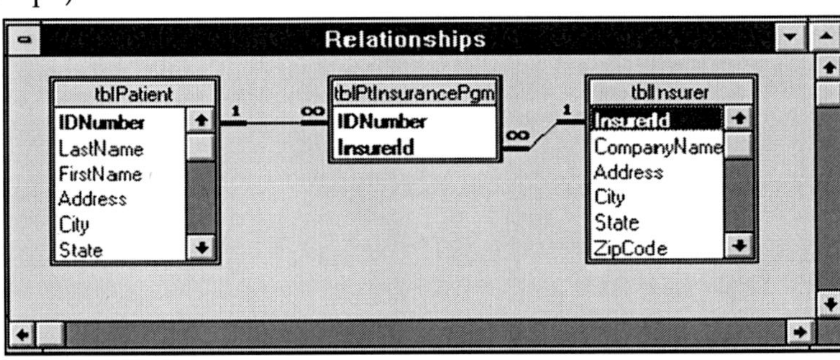

Fig. A Linking Table, tblPtInsurancePgm, is used to Model the Many-to-many Relationship between tblPatient and tblInsurer.

In Microsoft Access, you specify relationships using the Edit-Relationships command. In addition, you can create ad-hoc relationships at any point, using queries.

Normalisation

As mentioned earlier in this chapter, when designing databases you are faced with a series of choices. How many tables will there be and what will they represent? Which columns will go in which tables? What will the relationships between the tables be? The answers each to these questions lies in something called normalisation.

Normalisation is the process of simplifying the design of a database so that it achieves the optimum structure. Normali-sation theory gives us the concept of normal forms to assist in achieving the optimum structure. The normal forms are a linear progression of rules that you apply to your database, with each higher normal form achieving a better, more efficient design.

The normal forms are:

- First Normal Form
- Second Normal Form
- Third Normal Form
- Boyce Codd Normal Form
- Fourth Normal Form
- Fifth Normal Form.

Before First Normal Form: Relations

The Normal Forms are based on relations rather than tables. A relation is a special type of table that has the following attributes:

- They describe one entity.
- They have no duplicate rows; hence, there is always a primary key.
- The columns are unordered.
- The rows are unordered.

Microsoft Access doesn't require you to define a primary key for each and every table, but it strongly recommends it. Needless to say, the relational model makes this an absolute requirement. In addition, tables in Microsoft Access generally meet attributes 3 and 4. That is, with a few exceptions, the manipulation of tables in Microsoft Access doesn't depend upon a specific ordering of columns or rows.

First Normal Form

Table: tblOrder1

OrderId	CustomerId	Items
1	4	5 hammer, 3 screwdriver, 6 monkey wrench
2	23	1 hammer
3	15	2 deluxe garden hose, 2 economy nozzle
4	2	15 10' 2x4 untreated pine board
5	23	1 screwdriver
6	2	5 key

Record: 1 of 6

Fig. tblOrder1 Violates First Normal Form because the Data Stored in the Items Column is not Atomic.

First Normal Form (1NF) says that all column values must be atomic. The word atom comes from the Latin atomis, meaning indivisible (or literally "not to cut"). 1NF dictates that, for every row-by-column position in a given table, there exists only one value, not an array or list of values. The benefits from this rule should be fairly obvious. If lists of values are stored in a single column, there is no simple way to manipulate those values. Retrieval of data becomes much more laborious and difficult to generalise. tblOrder1, used to store order records for a hardware store, would violate 1NF:

A difficult time retrieving information from this table, because too much information is being stored in the Items field. Think how difficult it would be to create a report that summarised purchases by item. 1NF also prohibits the presence of repeating groups, even if they are stored in composite (multiple) columns. For example, the same table might be improved upon by replacing the single Items column with six columns: Quant1, Item1, Quant2, Item2, Quant3, Item3.

Table: tblOrder2

OrderId	CustomerId	Quant1	Item1	Quant2	Item2	Quant3	Item3
1	4	5	hammer	3	screwdriver	6	monkey wrench
2	23	1	hammer				
3	15	2	deluxe garden hose	2	economy nozzle		
4	2	15	10' 2x4 untreated pine board				
5	23	1	phillips screwdriver				
6	2	5	key				

Record: 1 of 6

Figure: A Better, but Still Flawed, Version of the Orders Table, tblOrder2. The Repeating Groups of Information Violate First Normal Form.

While this design has divided the information into multiple fields, it's still problematic. For example, how would you go about determining the quantity of hammers ordered by all customers during a particular month? Any query would have to search all three Item columns to determine if a hammer was purchased and then sum over the three quantity columns. Even worse, what if a customer ordered more than three items in a single order? You could always add additional columns, but where would you stop? Ten items, twenty items? Say that you decided that a customer would never order more than twenty-five items in any one order and designed the table accordingly.

That means you would be using 50 columns to store the item and quantity information per record, even for orders that only involved one or two items. Clearly this is a waste of space. And someday, someone would want to order more than 25 items.

Tables in 1NF do not have the problems of tables containing repeating groups. tblOrder3, is 1NF since, each column contains one value and there are no repeating groups of columns. In order to attain 1NF, I have added a column, OrderItem#. The primary key of this table is a composite key made up of OrderId and OrderItem#.

Table: tblOrder3

OrderId	CustomerId	OrderItem#	Quantity	Item
1	4	1	5	hammer
1	4	2	3	screwdriver
1	4	3	6	monkey wrench
2	23	1	1	hammer
3	15	1	2	deluxe garden hose
3	15	2	2	ecomomy nozzle
4	2	1	15	10' 2x4 untreated pine board
5	23	1	1	screwdriver
6	2	1	5	key

Record: 1 of 9

Fig. The tblOrder3 Table is in First Normal Form.

You could now easily construct a query to calculate the number of hammers ordered. The query in Figure below is an example of such a query.

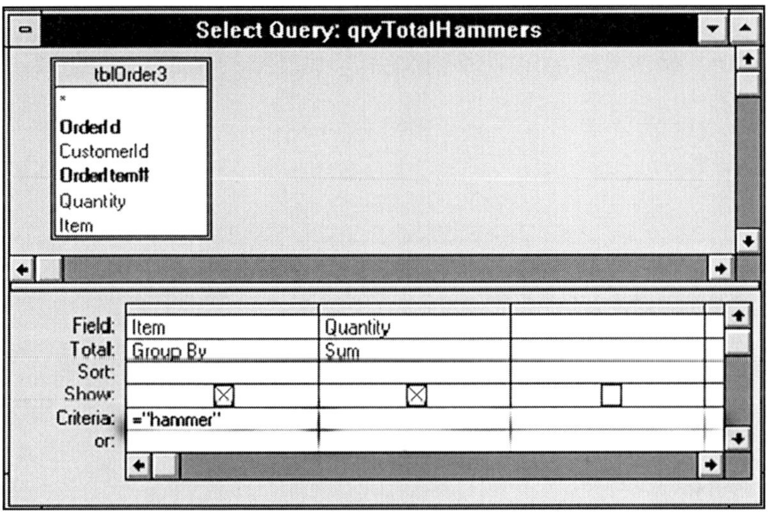

Fig. Since, tblOrder3 is in First Normal Form, you can easily Construct a Totals Query to Determine the Total Number of Hammers Ordered by Customers.

Second Normal Form

Table: tblOrder4

OrderId	CustomerId	OrderDate	OrderItem#	Quantity	ProductId	ProductDescription
1	4	5/1/94	1	5	32	hammer
1	4	5/1/94	2	3	2	screwdriver
2	23	5/9/94	1	1	32	hammer
3	15	7/4/94	1	2	113	deluxe garden hose
3	15	7/4/94	2	2	121	economy nozzle
4	2	8/1/94	1	15	1024	10' 2x4 untreated pine boards
5	23	8/2/94	1	1	2	screwdriver
6	2	8/2/94	1	5	52	key

Record: 1 of 8

Fig. The tblOrder4 Table is in First Normal Form. Its Primary Key is a Composite of OrderId and OrderItem#.

A table is said to be in Second Normal Form (2NF), if it is in 1NF and every non-key column is fully dependent on the (entire) primary key. Put another way, tables should only store data relating to one "thing" (or entity) and that entity should be described by its primary key. To determine if tblOrder4 meets 2NF, you must first note its primary key. The primary key is a composite of OrderId and OrderItem#. Thus, in order to be 2NF, each non-key column (*i.e.,* every column other than OrderId and OrderItem#) must be fully dependent on the primary key. In other words, does the value of OrderId and OrderItem# for a given record imply the value of every other column in the table? The answer is no. Given the OrderId, you know the customer and date of the order, without having to know the OrderItem#. Thus, these two columns are not dependent on the entire primary key which is composed of both OrderId and OrderItem#. For this reason tblOrder4 is not 2NF.

You can achieve Second Normal Form by breaking tblOrder4 into two tables. The process of breaking a non-normalised table into its normalised parts is called decomposition. Since, tblOrder4 has a composite primary key, the decomposition process is straightforward. Simply put everything that applies to each order in one table and everything that applies to each order item in a second table. The two decomposed tables, tblOrder and tblOrderDetail, are shown in Figure below.

Table: tblOrder

OrderId	CustomerId	OrderDate
1	1	5/1/94
2	3	5/9/94
3	1	7/4/94
4	2	8/1/94
5	1	8/2/94
6	2	8/2/94

Record: 1 of 6

Table: tblOrderDetail

OrderId	OrderItem#	Quantity	ProductId	ProductDescription
1	1	5	32	hammer
1	2	3	2	screwdriver
2	1	1	32	hammer
3	1	2	113	deluxe garden hose
3	2	2	121	ecomomy nozzle
4	1	15	1024	10' 2x4 untreated pine boards
5	1	1	2	screwdriver
6	1	5	52	key

Record: 1 of 8

Fig. The tblOrder and tblOrderDetail Tables Satisfy Second Normal Form. OrderId is a Foreign Key in tblOrderDetail that you can use to Rejoin the Tables.

Two points are worth noting here.

- When normalising, you don't throw away information. In fact, this form of decomposition is termed non-loss decomposition because no information is sacrificed to the normalisation process.
- You decompose the tables in such a way as to allow them to be put back together again using queries. Thus, it's important to make sure

that tblOrderDetail contains a foreign key to tblOrder. The foreign key in this case is OrderId which appears in both tables.

Third Normal Form

A table is said to be in Third Normal Form (3NF), if it is in 2NF and if all non-key columns are mutually independent. An obvious example of a dependency is a calculated column. For example, if a table contains the columns Quantity and PerItemCost, you could opt to calculate and store in that same table a TotalCost column (which would be equal to Quantity*PerItemCost), but this table wouldn't be 3NF. It's better to leave this column out of the table and make the calculation in a query or on a form or a report instead. This saves room in the database and avoids having to update TotalCost, every time Quantity or PerItemCost changes.

Dependencies that aren't the result of calculations can also exist in a table. The tblOrderDetail table, for example, is in 2NF because all of its non-key columns (Quantity, ProductId and ProductDescription) are fully dependent on the primary key. That is, given an OderID and an OrderItem#, you know the values of Quantity, ProductId and ProductDescription. Unfortunately, tblOrderDetail also contains a dependency among two if its non-key columns, ProductId and ProductDescription.

Dependencies cause problems when you add, update, or delete records. For example, say you need to add 100 detail records, each of which involves the purchase of screwdrivers. This means you would have to input a ProductId code of 2 and a ProductDescription of "screwdriver" for each of these 100 records. Clearly this is redundant. Similarly, if you decide to change the description of the item to "No. 2 Phillips-head screwdriver" at some later time, you will have to update all 100 records. Another problem arises when you wish to delete all of the 1994 screwdriver purchase records at the end of the year. Once all of the records are deleted, you will no longer know what ProductId of 2 is, since, you've deleted from the database both the history of purchases and the fact that ProductId 2 means "No. 2 Phillips-head screwdriver." You can remedy each of these anomalies by further normalising the database to achieve Third Normal Form.

Note: An Anomaly is simply an error or inconsistency in the database. A poorly designed database runs the risk of introducing numerous anomalies.

There are three types of anomalies:

- *Insertion*: An anomaly that occurs during the insertion of a record. For example, the insertion of a new row causes a calculated total field stored in another table to report the wrong total.
- *Deletion*: An anomaly that occurs during the deletion of a record. For example, the deletion of a row in the database deletes more information than you wished to delete.
- *Update*: An anomaly that occurs during the updating of a record. For

example, updating a description column for a single part in an inventory database requires you to make a change to thousands of rows.

The tblOrderDetail table can be further decomposed to achieve 3NF by breaking out the ProductId-ProductDescription dependency into a lookup table. This gives you a new order detail table, tblOrderDetail1 and a lookup table, tblProduct. When decomposing tblOrderDetail, take care to put a copy of the linking column, in this case ProductId, in both tables. ProductId becomes the primary key of the new table, tblProduct, and becomes a foreign key column in tblOrderDetail1. This allows you to easily join together the two tables using a query.

Table: tblOrderDetail1

OrderId	OrderItem#	Quantity	ProductId
1	1	5	32
1	2	3	2
2	1	1	32
3	1	2	113
3	2	2	121
4	1	15	1024
5	1	1	2
6	1	5	52

Record: 1 of 8

Table: tblProduct

ProductId	ProductDescription
2	screwdriver
32	hammer
52	key
113	deluxe garden hose
121	ecomomy nozzle
1024	10' 2x4 untreated pine boards

Record: 1 of 6

Fig. The tbOrderDetail1 and tblProduct Tables are in Third Normal Form. The ProductId Column in tblOrderDetail1 is a Foreign Key Referencing tblProduct.

Higher Normal Forms

After Codd defined the original set of normal forms it was discovered that Third Normal Form, as originally defined, had certain inadequacies. This led to several higher normal forms, including the Boyce/Codd, Fourth and Fifth Normal Forms.

We will not be covering these higher normal forms, instead, several points are worth noting here:

- Every higher normal form is a superset of all lower forms. Thus, if your design is in Third Normal Form, by definition it is also in 1NF and 2NF.

- If you've normalised your database to 3NF, you've likely also achieved Boyce/Codd Normal Form (and maybe even 4NF or 5NF).
- To quote C.J. Date, the principles of database design are "nothing more than formalised common sense."
- Database design is more art than science.

This last item needs to be emphasised. While it's relatively easy to work through the examples in this article, the process gets more difficult when you are presented with a business problem (or another scenario) that needs to be computerised (or downsised). An approach to take later in this chapter, but first the subject of integrity rules.

INTEGRITY RULES

The relational model defines several integrity rules that, while not part of the definition of the Normal Forms are nonetheless a necessary part of any relational database. There are two types of integrity rules: general and database-specific.

General Integrity Rules

The relational model specifies two general integrity rules. They are referred to as general rules, because they apply to all databases. They are: entity integrity and referential integrity. The entity integrity rule is very simple.

It says that primary keys cannot contain null (missing) data. The reason for this rule should be obvious. You can't uniquely identify or reference a row in a table, if the primary key of that table can be null. It's important to note that this rule applies to both simple and composite keys. For composite keys, none of the individual columns can be null. Fortunately, Microsoft Access automatically enforces the entity integrity rule for you. No component of a primary key in Microsoft Access can be null.

The referential integrity rule says that the database must not contain any unmatched foreign key values. This implies that:

- A row may not be added to a table with a foreign key unless the referenced value exists in the referenced table.
- If the value in a table that's referenced by a foreign key is changed (or the entire row is deleted), the rows in the table with the foreign key must not be "orphaned."

In general, there are three options available when a referenced primary key value changes or a row is deleted. The options are:

- *Disallow.* The change is completely disallowed.
- *Cascade.* For updates, the change is cascaded to all dependent tables. For deletions, the rows in all dependent tables are deleted.
- *Nullify.* For deletions, the dependent foreign key values are set to Null.

Microsoft Access allows you to disallow or cascade referential integrity updates and deletions using the Edit | Relationships command. Nullify is not an option.

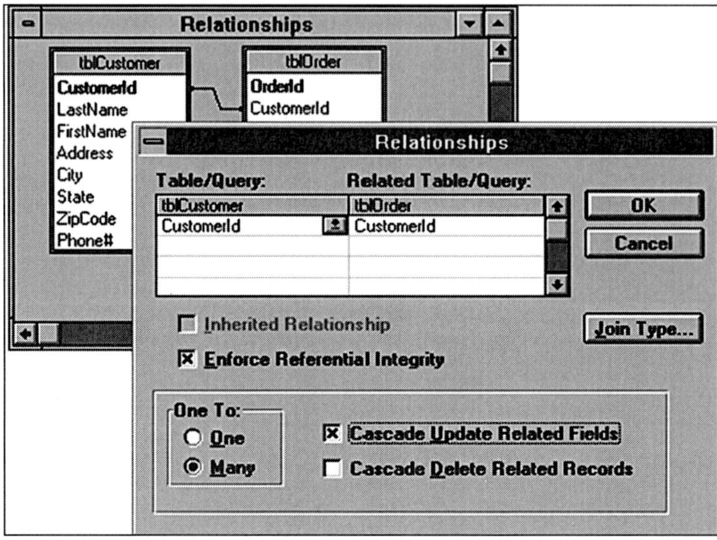

Fig. Specifying a Relationship with Referential Integrity between the tblCustomer and tblOrder Tables using the Edit | Relationships Command. Updates of CustomerId in tblCustomer will be Cascaded to tblOrder. Deletions of Rows in tblCustomer will be Disallowed if Rows in tblOrders would be Orphaned.

Note: When you wish to implement referential integrity in Microsoft Access, you must perform one additional step outside of the Edit | Relationships dialogue: in table design, you must set the Required property for the foreign key column to Yes. Otherwise, Microsoft Access will allow your users to enter a Null foreign key value, thus violating strict referential integrity.

Database-Specific Integrity Rules

All integrity constraints that do not fall under entity integrity or referential integrity are termed database-specific rules or business rules. These type of rules are specific to each database and come from the rules of the business being modelled by the database. It is important to note that the enforcement of business rules is as important as the enforcement of the general integrity rules.

Note: Rules in Microsoft Access 2.0 are now enforced at the engine level, which means that forms, action queries and table imports can no longer ignore your rules. Because of this change, however, column rules can no longer reference other columns or use domain, aggregate, or user-defined functions.

Without the specification and enforcement of business rules, bad data will get in the database. The old adage, "garbage in, garbage out" applies aptly to the application (or lack of application) of business rules.

For example, a pizza delivery business might have the following rules that would need to be modelled in the database:

- Order date must always be between the date the business started and the current date.
- Order time and delivery time can be only during business hours.
- Delivery time must be greater than or equal to Order time.
- New orders cannot be created for discontinued menu items.
- Customer zip codes must be within a certain range-the delivery area.
- The quantity ordered can never be less than 1 or greater than 50.
- Non-null discounts can never be less than 1 per cent or greater than 30 per cent.

Microsoft Access 2.0 supports the specification of validation rules for each column in a table. For example, the first business rule from the above list has been specified in Figure below.

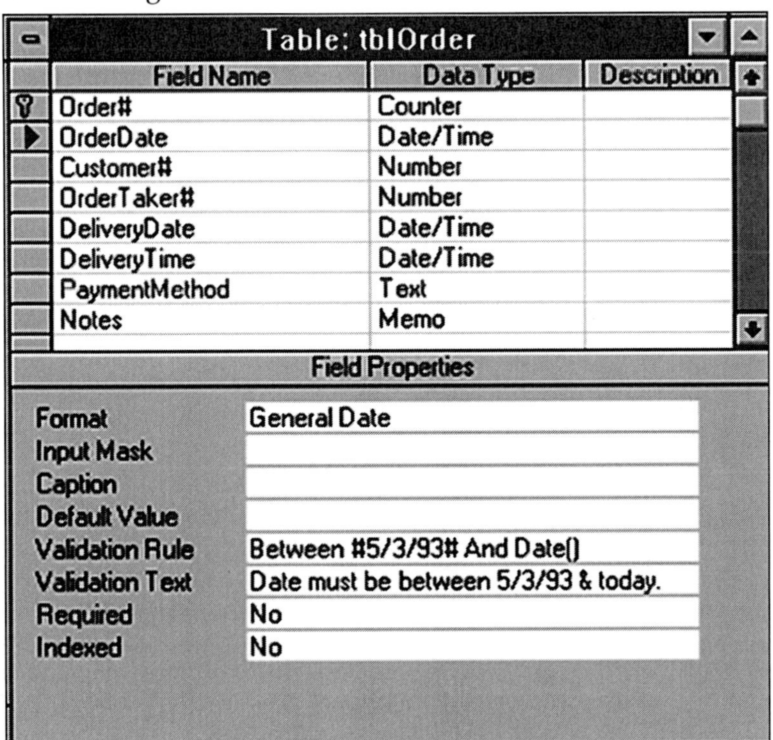

Fig. A Column Validation Rule has been Created to Limit all Order Dates to Some Time between the First Operating Day of the Business and the Current Date.

Microsoft Access 2.0 also supports the specification of a global rule that applies to the entire table. This is useful for creating rules that cross-reference columns. Unfortunately, you're only allowed to create one global rule per table, which could make for some awful validation error messages (*e.g.*, "You have violated one of the following rules: 1. Delivery Date > Order Date. 2. Delivery Time > Order Time....").

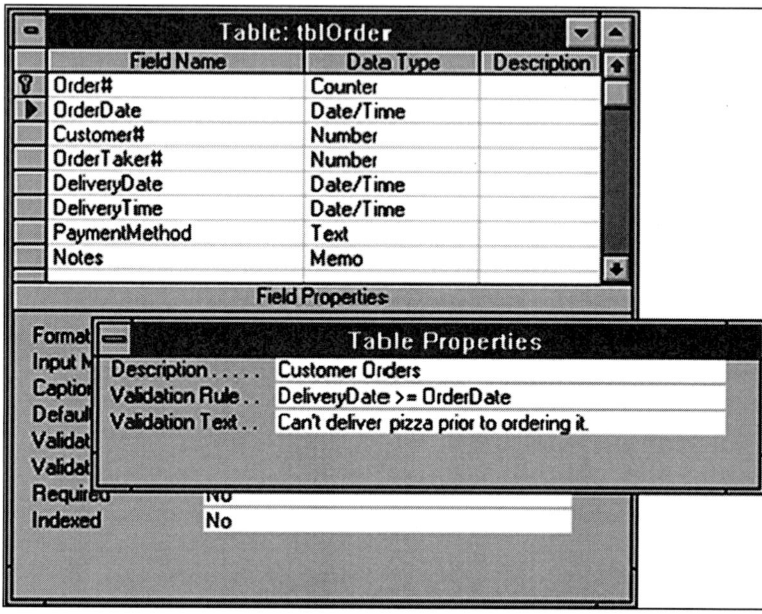

Fig. A Table Validation Rule has been Created to Require that Deliveries be Made on or After the Date the Pizza was Ordered.

Although Microsoft Access business-rule support is better than most other desktop DBMS programmes, it is still limited (especially the limitation of one global table rule), so you will typically build additional business rule logic into applications, usually in the data entry forms. This logic should be layered on top of any table-based rules and can be built into the application using combo boxes, list-boxes and option groups that limit available choices, form-level and field-level validation rules, and event procedures. These application-based rules, however, should be used only when the table-based rules cannot do the job.

The more you can build business rules in at the table level, the better, because these rules will always be enforced and will require less maintenance.

A PRACTICAL APPROACH TO DATABASE DESIGN

As mentioned earlier in this chapter, database design is more art than science. While it's true that a properly designed database should follow the normal forms and the relational model, you still have to come up with a design that reflects the business you are trying to model. Relational database design theory can usually tell you what not to do, but it won't tell you where to start or how to manage your business. This is where it helps to understand the business (or other scenario) you are trying to model. A well-designed database requires business insight, time, and experience. Above all, it shouldn't be rushed.

To assist you in the creation of databases, we've outlined the following 20-step approach to sound database design:

- Take some time to learn the business (or other system) you are trying to model. This will usually involve sitting down and meeting with the people who will be using the system and asking them lots of questions.
- On paper, write out a basic mission statement for the system. For example, you might write something like "This system will be used to take orders from customers and track orders for accounting and inventory purposes." In addition, list out the requirements of the system. These requirements will guide you in creating the database schema and business rules. For example, create a list that includes entries such as "Must be able to track customer address for subsequent direct mail."
- Start to rough out (on paper) the data entry forms. (If rules come to mind as you lay out the tables, add them to the list of requirements outlined in step 2.) The specific approach you take will be guided by the state of any existing system.
  - If this system was never before computerised, take the existing paper-based system and rough out the table design based on these forms. It's very likely that these forms will be non-normalised.
  - If the database will be converted from an existing computerised system, use its tables as a starting point. Remember, however, that it's very likely that the existing schema will be non-normalised. It's much easier to normalise the database now rather than later. Print out the existing schema, table by table, and the existing data entry forms to use in the design process.
  - If you are really starting from scratch (*e.g.*, for a brand new business), then rough out on paper what forms you envision filling out.
- Based on the forms, you created in step 3, rough out your tables on paper. If normalisation doesn't come naturally (or from experience), you can start by creating one huge, non-normalised table per form that you will later normalise. If you're comfortable with normalisation theory, try and keep it in mind as you create your tables, remembering that each table should describe a single entity.
- Look at your existing paper or computerised reports. For existing systems that aren't currently meeting the user needs, it's likely that key reports are missing. Create them now on paper.

- Take the roughed-out reports from step 5 and make sure that the tables from step 4 include this data. If information is not being collected, add it to the existing tables or create new ones.
- On paper, add several rows to each roughed-out table. Use real data if at all possible.
- Start the normalisation process. First, identify candidate keys for every table and using the candidates, choose the primary key. Remember to choose a primary key that is minimal, stable, simple, and familiar. Every table must have a primary key! Make sure that the primary key will guard against all present and future duplicate entries.
- Note foreign keys, adding them if necessary to related tables. Draw relationships between the tables, noting if they are one-to-one or one-to-many. If they are many-to-many, then create linking tables.
- Determine whether the tables are in First Normal Form. Are all fields atomic? Are there any repeating groups? Decompose if necessary to meet 1NF.
- Determine whether the tables are in Second Normal Form. Does each table describe a single entity? Are all non-key columns fully dependent on the primary key? Put another way, does the primary key imply all of the other columns in each table? Decompose to meet 2NF. If the table has a composite primary key, then the decomposition should, in general, be guided by breaking the key apart and putting all columns pertaining to each component of the primary key in their own tables.
- Determine if the tables are in Third Normal Form. Are there any computed columns? Are there any mutually dependent non-key columns? Remove computed columns. Eliminate mutual dependent columns by breaking out lookup tables.
- Using the normalised tables from step 12, refine the relationships between the tables.
- Create the tables using Microsoft Access (or whatever database programme you are using). If using Microsoft Access, create the relationships between the tables using the Edit | Relationships command. Add sample data to the tables.
- Create prototype queries, forms, and reports. While creating these objects, design deficiencies should become obvious. Refine the design as needed.
- Bring the users back in. Have them evaluate your forms and reports. Are their needs met? If not, refine the design. Remember to re-normalise if necessary.
- Go back to the table design screen and add business rules.
- Create the final forms, reports, and queries. Develop the application. Refine the design as necessary.

- Have the users test the system. Refine the design as needed.
- Deliver the final system.

This list doesn't cover every facet of the design process, but it's useful as a framework for the process.

BREAKING THE RULES: WHEN TO DENORMALISE

Sometimes it's necessary to break the rules of normalisation and create a database that is deliberately less normal than it otherwise could be. You'll usually do this for performance reasons or because the users of the database demand it. While this won't get you any points with database design purists, ultimately you have to deliver a solution that satisfies your users.

If you do break the rules, however, and decide to denormalise you database, it's important that you follow these guidelines:

- Break the rules deliberately; have a good reason for denormalising.
- Be fully aware of the tradeoffs this decision entails.
- Thoroughly document this decision.
- Create the necessary application adjustments to avoid anomalies.

This last point is worth elaborating on. In most cases, when you denormalise, you will be required to create additional application code to avoid insertion, update, and deletion anomalies that a more normalised design would avoid. For example, if you decide to store a calculation in a table, you'll need to create extra event procedure code and attach it to the appropriate event properties of forms that are used to update the data on which the calculation is based.

The considering denormalising for performance reasons, don't always assume that the denormalised approach is the best. Instead, you first fully normalise the database (to Third Normal Form or higher) and then denormalise only if it becomes necessary for reasons of performance.

The considering denormalising because your users think they need it, investigate why. Often they will be concerned about simplifying data entry, which you can usually accomplish by basing forms on queries while keeping your base tables fully normalised.

Here are several scenarios where you might choose to break the rules of normalisation:

- You decide to store an indexed computed column, Soundex, in tblCustomer to improve query performance, in violation of 3NF (because Soundex is dependent on LastName). The Soundex column contains the sound-alike code for the LastName column. It's an indexed column (with duplicates allowed) and is calculated using a user-defined function. If you wish to perform searches on the Soundex column with any but the smallest tables, you'll find a significant performance advantage to storing the Soundex column in the table and indexing this computed column. You'd likely use an event procedure attached to a form to perform the Soundex calculation and store the result in the Soundex column. To avoid update anomalies, you'll want to ensure that this column cannot be updated by the user and that it is updated every time LastName changes.

- In order to improve report performance, you decide to create a column named TotalOrderCost that contains a sum of the cost of each order item in tblOrder. This violates 2NF because TotalOrderCost is dependent on the primary key of tblOrderDetail, not on tblOrder's primary key. TotalOrderCost is calculated on a form by summing the column TotalCost for each item. Since, you often create reports that need to include the total order cost, but not the cost of individual items, you've broken 2NF to avoid having to join these two tables every time this report needs to be generated. As in the last example, you have to be careful to avoid update anomalies. Whenever a record in tblOrderDetail is inserted, updated, or deleted, you will need to update tblOrder, or the information stored there will be erroneous.
- You decide to include a column, SalesPerson, in the tblInvoice table, even though SalesId is also included in tblInvoice. This violates 3NF because the two non-key columns are mutually dependent, but it significantly improves the performance of certain commonly run reports. Once again, this is done to avoid a join to the tblEmployee table, but introduces redundancies and adds the risk of update anomalies.

STORAGE IN A RELATIONAL DATABASE MANAGEMENT SYSTEM

A multiuser geodatabase utilises a multitier architecture that implements advanced logic and behaviour in the application tier (*e.g.,* ArcGIS software) on top of a storage tier. The responsibility for managing geographic data in a multiuser geodatabase is shared between ArcGIS and the RDBMS software. A relational database management system provides a straightforward formal structure for storing and managing information in tables. Data storage and retrieval are implemented with simple tables. The multiuser geodatabase utilises the power of the RDBMS. Certain characteristics of geographic data management, such as disk-based storage, definition of attribute types, query processing, and multiuser transaction processing, are delegated to the RDBMS.

The multiuser geodatabase uses an RDBMS to provide you with:

- Flexibility to store your data in a supported RDBMS of your choice
- Ability to apply your existing IT knowledge and experience to manage the environment through common RDBMS practices
- Spatial types to enhance data storage and interoperability.

ARCSDE TECHNOLOGY

Prior to ArcGIS 9.2, Esri sold ArcSDE as a core product. At ArcGIS 9.2, ArcSDE is no longer a separate product. It is now ArcSDE technology and integrated into ArcGIS for Desktop and ArcGIS for Server products.

ArcSDE technology serves as the gateway between GIS clients and the RDBMS. It enables you to easily store, access, and manage spatial data within an RDBMS package such as:

- DB2
- Informix
- Oracle
- PostgreSQL
- SQL Server and SQL Server Express.

ArcSDE technology is critical when you need to manage long transactions and versioned-based workflows such as:

- Support for multiuser editing environments
- Distributed editing
- Federated replicas managed across many RDBMS architectures
- Managing historical archives.

The responsibility for defining the specific RDBMS schema used to represent geographic data and for application logic is retained in ArcGIS, which provides the behaviour, integrity, and utility of the underlying records.

Geodatabase Application Logic

While the RDBMS manages simple data types and tables and ArcSDE technology enables communication between GIS clients and the RDBMS, additional application logic is required to implement more complex object behaviour and integrity constraints.

ArcObjects is an example of application logic that enables the behaviour in a geodatabase. ArcObjects is a library of software components that make up the foundation of ArcGIS.

Spatial Types

A spatial type is an object type that describes and supports spatial data such as points, lines, and polygons. It allows you to create columns capable of storing spatial data such as the location of a landmark, a street, or a parcel of land.

A spatial type:

- Provides a spatial index that supports spatial queries, functions, and predicates
- Is a seamless component of your GIS data
- Provides the flexibility that enables you to issue SQL-level spatial queries.

RDB: A RELATIONAL DATABASE MANAGEMENT SYSTEM

A good question one could ask is "With all the relational database management systems available today, why do we need another one?"

There are five reasons. They are:

- RDB is easy to use by non-computer people. The concept is straight forward and logical. To select rows of data, the 'row' operator is used; to select columns of data, the 'column' operator is used.
- The data is highly portable to and from other types of machines, like Macintoshes or MSDOS computers.
- The system will run on any UNIX machine (that has the PERL Programming Language).
- The system can work on intermediate data, which will later be put into a commercial RDBMS, like INGRES.
- RDB essentially has no arbitrary limits, and can work where INGRES can't. For example there is no limit on data field size, the number of columns, or file size.

A more through discussion of why this type of relational database structure makes sense is found in the book, "UNIX Relational Database Management". It is assumed that the reader has at least a minimum knowledge of the UNIX Operating System, including knowledge of Input/Outout redirection (*e.g.*, STDIN, STDOUT, pipes). The RDB system was implemented in the PERL programming language on a SUN Sparc I computer.

This document presents information in the following order: The DATA section describes the structure of the data, with examples. There is a general discussion about operators in the section on OPERATORS, followed by several sub-sections, one for each operator in alphabetic order. Each has detailed instructions for use, and examples. There are sections describing selection of information using multiple operators, producing reports, and generating new rdbtables (data files in RDB format).

DATA (RDBTABLE)

The data is contained in regular UNIX, ASCII files and therefore can be manipulated by regular UNIX utilities, *e.g.* grep, ls, wc, mv, cp, cat, more, less, head, RCS, and editors like the RAND editor 'e', vi, etc. A good way to view the data of course, would be to use the RDB operator that prints such datafiles 'ptbl'.

The relation, or table structure is achieved by separating the columns with ASCII TAB characters, and terminating the rows with ASCII NEWLINE characters. That is, each row of data in a file contains the data values (a data field) separated by TAB characters and terminated with a NEWLINE character. Therefore a fundamental rule is that data values must NOT contain TAB characters.

In the earlier mention of the file, called the header, contains the file structure information used by the operators. The header also contains optional embedded documentation relating to the entire datafile (table documentation) and/or each data column (column documentation). The rest of the file, called the body, contains the actual data values. A file of data, so structured, is said to be an 'rdbtable'.

The header consists of two or more lines. There is an optional number (zero or more) of lines of table documentation followed by exactly two lines that contain the structure information: the column name row and the column definition row. The table documentation lines start with either a sharp sign (#) followed by a space character, or one or more space characters followed by a sharp sign (#). The rest of each line may contain any documentation desired. Note that the table documentation lines are the only lines in an rdbtable that are not required to conform to the table structure defined above. The fields in the column name row contain the names of each column. The fields in the column definition row contain the data definitions and optional column documentation for each column.

The column names are case sensitive, *i.e.*, 'COUNT' is different from 'Count'. The guideline for characters that may be used in column names is that alphabetic, numeric, and non-alphanumeric characters that are not special to the UNIX shell are good choices. Column names must include at least one alphabetic character. It is highly recommended (but not required) that column names start with an alphabetic or numeric character.

Non-alphanumeric characters that are acceptable in column names are the per cent sign (%) colon (:) at sign (@) equals (=) comma (,) and dot (.). The sharp sign (#) underscore (_) and dash (-) characters may also be used but they must not be the first character in a column name. The TAB character must never be used in column names, nor should internal spaces or UNIX I/O redirection characters (<,>,|) be used.

The data definitions include column width, data type, and justification. The column width must be explicitly specified; the others are optional and are frequently specified by default. The data definitions are specified by adjacent characters in a single word. The width of each field is specified by a numeric count. The type of data is "string", "numeric", or "month". The types are specified by an 'S', 'N', or 'M' respectively, and the default is type string. Printout justification is 'left', or 'right', and is specified by an '<' or '>' character respectively. If not specified, data types string and month will be left justified and type numeric will be right justified.

Note that column width is used primarily by the operator 'ptbl' and in no way limits the actual data size. It is not an error if some actual data in a column is wider than the defined width; a listing produced with 'ptbl' may be out of alignment however. The optional documentation for each column follows the data definition word in the field. There must be one or more space characters after the data definition word and before the column documentation; the column documentation may be as long as necessary.

OPERATORS

The operators are separate programme modules that each perform a unique function on the data. They can be grouped into data movers, report generators, and utilities. The data movers are operators that extract or rearrange the data in some way. They each read an rdbtable via STDIN and write a rdbtable via STDOUT and so are frequently connected using the UNIX pipe function to form a larger task. Each operator in such a "pipeline" style of operation gets its input from the output of the previous operator in the "pipeline".

The data movers include:

- Row- Selects rows based on arbitrary expressions.
- Column- Selects columns by name, outputs columns in listed order.
- Search- Selects rows based on a multi-column key of a sorted or indexed rdbtable.
- Sorttbl- Sorts a datafile by one or more columns.
- Jointbl- Natural or "Master/Detail" join of two rdbtables.
- Mergetbl- Merges two like rdbtables.
- Compute- Computes an arbitrary expression using column names.
- Uniqtbl- Makes an rdbtable unique on specified columns.
- Subtotal- Lists subtotals of specified columns.

The report generators each read an rdbtable via STDIN and produce a report on STDOUT, so when they are in a "pipeline" of operators they will be the operator at the end.

The report generators are:

- ptbl- Quick and easy printing of output formatted from information in the header.
- Reporttbl- Best form of output, with definable format.
- Summ- Summary/Statistical information about data values in an rdbtable.

The utilities are used for manipulating the structure and content of rdbtables and are generally used as separate tasks.

The utilities are:

- Headchg- Generates and replaces (or removes) the header of an rdbtable.
- Dataent- An interactive capability for entering data into an rdbtable.
- etbl- Uses an editor to allow modifications to an rdbtable.
- Valid- Verifies the structure of an rdbtable.
- Repair- Attempts to repair candidate RDB datafiles.

All operators take a '-help' option to show details of operation online. Following is a sub-section for each operator, in alphabetic order.

GENERATING NEW RDBTABLES

Any editor may be used to construct or modify an rdbtable, since, it is a regular UNIX file, and this 'direct editing' method is occasionally used, especially for small amounts of data. However, avoid using an editor that destroys TAB characters, like the RAND 'e' editor.

To generate a new rdbtable the best plan (and usually the safest one) is to first generate a template file, then convert it to rdbtable format and add the rows of data. Any convenient editor may be used to generate a template file. To convert it to an rdbtable the command 'headchg -gen' may be used, which will produce an empty rdbtable. Next use the operator 'etbl' to edit in rows of data.

An alternate method is to generate a template file with an editor and then use the command 'dataent -init template_file' to enter the rows of data.

A typical template file is shown below:

```
#   These are lines of table documentation. They can
be of any length,
# and any number of such lines may exist.
# Each line must start correctly, e.g. with "# " or " #".
Any number of
#   space characters may preceed the sharp sign in the
  second case above.
0           Name  24   Name of item
1           Type  1    Type: 1,2,3,7,9,A,B,X
2          Count  3N   Number of items
3              K  1    Constant modifier
4            SS7  2    Special status for type 7
5          Size   12N  In Kilobytes
```

It makes sense to have all significant or critical documentation about an rdbtable embedded in the rdbtable, rather than in some other place. The above template file contains the usual elements to describe a table of six columns: table documentation (the comment lines that each start with a sharp sign '#'), index number (the first number on each of the column lines), column name ("Name", "Type", "Count"...), column definition ("24", "1", "3N"...), and column documentation for each column (the text at the end of each column line).

Note that the index number, column name, and column definition all consist of contiguous characters, each forming a word separated by whitespace. Also note that there is one or more space characters after the column definition and before the column documentation. That is, the column documentation starts with the fourth word on the line. When the template file is converted into an rdbtable, all documentation will remain in the header (although the column documentation may be hard to read if there are many columns). At any time the entire header, including documentation, can be viewed by using the command 'valid -templ < rdbtable' (or 'headchg -templ <

rdbtable). The output from either command will be essentially like the above example.

Modifying Existing RDBtables

Basically there are three ways to modify an existing rdbtable: Use 'dataent', 'etbl', or 'mergetbl'. The operator 'dataent' can only add new rows of data, and they are added at the end of the existing table. Therefore the table may need sorting after the modification process is done. The following command might be used to update an rdbtable using 'dataent':

```
Dataent rdbtable
```

The operator 'etbl' can be used to add new rows, change existing rows, or delete existing rows of data in an rdbtable. To modify an rdbtable 'etbl' can be used in either column or list form.

The choice of form to use depends somewhat on the structure of the rdbtable. If the rdbtable has several columns of relatively narrow data (that will all fit in the width of the current window or terminal) and also several very wide columns (none of which will fit) and changes need to be made to some of the narrow columns, then it makes sense to use 'etbl' on the desired narrow columns in 'column' form, as in:

```
etbl table narrow_cola narrow_colb...
```

If changes need to be made to some of the wide columns then use 'etbl' in 'list' form on the wide columns, plus any key columns necessary, as in:

```
etbl -list table control_col... wide_cola wide_colb...
```

After editing an rdbtable it is always recommended that the structure of the rdbtable be checked with the operator 'valid'. If there are data values that are longer than the defined column width, use the command 'valid -n' to avoid many warning messages. The 'mergetbl' process actually involves other operators like 'search', and 'etbl', and works only when the existing rdbtable is sorted on one or more columns (which is a fairly common case). The process includes selecting rows from an existing sorted rdbtable (using 'search') into a small rdbtable which is easy to edit (using 'etbl') and then combining the two rdbtables again (using 'mergetbl'). Since, 'etbl' is used modifications may include changes, additions, or delitions of rows. Also note that 'mergetbl' keeps the final table in sort order.

The difference is that 'search' is much faster than 'row' or 'etbl', the editing is done on a table of conveniently small size, and that the 'mergetbl' operation can be done in the background. Remember that whether one uses 'mergetbl' or 'etbl', putting the data back together after editing requires the entire original table to be passed, which can take some time if the original rdbtable is large.

Concatenating RDBtables

The need to concatenate rdbtables comes up every so often and although it is simple to do it may not be obvious. The UNIX 'cat' command can not be used as it would result in duplicating the header and thus make an invalid rdbtable. And of course, only rdbtables with the same header should be concatenated, otherwise an invalid rdbtable would result (in this case it could be a gross inconsistency if the number of columns were different). If we have two rdbtables, TABA and TABB, then to concatenate TABB onto the end of TABA we use the command:

```
headchg -del < TABB >> TABA
```

This avoids duplicating the header. Note also that in this case the operator 'headchg' does not use a template file.

The operator 'mergetbl' may be used to merge two like rdbtables based on a key of one or more columns. In this case however the two rdbtables must be sorted on the key.

EXTRACTING INFORMATION FROM RDBTABLES

The following shows some examples of how the system is usually used, which involves a combinations of operators. Using the rdbtable named 'sample' the command:

```
column NAME OTHER TYP AMT < sample | sorttbl TYP AMT | ptbl
```

gives the output:

```
------  -----------------
NAME    OTHER    TYP AMT
------  -----------------
Hansen  One      A   23
Bush    Another  A   133
Perry   And      B   244
Hart    SoD          1111
Holmes  OnD          1111
Jones   HereX        77
------  -----------------
```

Note that columns COUNT and RIGHT were excluded by the 'column' oper, and that the order of the selected columns was changed from that in the rdbtable. Of course to save the output in a file, (redirection of STDOUT into a file) something like the following is used:

column... < sample | sorttbl... | ptbl > file.out

An example using the operator 'row' on the rdbtable sample is:

```
row AMT lt 900 < sample | column NAME AMT TYP RIGHT |\
sorttbl 1 NAME | ptbl
```

Note that the '\' character at the end of the first line of the above command is the signal to the UNIX shell that the command is continued on the next line. Here we select some rows using 'row', select some columns using 'column', sort what we have with 'sorttbl', and print with 'ptbl'. The output is:

```
------ ----- ------------
NAME    AMT   TYP   RIGHT
------ ----- ------------
Bush    133   A   This
Hansen  23    A   Is
Jones   77    X   On
Perry   244   B   The
------ ----- ------------
```

A Real World Problem

The following shell script shows how the RDB operators and other UNIX utilities can be fitted together to solve a real world problem. The problem was to find out if the rows in a large rdbtable were unique over four columns. Since, 'summ' will tell us whether the rows of an rdbtable are unique on a single column, we need to construct a temporary tdbtable.

To illustrate the solution on a small rdbtable, the script below works on an rdbtable like 'sample' but with some rows repeated. First the script selects four columns and adds a dummy column named 'uniq' (using 'column'). It then puts the combined values of the four columns into the dummy column (using 'compute'). Next it examines the value of the dummy column 'uniq' for uniquness (using 'summ') and then uses the UNIX command 'egrep' to show only the lines of interest, *e.g.*, those lines that start with something other than a '1'.

```
column < table.rdb Unit Day Time MSN -a uniq 12 |\
compute uniq = Unit. Day. Time. MSN |\
summ -cuu uniq |\
egrep -v '^ *1'
```

The output was like the following:

```
Rows: 9
Unique values for uniq: 6
          2 Jones77X77
          3 Perry77B244
```

meaning that there were (in this example) two rows that had duplicates over the four columns with one set of values, and three rows that had duplicate with another set of values.

DATA ACCESS CONTROL

Since, rdbtables are regular UNIX files, we have so far found no need to implement, and have the associated overhead of, general data access controls in RDB. Setting the UNIX permissions on files or directory has proven very useful and effective. This is another example of how the RDB system works "with" UNIX, not in addition to it, *e.g.*, not duplicating UNIX functions. The Revision Control System (RCS) is one of the best configuration management tools available and is in use here at RAND for version control of many types of files, including rdbtables. The operator 'etbl' will automatically check out an rdbtable for editing, and then check the new version back into RCS. Other operators can utilise rdbtables that are under RCS control by using commands like:

```
co -p table | row... | column... | ptbl
```

Note that this checks out an rdbtable, sends it to 'row', then to 'column', and finally prints the data with 'ptbl'. In general, any series of commands necessary can be constructed to do a given task even if the rdbtables are checked into RCS.

Write Concurrency Control

When either of the two utility operators 'etbl' or 'dataent' is used (which modify an rdbtable in place) there could be a possibility of silmultaneous writing of an rdbtable by multiple users. That is, if two or more users, on the same computer or perhaps on different computers on a network, attempted to modify a given rdbtable with either 'etbl' or 'dataent' at the same time the rdbtable could become corrupted. To prevent this, write concurrency control is provided by the use of a lockfile, and is in effect when either of the two utility operators is used.

The name of the lockfile is the name of the rdbtable being modified with a suffix of ".LCK". For example an rdbtable named "main.rdb" would have a lockfile named "main.rdb.LCK". The lockfile is placed in the same directory as the rdbtable and is normally removed after the modification process is complete, even if the operation is aborted with an INTERRUPT signal (CONTROL-C or <DEL>). However in the event of an emergency such as a computer system crash the lockfile could be left in place, preventing the use of 'etbl' or 'dataent' when the computer system is again operable. When an attempt to use either utility operator is made an there is and existing lockfile associated with the referenced rdbtable an online message is produced and the operator dies. In this case simply remove the lockfile with the UNIX command 'rm' and proceed. If an emergency has not occurred appropriate caution should be exercised before removing a lockfile, due to the possibility of data corruption.

Fast Access Methods

The RDB operator 'search' may be used to execute one of two fast access methods (binary or hashtable search, although currently only binary search is implemented). These methods are useful when the key field values of a number of rows in an existing, large rdbtable is known in advance, a common situation. One example of updating an rdbtable using these methods is as follows. First, 'search' is used to quickly obtain a new, small rdbtable consisting of the desired rows from the existing, large rdbtable. Then 'etbl' is used to update the data in the new rdbtable, including generating new rows, changing some rows, and marking certain rows for deletion, if desired. The next stage would be to use 'mergetbl' to combine the new and old rdbtables into a new, large rdbtable, which will still be in sort order (both the old rdbtable and the new, small one will still exist for backup and/or journaling purposes). Note that the last step could be done in the background.

Limits, A Few Minor Ones

The following limits apply.

- There must not be any ASCII TAB characters in the data. This is the primary limit as the ASCII TAB character is the delimiter in rdbtables.
- There must not be any pipe characters `|` used or entered as data when using the operator 'etbl'.
- All of the Compare operators and Logical constructors are reserved and should not be used as column names (they are all lower case and four characters or less). They are: 'gt', 'ge', 'lt', 'le', 'eq', 'ne', 'or', 'and', 'null', 'mat', and 'nmat'.

7

Distributed Database Management System and Architecture

The architecture of different distributed systems such as client/server system and peer-to-peer distributed system. Owing to the diversity of distributed systems, it is very difficult to generalise the architecture of distributed DBMSs.

Different alternative architectures of the distributed database systems and the advantages and disadvantages of each system. This chapter also introduces the concept of a multi-database system (MDBS), which is used to manage the heterogeneity of different DBMSs in a heterogeneous distributed DBMS environment. The classification of MDBSs and the architecture of such databases.

INTRODUCTION

The architecture of a system reflects the structure of the underlying system. It defines the different components of the system, the functions of these components and the overall interactions and relationships between these components.

This concept is true for general computer systems as well as for software systems. The software architecture of a programme or computing system is the structure or structures of the system, which comprises software elements or modules, the externally visible properties of these elements and the relationships between them.

Software architecture can be thought of as the representation of an engineering system and the process(es) and discipline(s) for effectively implementing the design(s) of such a system. A distributed database system can be considered as a large-scale software system; thus, the architecture of a distributed system can be defined in a manner similar to that of software systems.

This chapter introduces the different alternative reference architectures of distributed database systems such as client/server, peer-to-peer and MDBSs.

CLIENT/SERVER SYSTEM

In the late 1970s and early 1980s smaller systems (mini computer) were developed that required less power and air conditioning. The term client/ server was first used in the 1980s, and it gained acceptance in referring to personal computers (PCs) on a network. In the late 1970s, Xerox developed the standards and technology that is familiar today as the Ethernet. This provided a standard means for linking together computers from different manufactures and formed the basis for modern local area networks (LANs) and wide area networks (WANs). Client/server system was developed to cope up with the rapidly changing business environment.

The general forces that drive the move to client/server systems are as follows:

- A strong business requirement for decentralised computing horsepower.
- Standard, powerful computers with user-friendly interfaces.
- Mature, shrink-wrapped user applications with widespread acceptance.
- Inexpensive, modular systems designed with enterprise class architecture, such as power and network redundancy and file archiving network protocols, to link them together.
- Growing cost/performance advantages of PC-based platforms.

PEER-TO-PEER DISTRIBUTED SYSTEM

The peer-to-peer architecture is a good way to structure a distributed system so that it consists of many identical software processes or modules, each module running on a different computer or node. The different software modules stored at different sites communicate with each other to complete the processing required for the execution of distributed applications. Peer-to-peer architecture provides both client and server functionalities on each computer. Therefore, each node can access services from other nodes as well as providing services to other nodes. In contrast with the client/server architecture, in a peer-to-peer distributed system each node provides user interaction facilities as well as processing capabilities.

Considering the complexity associated with discovering, communicating with and managing the large number of computers involved in a distributed system, the software module at each node in a peer-to-peer distributed system is typically structured in a layered manner. Thus, the software modules of peer-to-peer applications can be divided into the three layers, known as the base overlay layer, the middleware layer, and the application layer. The base overlay layer deals with the issue of discovering other participants in the system and creating a mechanism for all nodes to communicate with each other. This layer ensures that all participants in the network are aware of other participants. The middleware layer includes additional software components that can be potentially reused by many different applications. The functionalities provided by this layer include the ability to create a distributed index for information in the system, a publish/subscribe facility and security services. The functions provided by the middleware layer are not necessary for all applications, but they are developed to be reused by more than one application.

The application layer provides software packages intended to be used by users and developed so as to exploit the distributed nature of the peer-to-peer infrastructure. There is no standard terminology across different implementations of the peer-to-peer system, and thus, the term "peer-to-peer" is used for general descriptions of the functionalities required for building a generic peer-to-peer system. Most of the peer-to-peer systems are developed as single-application systems.

MULTI-DATABASE SYSTEM (MDBS)

In recent years, MDBS has been gaining the attention of many researchers who attempt to logically integrate several different independent DDBMSs while allowing the local DBMSs to maintain complete control of their operations. Complete autonomy means that there can be no software modifications to the local DBMSs in a DDBMS. Hence, an MDBS, which provides the necessary functionality, is introduced as an additional software layer on top of the local DBMSs.

An MDBS is a software that can be manipulated and accessed through a single manipulation language with a single common data model (*i.e.,* through a single application) in a heterogeneous environment without interfering with the normal execution of the individual database systems. The MDBS has developed from a requirement to manage and retrieve data from multiple databases within a single application while providing complete autonomy to individual database systems. To support DBMS transparency, MDBS resides on top of existing databases and file systems and presents a single database to its users. An MDBS maintains a global schema against which users issue queries and updates, and this global schema is constructed by integrating the schemas of local databases. To execute a global query, the MDBS first translates it into a number of subqueries, and converts these subqueries into appropriate local queries for running on local DBMSs. After completion of execution, local results are merged and the final global result for the user query is generated. An MDBS controls multiple gateways and manages local databases through these gateways.

WEB AND DBMS INTEGRATION ARCHITECTURE

The web is connecting together data sources at a fantastic rate. Many data sources including DBMS systems that were formerly inaccessible and write-only are or could soon become accessible. There is increased incentive in enterprises to make more information available not just within the organisation but to customers as well. The Internet Tools Survey is to identify software architecture approaches for integration of the Web with DBMS systems. A companion section of the survey covers Web + Object (middleware) Integration. So far we have not surveyed Object Middleware + DBMS integration. Background sections cover the current Web Architecture and OMG-based object frameworks.

DESIGN SPACE

There are currently many variants of how to connect the Web to DBMS systems. The range of design choices. A design space is a category scheme of design choices that covers a range of variations in approaches. A collection of systems or examples is reviewed and the design space captures the main design dimensions and alternative choices within each dimension. The approach can lead to more general solutions which can emerge from viewing the main design choices. Then, specific systems can evolve towards more general solutions.

The evolution of features to support information accessibility on the web, and then the kinds of databases that are now or will likely be available through the web. As data is stored using different data models, concerns about a common data model, sharing of complex (and multimedia) data types, and how multiple data sources can be connected together with DBMS glueware. The two- and three-tier architectures we can build with databases, then useful web-related database functionality, and finally, proprietary and standards concerns.

Web, OO Middleware, and DBMSs

At a high level, the Web provides client and server interfaces that each allow connection to any kind of service, including middleware services (*e.g.*, CORBA services) or database services (*e.g.*, database access). Similarly, middleware services often connect to DBMS systems.

Web Generations

Some view the web as rapidly evolving through several generations of increasingly general functionality.

Web + DBMS systems vary in the way they connect together.

- Static HTML. The first generation web only supported browsing of static HTML pages.
- CGI plus Scripting. A second generation used the Web's Common Gateway Interface (CGI) plus web programmer-designed, proprietary, and idiosyncratic scripts written in scripting languages like Perl or programming languages like C to dynamically construct custom and application-specific HTML on-the-fly.
- Extended CGI and Application Generation. From a DBMS point of

view, a third generation on the server side makes application construction higher level via recourse to higher level application generation tools (*e.g.*, object modelling, CASE, DBMS). DBMS vendors (and in general vendors of client-server software) are providing ways of connecting Web interfaces (mostly based on CGI and now Java) to existing DBMS data and client-server functionality. These provide a third generation of integration in that higher level tools or techniques can be used to limit the amount of custom code that must be developed. Some specific Web extensions and techniques to handle sessions (*e.g.*, Netscape's cookies) are a step in the directions of extending stateless CGI capabilities for applications that depend on stateful sessions.

- Client-side DBMS Connections. A forth generation (the current generation), downloaded client-side Java applets, are now providing direct client-side connections to middleware, DBMS gateways and systems and bypassing the Web server and its CGI API. With this architecture, applications are downloaded to "thin Web clients" on a just-in-time basis. This permits richer transactional and session-based interfaces than pre-Java stateless forms-based interfaces that could reside on the client side. JavaSoft's JDBC API provides a Java class library for interfacing applications to DBMS clients including ODBC.

Kinds of DBMS

A principal dimension of categorisation is the kind of data source connected to a Web system. In the last few years, the Web has quickly become a universal publishing medium for unstructured and semi-structured information. Now, there is a rush to use the Web to connect once closed and write-only DBMS systems and databases to internal and external customers. If successful, this would extend the reach of the Web to also subsume structured information.

Of course, a useful goal would be to develop middleware technology to provide transparent access to data regardless of its source.

- File systems — File systems contain the bulk of information. There are billions of application-specific file-formats and thousands of standardised file formats. File systems are relatively light weight and provide varying services (storing and naming persistent opaque large objects (blobs), sometimes security, versioning, and replication). First and later Web architectures depend on access to HTML usually stored in files.
- Information Retrieval Systems — After years of playing a back seat role to DBMSs, information retrieval in the form of web crawlers has become a basic ingredient in browsing the Web. These systems

(*e.g.*, Lycos, AltaVista) generate indexes of the information stored on the internet. We cover these separately in the internet tools survey on Searching and indexing.

- COBOL, Navigational and Hierarchic DBMS — Significant amounts of data are stored within these and other types of legacy systems. Many of these systems are still in operation today (*e.g.*, a part of one major U.S., airline's system is still running on pre-ANSI FORTRAN).
- Relational DBMS — Relational DBMS systems are mature in the market (but only since, the late 1980s). Dominant vendors are Oracle, Sybase, Informix, IBM, and Microsoft but there are many more (not listed).
- Object DBMS systems are the perpetual runners up. Object Database Management Group (ODMG) is a consortium of vendors of many of the object-oriented DBMS systems. ODMG-93 is their standard specification (latest release 1.2, December 1995). Voting members of ODMG are GemStone Systems (formerly Servio), IBEX Computing, O2 Technology, Object Design, Objectivity, POET Software, UniSQL, and Versant Object Technology. Related information is available here.
- Object-Relational — Object-Relational is a term for systems that support both relational (table-based) SQL queries and object data types. At this point, most ODBMSs offer a relational query capability and some RDBMS' provide some ADT capabilities so differences are in the details.
- Componentware DBMSs — OMG CORBAServices provide services for data modelling, persistence, transactions, queries, and several other DBMS functions and provide an alternative middleware approach to exporting DBMS function. So far, there are few vendors of CORBAServices and so it is early to say whether DBMS functionality will appear in componentware form though some promising experiments demonstrate this approach (*e.g.*, the TI Open OODB system) and some interested products are on the horizon (*e.g.*, Microsoft OLE/DB).

Data Model is Supported

Different DBMS systems provide native support for different data models. To date, the relational DBMS community supports tables. SQL2 is the current standard ISO/ANSI X3H2 SQL. SQL3 is an upwards compatible specification that adds objects via abstract data types (ADTs), which are unfortunately not the same as OMG IDL objects (meaning that unfortunately the world will have two competing incompatible modelling languages for sharing complex objects. The SQL community is also specifying standard libraries for GIS, multimedia types, etc. as is OMG, again incompatibly. Several ODBMS vendors support C++ and Java, others support Smalltalk, some support all three. The ODMG standard defines ODL (Object Definition Language), a superset of OMG's IDL, which also includes a specific class library that defines collections among other data types. ODMG also defines a not-very-seamless "binding" to C++.

ODMG OQL is an object variant of SQL3 but uses the ODL object model in place of SQL3 ADTs. The potential is there for OMG, SQL3, and ODMG to converge on a common object model but this does not appear to be happening (although there are efforts within the ODMG and X3H2 to attempt to merge OQL and the query portion of SQL, but it is difficult at this point to say how successful these efforts will be).

Complex and Multimedia Data Types

DBMS vendors are beginning to provide more or less support for extensibility of new data types and integration with existing data stores. Sybase provides separate, unintegrated servers for geospatial data and relational data. Other DBMS systems (*e.g.*, Oracle, Informix/Illustra, IBM DB2, Object Design) provide "data blades" or Database Extenders, that is, well supported (class) libraries for some useful data types like text, audio, images, video, spatial, time-series, HTML, Java, and other data types. Some of these libraries are application-developer extensible but they are tied to particular DBMS products and not portable though it appears that they could be made portable. ODI's libraries appear to be C++ libraries that are made persistent, versionable, and event-driven via ODI's C++ processing.

In the short term, media class libraries are much better than each programmer developing idiosyncratic media types. In the longer term, standard media libraries and/or porting standards could be developed to make applications developed using one DBMS system portable to another. In fact, there is no real reason why these libraries should be only useful to DBMS applications. They could be useful to any multimedia web application.

DBMS Glueware

There are some tools, techniques, standards, and glueware for connecting DBMS systems together with loose or tight coupling.

- Federated DBMS architectures create a front-end DBMS that maps queries to any of several possibly heterogeneous backend DBMSs. In spite of several years of DBMS research on heterogeneous DBMS systems, many DBMS research puzzles remain.
- RDA and ODBC provide DBMS gateways so applications connected to ODBC can be connected to any of several backend DBMSs. JDBC API is a standard SQL database access interface from JavaSoft that provides a Java class library for interfacing to DBMSs in a standards way, including a JDBC-ODBC mapping.

- Vendors like Persistence Software Inc., Object Design Inc. (ObjectStore DBConnect), Rogue Wave Software Inc. (Dbtools.h++) and ParcPlace (VisualWave) provide differing ways to provide OO front-ends (*e.g.*, C++ class libraries) to relational DBMS systems.
- X/Open XA defines protocols for transaction commit coordination protocol to insure that a parent transaction only commits if all child transactions in separate DBMS systems commit.
- Microsoft OLE-DB is a library of interfaces that componentises some useful DBMS query interfaces.

Two- and Three-tier Architectures

Traditional client-server architectures are called two-tier or fat client since, application logic resides in the client and the server provides a generic service. Since, many servers provide overlapping middleware capabilities and thinner clients are desirable, some newer Web and middleware systems use so-called three tier architectures with a thin client connected to a server which connects to other servers as needed.

CORBA provides an extensible way of doing this but many systems have specialised capabilities. For instance, a federated DBMS might be viewed as a parent DBMS engine that coordinates and accesses other DBMS engines. There are many ways in which DBMS systems are currently being hooked to the Web. At present, most products use CGI, and some are compatible with NSAPI, ISAPI, and WRBAPI.

These typically connect to one of the following: a DBMS client directly, an analysis or decision support system, a caching scheme for caching multiple DBMS connections, ODBC so many DBMS systems can plug in, or CORBA which then connects to a DBMS. Alternatively, some new systems are downloading Java applets that then interface to a library like JDBC or a CORBA client which then interfaces directly to a DBMS client or ODBC or various CORBA services.

DBMS Functionality

Web systems can connect to DBMS to show off more or less of the DBMS functionality. Both file and DBMS systems provide local stores of information. DBMS systems compete with file systems in supporting a richer collection of services (good performance, fine-grained persistence, sharing, concurrency, transactions, queries, updates, optimisation, referential integrity, sometimes relationships, distribution, replication, security, interfaces to and federation with other DBMSs). While DBMS systems are often built on top of file systems, they do not necessarily support integration with file systems though many applications might use both DBMS and file storage in an integrated but customised way. Different Web + DBMS systems handle different kinds of functional extensions.

Transactions and Sessions

Web servers are memoryless - they do not store state from one simple web transactions (page or CGI access) to the next. Therefore it is difficult to build session-based transactional applications that depend on context or state.

Solution approaches are:

- Pass state back and forth from client to server and back on every web access - Netscape's cookies is one way to do this.
- Cache connections in a CGI connection server so that connections can be continued in other processes without slowing down the Web server.
- Download applets to Web clients running Java and let these communicate directly with DBMS or other session-based APIs.

Query Interfaces

Web applications that access DBMS systems do so mostly via fixed forms and canned queries. A next generation web-DBMS interface will make dynamic query interfaces an option. There are many kinds of these (*e.g.*, typein, forms and menu-driven, graphical, spatial, natural language, speech) and they are reasonably well understood. Client side scripting languages will enable a new generation of these over the next few years. An ever present challenge for these interfaces is the ease with which the end-user can ask complex queries that bring the DBMS system to its knees since, many DBMS systems are carefully optimised for certain mixes of queries. Better support for prediction of how long a query will take and other forms of cooperative response (*e.g.*, providing intermediate answers, related answers, telling why a complex query fails) will be needed.

Indexing DBMS Content

Internet search engines index actual pages but cannot index pages constructed on the fly by CGI-based applications including applications materialising pages from DBMS systems. That leaves DBMS systems, which are often internally indexed, unreachable by today's search engines because DBMS systems do not expose their indices. A challenge is to identify new ways to expose and advertise information locked in DBMS systems to search engines.

Meta Data

A related problem is advertising the existence and content of DBMS systems that become accessible on line. At present, there are no standard ways of publishing the existence and meta data content of DBMS systems though there are standards for relational DBMS catalogues (and CORBA interface repositories) and also proposals for standards for ODMG meta data catalogues. Some communities view this as the repository problem and much effort has been expended in this area (*e.g.*, ANSI X3H4) though not in a web context.

Global Object Base

There is the potential for rethinking how DBMS systems, file systems, the Web, and object frameworks can provide a better, closer coupled longer-term infrastructure that supports today's "legacy information systems" and provides a route to a more universal objectbase in the future. Indeed, one of the visions of Object-Internet integration views the Web as a giant decentralised object DBMS. It appears that object technology like that of OMG and/or Microsoft may provide the right infrastructure glue.

Application Partitioning

With Java applets and mobile code, applications are statically partitioned from client to server. With ODBMS client-side caching of objects and middleware like OMG, there is the potential of moving objects from server to client and middleware services from server to client, which could result in more seamless dynamic application partitioning and load balancing.

What's Proprietary? What's Standard?

In Web + DBMS architectures, it is appropriate to look at different approaches to connecting the web and DBMSs and ask whether standards are being used and whether additional standards can be identified. If they can, it could mean much greater interoperability among data sources. The alternative is many variant ways to connect data sources. At present, the state of practice is that there are a handful of approaches to Web + DBMS integration and that even when the same approach is followed, details differ from vendor to vendor so that current solutions are vendor proprietary and non-portable. The potential now exists for adopting standards in this area to decouple DBMS access from the engine providing the data. But it may still be a few years premature for these standards since, solution approaches (*e.g.*, client-side applets connected to DBMSs, better support for transactions and sessions, next generations of CGI) are still evolving.

CONNECTION FOR JAVA (OPEN HORIZON INC.)

Connection for Java is a Java applet (client side) that connects directly to the client (also on the client's machine) of Open Horizon's existing Connection Enterprise Broker server. A Web server is not needed (other than to download the applet) as long as the client can run Java applets. Connection for Java is built on Java DataBase Connectivity.

The Connection Server provides access to:

- DBMS servers (DB2, Informix, Oracle, Sybase)
- TP monitors (CICS, Encina, Top End, Tuxedo)
- server-resident application generators
- forthcoming Java development environments from Sybase (Powersoft), Oracle, Gupta (Centura), and Borland.

COMPONENTWARE CONSORTIUM

Bruce Cottman (I-Kinetics) made a presentation on the DARPA TRP ComponentWare Consortium during the OMG Internet SIG held in San Diego, California, in January 1996. He described a CORBA DB Component. Today, the Web interface is exported to the Desktop client. The object executable (process) resides on a remote server. Methods are invoked by client on server. In his example, to retrieve the value from an array cell, a remote call is executed.

This is unacceptable in today's Internet. Thus the need for Object migration. The CWDynaset is migrated to the client. Object method calls and properties are executed locally, while the CWDatabase object is local to the legacy database it wraps. Bruce described security and component groups (useful for replication) as two middleware functions that reside on the object network, not necessarily bundled inside the DBMS. He described ObjectPump, an input/output wrapper that captures I/O of production systems that themselves cannot be perturbed. It is interoperable with OLE/COM. So a legacy application wrapped with CORBA can now talk to Excel on a PC. ObjectPump can be used to wrap data sources like DBMS systems.

DB2 WWW CONNECTION (IBM)

DB2 WWW Connection is an Internet gateway to IBM's DB2 relational DBMS. A CGI programme macro file format provides "cross-language variable substitution," enabling the application developer to use the standard capabilities of HTML and dynamic SQL for creation of query forms, reports, and updates. The macro file is general purpose and can also be used to allow an application to access data on remote servers using Distributed Database Connection Services (DDCS) or DataJoiner, which can connect to Oracle, Sybase, Microsoft SQL Server or other relational and non-relational data sources. Data security is handled via: DB2 login and password; login and password variables in DB2 WWW Connection that link to the DB2 authentication mechanisms; the Web server's security mechanisms, when configured to protect DB2 server directories; and IBM Internet Connection Secure Servers that support S-HTTP and SSL standards, which encrypt requests and results.

DataFountain (Dimensional Insight Inc.)

Not reviewed.

DataRamp(DataRamp, Inc.)

DataRamp provides RSA-secure access to ODBC-compliant databases over the internet. It provides a codeless development environment with support for forms definitions for data access and manipulation. Supports Microsoft Windows user interfaces/applications (*e.g.*, applications built with

MS Access, Visual Basic, Visual C++, PowerBuilder, Delphi, Crystal Reports, etc.) without alteration. These applications require a DataRamp ODBC client driver, and can then connect to any ODBC-compliant RDBMS via a DataRamp server. A DataRamp Java client is also available.

dbWeb (Microsoft)

Microsoft dbWeb is a connectivity tool between Microsoft ODBC and Microsoft Internet Information Server (IIS) to publish ODBC-database data on the internet. Web clients connect to a Microsoft IIS which communicates with a dbWeb ISAPI client. The dbWeb client submits the queries to the dbWeb Service which returns the dynamically-generated HTML results.

DSS Web (MicroStrategy Inc.)

DSS Web interposes decision support analytic capabilities between a Web server and any of several DBMS systems.

Empress Hypermedia Web HTML Toolkit (Empress Software Inc.)

Not reviewed.

HAHTSITE (HAHT Software Inc.)

HAHTSITE is an integrated development environment that provides tools for building Web sites and applications. Tools include: an editor and page authoring environment, a debugger, site management tools, ODBC access to data sources, and interfaces to version control software.

HyperStar Web Developer's Kit (Vmark Software Inc.)

Not reviewed.

iResults DataWeb 2.0(Integral Results Inc.)

Not reviewed.

Internet Assistant for Access (Microsoft)

Internet Assistant for Microsoft Access 95 is a free add-in that allows users of Microsoft Access to create HTML documents from structured data stored in Access or any ODBC-compliant data source and share it over the Internet. It requires an HTML browser that supports Tables.

InfoHarness (Bell Communications Research and University of Georgia)

This research project seeks to provide an extensible way to define meta data that can provide access to unstructured, semi-structured, or structured data. The data itself is not relocated, reformatted, or restructured. Instead, a meta data description language (declarative repository definition language) is defined and a library of meta data extractors (a repository generator) are used to populate it. Examples show how InfoHarness can be used to view the same file of C++ functions from different views. A companion project InfoQuilt is working on information correlation in content descriptive domain specific meta data.

Informix

Informix recently bought Illustra. In addition, Informix provides two free interface kits to connect databases to the Web from Informix-4GL applications and ESQL/C applications using CGI. Examples are provided.

JAM/WEB (Prolifics)

Transactional web-based (codeless) applications development environment. Includes high-level visual editor (eliminates need to know HTML, SQL, CGI, Perl, etc.), support for Javascript, dynamic HTML, and report generation.

Java DataBase Connectivity (JavaSoft)

The JDBC API is a standard SQL database access interface under development at JavaSoft. JDBC is similar in purpose to Microsoft's ODBC but provides an object-oriented interface. A number of companies have endorsed the JDBC database access API. A 114-page spec (available here in postscript) is undergoing public review through June 8, 1996. The API defines Java classes that allow a Java application developer to create database connections to (possibly multiple) DBMSs, issue SQL statements, and process results.

The JDBC API is implemented as a driver manager that can support multiple drivers that are connected to different DBMS systems. JavaSoft and Intersolv are developing a JDBC-ODBC driver that will run existing ODBC drivers. JDBC drivers can be written in Java so they can be downloaded as part of an applet or they can be implemented using native methods to access existing DBMS access libraries.

JetConnect/JetAssist (XDB Systems Inc.)

JETConnect (JET = Java Enterprise Tools) is a set of class libraries and drivers that connects Java to any ODBC DBMS. JET eliminates performance and usage problems of CGI by maintaining persistent connections between the client and the DBMS. JetAssist is a Java applet (codeless) development environment which provides the features of JETConnect in a GUI.

JTF/ATD Data Server (SAIC) (password protected) and more

JTF/ATD is a major U.S DoD Command and Control architecture that several defence contractors are working on. The architecture rests on a distributed object foundation at the bottom, several "servers" (services) for data, webs (hypergraphs), maps, and situations. Rick Goodwin described the

JTF/ATD Data Server at the OMG ISIG meeting in January 1996. The problem involves linking together many data sources and getting information to flow between them. CORBA is the backplane hooking information sources together. This includes wrappers for SQL-based relational DBMS systems, OSQL-based ODBMSs (Objectivity sql++ queries and getfirstobject, getnextobject, and getallobjects), and flat files as well as "mediators" which federate multiple data sources. They have developed login, data location, and schema services including a shared Command and Control schema in IDL. Legacy DBMS systems do not know about objects. The IDL-based schema contains mappings to data source objects. Queries result in in-memory collections of in-memory fine-grained C++ objects, which are needed for applications like simulations. Refinements include: query scheduling, notification, caching, triggers, and comm. bandwidth adaptivity.

JTF is an early adopter of ORB technology - "before ORB technology was ready." They are working on moving query and collection classes from Orbix to ObjectBroker to HP Orbplus. Now they want a global yellow pages. Also, they developed their own object services implementations for naming and transactions; some of these will be replaced when service providers provide these.

They are working with others in the ARPA community on distributed query optimisation and query relaxation. Steps for the next year are to focus on unstructured information sources including images, intelligent distribution and positioning of objects in video (working with CMU), working on natural language interfaces, information retrieval, GIS (working with Open GIS), updates. Goodwin introduced Mike Dean (BBN) who is working on the JTF map server. They need object views so different C2 roles (*e.g.*, staff, field) see different views of situations. They are working on CGI queries and have not yet moved to Java. They are working on a CASE tool to generate IDL and then map to OOPLs.

JRB

JRB, Java Relational Binding from O_2 Technology, generates a relational schema from Java classes including read and write access methods to the relations. The generated schema must correspond to a Sybase or ORACLE RDBMS schema, and is accessed via Sun Microsystem's JDBC.

LiveWire (Netscape)

LiveWire and LiveWire Pro are tools for web site management, on-line application creation (with JavaScript support), and access to RDBMS systems (with specific support for SQL access to Informix, Sybase, and Oracle; and, ODBC support to connect to most others). LiveWire Pro comes with a developer version of Informix's OnLine-Workgroup high-performance SQL database, and reporting software.

MORE System and More

MORE (Multimedia Oriented Repository Environment) is a research system developed at U Houston at Clear Lake. The system is used for asset management and provides a repository for meta data with a collection of built-in classes. It replaced an earlier prototype developed using X-Windows with a Web-based implementation using CGI scripts. The result was more accessible to users, more scaleable, easier to build, and less monolithic. Much of the design changed due to assumptions of a stateless server.

NetDynamics (NetDynamics, Inc.)

NetDynamics is representative of a no-code (codeless) application builder for web/database application development. In contrast to DBMS-vendor supplied Web integration, these are open systems solutions that work with any Web server, Web browser, HTML editor, major DBMS, ODBC-compliant DBMS, UNIX, and PC. The Web server can use CGI, Netscape's NSAPI, or Microsoft's ISAPI to communicate with the NetDynamics server. An architectural issue is, what sorts of functions are supplied by such a tool, which should be supplied by a DBMS (or other server), and which by a next generation Web.

In client/server applications a session begins when a user logs on (to a DBMS, for instance) and ends when a user logs off. Web sessions are defined differently (less intuitively, more scaleably perhaps). NetDynamics provides session management via secure session ids. NetDynamics must keep session state both on the server and client page. It automatically maintains user database login and password and user page privileges, generating an encrypted session ID for each page; the key is kept on a client page that is associated with data stored on the server. Cursor information can be kept associated with a page so operations to scroll through database tables can be supported even when a user leaves and returns later to a page. NetDynamics supports some transaction commit and rollback capabilities.

NetDynamics provides access privileges that interoperate with database security mechanisms. NetDynamics security bridge works as follows. The Web server provides user authentication and supplies NetDynamics with a WebID. NetDynamics provides navigation flow control for navigation through a NetDynamics application via defined paths; it provides support for defining user privileges for query, insert, etc., on a page-level basis; and it maps the WebID to the DBMS login. The DBMS server provides standard DBMS security.

The NetDynamics application server caches database connections, communicates through an optimised interface to CGI, ISAPI, or NSAPI, and can be scaled across multiple platforms and managed to provide automatic load balancing. A typical request follows the following route: web client - web server - [CGI NSAPI or ISAPI] - NetDynamics server - request broker to select one of the following - any free application server (these can run Java - if a DBMS operation continue) - request broker to select any of the following - any free data server.

ObjectStore ObjectForms and PSE (Object Design)

ODI is a client-server ODBMS with seamless support for C++. To support web applications, ODI has added seven products: six Object Managers (C++ class libraries designed to run with ObjectStore) that support text, audio, video, image, HTML data, and Java applets and a tool called ObjectStore ObjectForms. The image object manager developed by Virage Inc. supports query-by-content searches on images; the text object manager uses Verity Inc.'s full-text retrieval engine. The HTML and Java object managers support persistence, querying, and versioning of HTML and Java objects respectively. The ODI ODBMS supports relationships between these and programmer defined media types.

ObjectForms supports on-the-fly HTML page generation using template files, which are HTML files that include ODI-extended tags that extend standard HTML files. ObjectForms reads these tags to determine how to query or update ObjectStore and then dynamically generates HTML pages to display the results. Tags support HTML form generation and processing, environment variable setting, conditional HTML table generation, access to CGI variables, support for DBMS event trapping, display of query results, etc. WebConnect, a component of the ObjectForms, works with standard web servers via CGI. It consists of two parts, a CGI script that connects to ObjectForms or ObjectStore directly, and a Web Dispatcher that provides load balancing and high throughput for high volume web sites.

Other ODI products provide complementary capabilities: OpenAccess adheres to the ODBC standard and provides SQL access to ObjectStore databases. Inspector is a visual browser, editor, and query tool for ObjectStore databases.

ObjectStore's PSE (Persistent Storage Engine) is a single-user Java-based object repository for storing Java objects (*e.g.* applets). It comes in two versions, PSE, and PSE Pro. The PSE Pro version adds support for transactions. They can be used, for example, to support data storage for Java applications. This capability demonstrates the movement of database features to the client, specifically enabling clients to maintain private partitions of a larger globally-accessible database (checking Java objects in and out).

O2Web (O2)

O2 is a client-server ODBMS that conforms to the ODMG specification. O2 supports C++ and O2's 4th generation language O2C.

OQL is the ODMG object query language, a variant of SQL. In O2Web, OQL queries are mapped into HTTP URLs instead of physical file paths using a format http://host[:port]path?query. The query is evaluated on an O2 server. The O2 object that results from the query is sent a system-supplied print-yourself-in-HTML message. Complex objects and collections are recursively printed and primitive objects and some predefined classes like Date and Image are printed in a readable format. O2 programmers can overload print methods to customise the HTML returned and can include links and forms (using the POST method).

O2Web uses a variant of a 3-tier architecture to connect any web server via CGI to O2. The query is passed from the standard client to the standard HTTP server then via standard CGI to the O2 Web gateway which connects to the O2Web dispatcher (which tells the O2Web Gateway which O2Web server to connect to) and then connects to the O2Web server, which runs the query and transforms the result to HTML using O2 system or user supplied methods and the resulting HTML is sent back to the Web client.

R:Web (Microrim Inc.)

Internet-version of R:Base RDBMS for internet servers. R:Web converts R:Base forms to HTML, enabling users to view and modify a database.

Saphire/Web (Bluestone Inc.)

Visual web application development environment with support for ODBC and JDBC, as well as OLE, COM and CORBA.

WebDBC (Nomad Development Corp.)

WebDBC 2.5 is a Web/database application development tool. The WebDBC Connection Manager caches and reuses database connections to allow application control of the number of ODBC DBMS connections open.

WebDBC 2.5 supports custom user-authentication. WebDBC 2.5 can be invoked as a DLL, an NT Service, or via Microsoft/Process' ISAPI, Netscape's NSAPI, Spry's BGI, or CGI and provides the ability to support more simultaneous users. The former provide faster performance than traditional CGI (Common Gateway Interface) invocation.

Web-based "Instant Pages" are web-based wizards that allow users to quickly build and customise web page interfaces to their databases without knowing HTML or WebDBC commands.

Web DataBlade Module (Illustra)

Illustra is an object-relational DBMS. The company Illustra was recently acquired by Informix. Illustra has a number of interesting features (extensible support for new data types called data blades, type and table inheritance, optional archival no-overwrite storage that allows "time-travel" what if queries on past states of the DBM, rules and event notifications). An Illustra Web DataBlade enabled application is a collection of HTML pages stored in the

Illustra DBMS and that contain embedded SQL statements. As such, Illustra application programming is higher level than proprietary and hard to share CGI script-based applications written in C or Perl (though one could share CGI libraries

The Illustra Web DataBlade executes queries and processes results as follows: a standard web browser submits an HTML Query Page (form submission request or other query) to a standard web server. Using CGI the web server launches a Webdriver application, which connects to the specified Illustra server and then selects an Application Page stored as a row in a table. The Application page is HTML with embedded relational queries. A function called WebExplode that runs within the Illustra server parses the application page, executes embedded queries, and formats results. The expanded page is placed in the database memory and also returned via the Webdriver application and Web server to the web browser.

Application pages are HTML plus a small set of markup tags for:

- Specifying SQL and formatting instructions
- Managing variables within the Application Page
- Managing error processing within the Application Page
- Specifying calls to system services on the DBMS server
- Specifies conditionals controlling logical blocks of HTML.

The DataBlade module maintains transactional integrity (but only) within an Application Page, provides error reporting and logging, including providing click-stream analysis which allows analysis of application usage based on frequency of user link selections.

WebBuilder (VPE, Inc.)

WebBuilder is an internet application development environment that is used to build forms-based HTML applications. It supports concurrent access to multiple relational databases as well as state/session management on top of CGI, and a proprietary rules-based development language that can be used in forms design -- *e.g.,* for triggers (the event-driven rule engine exists on the server).

WebSystem 1.0 and 2.0 and PowerBrowser (Oracle)

The Oracle WebServer is an integration of three components: Oracle Web Listener, Oracle Web Agents, and Oracle7 Workgroup Server. Hypertext links in any HTML document can point directly to an Oracle stored procedure, written in Oracle's proprietary PL/SQL procedural extension to SQL. When the procedure is executed, a dynamic HTML page is returned. WebServer 2.0 provides Java capabilities on the server. It is built around Oracle Web Request Broker which bypasses high overhead CGI and provides a native custom connection to Oracle7. Web Request Broker API (WRB API) competes with Microsoft ISAPI, NetScape's NSAPI, and other HTTP server programmatic interfaces. A LiveHTML interpreter allows developers to user server-side-includes, which extend HTML pages to permit callouts to applications and to back-end servers.

Oracle has a forthcoming TextServer product that summarises content and a forthcoming VideoServer product. Currently, Web clients can access external systems either using WRB API by developing a Web Server "cartridge" or through the Java Interpreter. The Oracle Java Interpreter provides a Java class library that models Oracle's proprietary procedural extension to SQL PL/SQL as Java classes. Oracle is working on a Java-CORBA language binding to provide Internet access to CORBA from the WebServer. This involves developing a (DBMS-independent) Java language mapping for CORBA IDL and a Java-CORBA stub mapping that is ORB-independent-they see a need for a standard stub interface so all Java applets talk to ORBs the same way (required for portable applets).

Oracle's PowerBrowser[a] provides:

- Standard Web browser
- Personal Server[a], a personal Web HTTP 1.0 desktop server that is easy enough for novices to use and allows clients to publish and share web pages.
- Personal Publisher[a] an HTML 2.0 page authoring environment which allows drag and drop of controls such as buttons and text boxes and also supports tables, backgrounds, frames, and GIF animations.
- A BASIC interpreter for embedding scripts written in Oracle BASIC to HTML. The scripts can be run in the PowerBrowser to check forms arguments, for instance, or in the Personal Server to add server-side programming capabilities without resorting to CGI.
- Blaze, a local database
- A Database Wizard for accessing ODBC-compliant databases from Web applications (database-enabled Web applications).
- Add-ons SQL*Net and Oracle WebServer to access Oracle 7 or corporate DBMSs.
- Network Loadable Objects[a] (NLO) (formerly Client-Side Processing (CSP)) are compatible with Netscape 2.0 plug-ins and provide a standard interface and framework for running third-party-written network-resident applications on the same machine as the Web browser client. Examples are Java applets, VRML scripts, and various viewers (video player, sound player). Similar to CGI on the server, NLOs can be long-term tasks that keep state across network accesses and can provide direct access to user and client user interfaces.
- Provides a way to allow developers to integrate PowerBrowser features with OS-specific programme modules on the Web client.

- Software developer kits to provide examples of how to get started using NLO and CSP.
- Secure Sockets Layer (SSL) provides data encryption and authentication for both the browser and server.
- Support for Java applets (announced for May 1996).

web.works, web.sql, and PowerBuilder (Sybase)

web.works is an architecture encompassing Sybase's database, middleware, and tools products. Powerbuilder is a web server product supporting CGI/NSAPI/ISAPI and connections to databases. web.sql manages (caches) multiple open database connections. It evaluates HTML page templates with in-line database commands and Perl scripts to return HTML. Sybase also markets several visual components. WebViewer is an OLE Custom Control that adds HTML browsing to an application. Formula One/NET is an Excel-compatible spreadsheet plug-in for Navigator.

DISTRIBUTED DBMS MODEL TRANSACTIONS AND ARCHITECTURE

In the 1960s and 1970s, most efforts in operating system design were largely focused on the so-called traditional operating systems, which ran on stand-along computers with single processors. Thus, database system were generally implemented as an application on top of a general purpose operating system. Since, the requirement of a database system are different from those of a general purpose system, new functionality must be added to the operating system to efficiently support a database system. Sometimes, the new features might not be appropriate for an operating system and may have to be implemented in the user space at a much higher overhead.

Another approach is to write a new operating system which efficiently supports only the functions needed by database systems. Although such systems will have higher performance for database applications, their implementation from scratch might be expensive.

REQUIREMENTS OF A DATABASE OPERATING SYSTEM

Transaction Management

A user accesses a database system by executing a programme, called a transaction. A transaction is a sequence of read and write operations on the database. It is the unit of user interaction with the database system. A transaction maintains database consistency, even when several transactions are running concurrently (the problem of concurrency control). The system must ensure that a transaction either runs to completion or does not run at all (transaction atomicity). The system must ensure that in a case of system failure all partially completed transactions are either undone or are run to completion (failure recovery).

The operating system should support mechanisms to facilitate the implementation of the following properties in transactions:

- Concurrency control,
- Atomic commit, and
- Failure recovery.

Support for Complex, Persistent Data

A database system must support definition, efficient manipulation, and efficient storage on secondary devices of files with complex structures. Thus, an operating system must efficiently organise a file on secondary storage.

Buffer Management

Database systems are dominated by heavy I/O accesses and I/O traffic is usually a bottleneck. Data must be cached in buffers in the main memory to speed up the transactions. Thus, a database system requires mechanisms to perform the following operations efficiently: search the buffer to see if a page is present; select a page for replacement; and locate and retrieve the needed data page from secondary storage.

DATABASE SYSTEMS

A database system consists of a set of shared data objects that can be accessed by users. A database can be viewed as a collection of data objects.

A data object can be:

- A page,
- A file,
- A segment, or
- A record.

The state of a database is given by the values of its data objects. In a database, certain semantic relationships, called consistency assertions or integrity constraints must hold among its data objects. A database is said to be consistent if the values of its data objects satisfy all of its consistency assertions.

Transactions

A transaction is the unit of user interaction with the database. We assume the following properties about a transaction:

- A transaction preserves the consistency of a database.
- A transaction terminates in finite time.

If a transaction modifies at least one data object, then its called an update transaction, or an update. Otherwise its called a read-only transaction, or a query. The set of data objects that are read by a transaction are referred to as its readset and the set of data objects that are written by it as its writeset.

Conflicts

When transactions try to access the same data object then there is a conflict.

Transaction Processing

A transaction is executed by executing its actions one by one from the beginning to the end.

CONCURRENCY CONTROL MODEL

We can view a database system as consisting of three software modules: a transaction manager (TM), a data manager (DM), and a scheduler. The transaction manager supervises the execution of a transaction. It intercepts and executes all the submitted transactions. Thus, the TM is the interface between users and the database system.

The scheduler is responsible for enforcing concurrency control. It grands or releases locks on data objects as requested by a transaction. The data manager manages the database. It carries out the read-write requests issued by the transaction manager on behalf of a transaction by operating them on the database. It is also responsible for failure recovery. Thus, the DM is the interface between the scheduler and the database. The concurrency control model of a distributed database system.

THE PROBLEM OF CONCURRENCY CONTROL

In a typical database system, transactions are executed concurrently. Since, these transactions may access the same data objects, several anomalous situations may arise if the interleaving of actions is not controlled in some orderly way.

Inconsistent Retrieval

Inconsistent retrival occurs when a transaction reads some data objects of a database before another transaction has completed with its modification of those data objects.

Inconsistent Update

Inconsistent update occurs when many transactions read and write onto a common set of data objects of a database, leaving the database in an inconsistent state.

DISTRIBUTED RELATIONAL DATABASE ARCHITECTURE

Distributed Relational Database Architecture (TM) (DRDA) is a set of protocols that permits multiple database systems, both IBM(R) and non-IBM, as well as application programmes, to work together. Any combination of relational database management products that use DRDA(R) can be connected to form a distributed relational database management system. DRDA coordinates communication between systems by defining what must be exchanged and how it must be exchanged.

Unit of Work: A unit of work (UOW) is a single logical transaction. It consists of a sequence of SQL statements in which either all of the operations are successfully performed or the sequence as a whole is considered unsuccessful.

Distributed unit of Work: A distributed unit of work (DUOW), also known as multisite update, involves more than one database server within a unit of work.

A DUOW has the following characteristics:

- More than one database management server is updated per unit of work.
- The application directs the distribution of work, and initiates commit.
- There may be multiple requests per unit of work.
- There is one database management server per request.
- Commitment is coordinated across multiple database servers.

DISTRIBUTED DATABASE DESIGN CONCEPTS

In a distributed system, data are physically distributed among several sites but it provides a view of single logical database to its users. Each node of a distributed database system may follow the three-tier architecture like the centralised database management system (DBMS). Thus, the design of a distributed database system involves the design of a global conceptual schema, in addition to the local schemas, which conform to the three-tier architecture of the DBMS in each site. The design of computer network across the sites of a distributed system adds extra complexity to the design issue. The crucial design issue involves the distribution of data among the sites of the distributed system.

Therefore, the design and implementation of the distributed database system is a very complicated task and it involves three important factors as listed in the following.

- *Fragmentation-* A global relation may be divided into several non-overlapping subrelations called fragments, which are then distributed among sites.
- *Allocation-* Allocation involves the issue of allocating fragments among sites in a distributed system. Each fragment is stored at the site with optimal distribution.
- *Replication-* The distributed database system may maintain several copies of a fragment at different sites.

OBJECTIVES OF DATA DISTRIBUTION

In a distributed system, data may be fragmented, and each fragment can have a number of replicas to increase data availability and reliability. The following objectives must be considered while designing the fragmentation and allocation of these fragments to different sites in a distributed system (*i.e.,* during the design of data distribution).

- *Locality of reference-* To maximize the locality of references, whenever possible, data should be stored close to where it is used during data distribution. If a fragment is used at several sites, it may be beneficial to store copies of the fragment at different sites.
- *Improved availability and reliability of distributed data-* During data distribution, reliability and availability are improved by replication. A higher degree of availability can be achieved by storing multiple copies of the same information in different sites. Reliability is also achieved by storing multiple copies of the same information, since, it is possible to continue the normal operations of a particular site in case of site failure, by referencing the copy of the same information from other sites.
- *Workload distribution and improved performance-* Bad allocation may result in underutilisation of resources, and thereby system performance may degrade. Distributing the workload over the sites is an important feature of distributed database system. Workload distribution should be done to take advantage of system resources at each site and to maximize the degree of parallelism of execution of transactions. Since, workload distribution might negatively affect processing locality, it is necessary to consider the trade-off between them during the design of data distribution.
- *Balanced storage capacities and costs-* Database distribution must reflect the cost and availability of storage at different sites. The availability and cost of storage at each site must be considered so that cheap mass storage can be used, whenever possible. This must be balanced against locality of reference.
- *Minimal communication costs-* The cost of processing remote requests must be considered during data distribution. Retrieval cost is minimized when locality of reference is maximized or when each site has its own copy of the data. However, when replicated data are updated, the update has to be performed at all sites holding a replica, thereby increasing the communication costs.

DATA FRAGMENTATION

In a distributed system, a global relation may be divided into several non-overlapping subrelations and allocated to different sites, called fragments. This process is called data fragmentation. The objective of data fragmentation design is to determine non-overlapping fragments, which are logical units of allocation. Fragments can be designed by grouping a number of tuples or attributes of relations. Each group of tuples or attributes that constitute a fragment has the same properties.

Transparencies in Distributed Database Design

According to the definition of distributed database, one major objective is to achieve the transparency into the distributed system. Transparency refers to the separation of the higher-level semantics of a system from lower-level implementation issues. In a distributed system, transparency hides the implementation details from users of the system. In other words, the user believes that he or she is working with a centralised database system, and that all the complexities of a distributed database are either hidden or transparent to the user. A distributed DBMS may have various levels of transparency.

In a distributed DBMS, the following four main categories of transparency have been identified:

- Distribution transparency
- Transaction transparency
- Performance transparency
- DBMS transparency.

DESIGN ISSUES FOR MODELLING BEHAVIOUR IN DISTRIBUTED SYSTEMS

Many software engineering projects involve the automation of "real-world" systems, consisting of interacting entities that work together to perform specific tasks. These real-world systems often exhibit intrinsic qualities that parallel the inherent characteristics of distributed software systems.

One of these qualities is concurrency. A real-world system possesses this quality if it includes more than one entity at any time, which most do. For example, consider a system for shipping parcel packages around the world. At any time, this system may include many physical entities (*e.g.*, parcels, customers, and locations) and abstract concepts (*e.g.*, rates, origins, and destinations.) Each of these can exist independently and behaviour concurrently. Distributed software systems provide true concurrency by disbursing objects over a network of computing resources. In contrast, centralised (single-processor) systems can only simulate concurrency.

Another shared quality is partial failure. In real-world systems, a single entity, like a parcel or customer, can fail independent of the rest of the system. The same is true for distributed systems since, individual computing resources in the network can fail or become unreachable. In centralised systems, failure is usually treated as an all-or-nothing condition.

A third common quality is dynamic, incremental change. Real-world systems rarely require a complete shutdown to make changes in the way that its work is performed. In fact, change is often considered an integral part of a real-world system instead of an external process. Can you image a worldwide shipping company shutting down its entire operation every time an office needed to add a new piece of equipment or open up a new distribution channel? The same situation exists for distributed systems. Because of the impracticality of shutting down an entire distributed system, mechanisms for dynamic and incremental change are often built into the infrastructure. The similarities between real-world and distributed software systems, might lead one to conclude that an accurate conceptual model of the first could be easily transformed into a good design for the second. However, this is not true because of some subtle and not-so-subtle differences in what the models represent and because of additional design issues related to distributed systems.

CHALLENGES IN GOING FROM ANALYSIS TO DESIGN

In general, the process of going from analysis to design in software development has always involved mapping or transforming conceptual models. Models used during analysis, regardless of whether they are formal, informal or subconscious, aim to describe real-world systems from a problem-domain perspective. The concepts found in an analysis model should relate directly to concepts in the real-world system. Models used for software design, on the other hand, involve an additional level of abstraction and serve a different purpose. They describe software concepts, like objects, structures, and processes, that only indirectly relate to concepts from the problem-domain. The purpose of a design model is to provide a blueprint for implementation and a framework for subsequent evolution of the system.

Ideally, the conceptual distance between an analysis and a corresponding design should be kept to a minimum. This improves understandability, traceability, and maintainability. For distributed systems, however, there are several fundamental problems that tend to increase the conceptual distance and complicate the design process. Below is a summary of some of them:

Complex Mappings

The mapping between concepts in the analysis and those in the design is not one-to-one. A single real-world entity can be represented by many software objects. For example, to increase access time, a parcel-tracking system may include multiple software objects for a single parcel and distribute them across the network.

Fragmented Behaviour

A software object may represent only a portion of an entity described in the analysis. We will refer to such partial representations, as object fragments. The object fragments that represent a specific real-world object do not have to be uniform, as long as they collectively encapsulate the required information and behaviour. For example, in a client/server environment, client object fragments are often very lightweight and communicate with their server counterparts to provide users with the complete functionality.

Object Distribution

The distribution of software objects doesn't have to mirror the distribution of corresponding entities in the real-world. Just because a parcel is in Boston, doesn't mean that the software objects that represent it have to be in Boston. Decisions on how to distribute objects across system should consider other factors like performance, reliability, security, and fault tolerance.

Emergent Communications Play a Major Role

Distributed software systems involve many of different kinds of communications. Most of them, however, do not relate directly to communications in the problem domain. Some exist for house keeping reasons, like replica management, process and transaction synchronisation, name resolution, and service binding. Others exist as a consequence of using a particular communication architecture. In either case, these emergent communications play a significant role in design, and therefore, cannot be left out of a concept model.

Emergent Resource Sharing

Distribution can also introduce a significant amount of resource sharing that didn't exist in the analysis. For example, in the real-world parcel system, only one person is able to handling a given parcel at a time. In a distributed software system, many different users may be accessing and updating the software object(s) for that parcel at the same time.

Transparency

To help make a distributed system more open, extensible, and fault tolerant, designers attempt to shield users from issues dealing with the actual location of an object (or service), concurrent access, replication, migration, scaling, and failures. This principle is called transparency. Unfortunately, techniques for achieving transparency further increase the conceptual distance between analysis and design.

REQUIREMENTS FOR BETTER CONCEPTUAL MODELS

Although some of the problems mentioned above are due to inadequate development tools for distributed systems, it is not likely that better, more sophisticated tools will make a difference. In fact, they might even make the problems worse. Inappropriate use of a new tool could accidently increase the emergent communications and resource sharing, and thus, further complicate the design. A fully integrated and minimized collection of development tools could substantially reduce the complexity of distributed systems design. But, in an open market with a wide diversity of platforms and with a constant infusion of new technology, such a development environment is not realistic. Our best hope is to improve our conceptual models for distributed software systems.

Below are a few requirements, beyond those commonly found in existing conceptual models.

- Abstractions for mapping software objects (or object fragments) to entities described in the analysis.
- Abstractions for describing object fragmentation, especially for behaviour.
- Better mechanisms for specialising objects and object fragments in ways that don't violate inherited semantics.
- Abstractions for specifying and constraining object distribution, replication, and migration.
- Levelled abstractions for dealing with emergent communications and resource sharing.
- Abstractions for proven patterns or idioms that can help designer achieve transparency and other desirable properties.

These proposed abstractions should give software engineer control over design decisions, but allow them to hide the details when they are not pertinent to a particular discussion.

SEMANTIC DATA MANAGEMENT

During last years we have witnessed a tremendous increase in the amount of semantic data that is available on the Web in almost every field of human activity have been created and published online. Semantic data management refers to a range of techniques that can be employed for storing, querying, manipulating and integrating data based on its meaning. Current ISL activities in this area focus on two main topics: provenance and access control. Provenance means the origin of data, and refers from where and how the piece of data was obtained and it is critical in applications such as trust assessment, access control, data cleaning and data/information quality.

ISL activities in the domain of provenance for semantic web data target the following research activities:

- Development of annotation and abstract provenance models for Semantic Web Data
- Efficient storage and indexing schemes for the provenance of Semantic Web Data and
- Provenance manipulation languages.

One of the aspects of the problem of secure data management is to enforce access control policies that have been defined to protect data of sensitive nature. Addressing such security concerns mandates the development of generic, flexible access control frameworks that can effectively support a variety of policies for controlling access to Web data in an efficient and effective manner. ISL activities in the domain of secure data management target the following research activities:

- Specification languages for access control policies and formalisation of their semantics;
- Enforcement of access control policies; and
- Consistency checking and repairs of access control policies.

SEMANTIC DATA MODEL

A semantic data model in software engineering has various meanings:

- It is a conceptual data model in which semantic information is included. This means that the model describes the meaning of its instances. Such a semantic data model is an abstraction that defines how the stored symbols (the instance data) relate to the real world.
- It is a conceptual data model that includes the capability to express information that enables parties to the information exchange to interpret meaning (semantics) from the instances, without the need to know the meta-model. Such semantic models are fact oriented (as opposed to object oriented). Facts are typically expressed by binary relations between data elements, whereas higher order relations are expressed as collections of binary relations. Typically binary relations have the form of triples: Object-RelationType-Object. For example: the Eiffel Tower <is located in> Paris.

Typically the instance data of semantic data models explicitly include the kinds of relationships between the various data elements, such as <is located in>. To interpret the meaning of the facts from the instances it is required that the meaning of the kinds of relations (relation types) is known. Therefore, semantic data models typically standardise such relation types. This means that the second kind of semantic data models enable that the instances express facts that include their own meaning.

The second kind of semantic data models are usually meant to create semantic databases. The ability to include meaning in semantic databases facilitates building distributed databases that enable applications to interpret the meaning from the content. This implies that semantic databases can be integrated when they use the same (standard) relation types. This also implies that in general they have a wider applicability than relational or object oriented databases.

OVERVIEW OF DATABASE MANAGEMENT SYSTEM

The logical data structure of a database management system (DBMS), whether hierarchical, network, or relational, cannot totally satisfy the requirements for a conceptual definition of data, because it is limited in scope and biased towards the implementation strategy employed by the DBMS.

Therefore, the need to define data from a conceptual view has led to the development of semantic data modelling techniques. That is, techniques to define the meaning of data within the context of its interrelationships with other data. As illustrated in the figure. The real world, in terms of resources, ideas, events, etc., are symbolically defined within physical data stores. A semantic data model is an abstraction which defines how the stored symbols relate to the real world. Thus, the model must be a true representation of the real world.

According to Klas and Schrefl (1995), the "overall goal of semantic data models is to capture more meaning of data by integrating relational concepts with more powerful abstraction concepts known from the Artificial Intelligence field. The idea is to provide high level modelling primitives as integral part of a data model in order to facilitate the representation of real world situations".

History

The need for semantic data models was first recognised by the U.S. Air Force in the mid-1970s as a result of the Integrated Computer-Aided Manufacturing (ICAM) Programme. The objective of this programme was to increase manufacturing productivity through the systematic application of computer technology. The ICAM Programme identified a need for better analysis and communication techniques for people involved in improving manufacturing productivity.

As a result, the ICAM Programme developed a series of techniques known as the IDEF (ICAM Definition) Methods which included the following:

- IDEF0 used to produce a "function model" which is a structured representation of the activities or processes within the environment or system.
- IDEF1 used to produce an "information model" which represents the structure and semantics of information within the environment or system.
  - IDEF1X is a semantic data modelling technique. It is used to produce a graphical information model which represents the structure and semantics of information within an environment or system. Use of this standard permits the construction of semantic data models which may serve to support the management of data as a resource, the integration of information systems, and the building of computer databases.
- IDEF2 used to produce a "dynamics model" which represents the time varying behavioural characteristics of the environment or system.

During the 1990s the application of semantic modelling techniques resulted in the semantic data models of the second kind. An example of such is the semantic data model that is standardised as ISO 15926-2 (2002), which is further developed into the semantic modelling language Gellish (2005). The definition of the Gellish language is documented in the form of a semantic data model. Gellish itself is a semantic modelling language, that can be used to create other semantic models. Those semantic models can be stored in Gellish Databases, being semantic databases.

Applications

A semantic data model can be used to serve many purposes. Some key objectives include:

- *Planning of Data Resources*: A preliminary data model can be used to provide an overall view of the data required to run an enterprise. The model can then be analysed to identify and scope projects to build shared data resources.
- *Building of Shareable Databases*: A fully developed model can be used to define an application independent view of data which can be validated by users and then transformed into a physical database design for any of the various DBMS technologies. In addition to generating databases which are consistent and shareable, development costs can be drastically reduced through data modelling.
- *Evaluation of Vendor Software*: Since, a data model actually represents the infrastructure of an organisation, vendor software can be evaluated against a company's data model in order to identify possible inconsistencies between the infrastructure implied by the software and the way the company actually does business.
- *Integration of Existing Databases*: By defining the contents of existing databases with semantic data models, an integrated data definition can be derived. With the proper technology, the resulting conceptual schema can be used to control transaction processing in a distributed database environment. The U.S. Air Force Integrated Information Support System (I2S2) is an experimental development and demonstration of this type of technology applied to a heterogeneous DBMS environment.

CREATING NEW MODELS

The separation of functionality between the model/view components allows models to be created that can take advantage of existing views. This approach lets us present data from a variety of sources using standard graphical user interface components, such as QListView, QTableView, and QTreeView.

The QAbstractItemModel class provides an interface that is flexible enough to support data sources that arrange information in hierarchical structures, allowing for the possibility that data will be inserted, removed, modified, or sorted in some way. It also provides support for drag and drop operations. The QAbstractListModel and QAbstractTableModel classes provide support for interfaces to simpler non-hierarchical data structures, and are easier to use as a starting point for simple list and table models.

In this section, we create a simple read-only model to explore the basic principles of the model/view architecture. Later in this section, we adapt this simple model so that items can be modified by the user.

DESIGNING A MODEL

When creating a new model for an existing data structure, it is important to consider which type of model should be used to provide an interface onto the data. If the data structure can be represented as a list or table of items, you can subclass QAbstractListModel or QAbstractTableModel since, these classes provide suitable default implementations for many functions.

However, if the underlying data structure can only be represented by a hierarchical tree structure, it is necessary to subclass QAbstractItemModel. This approach is taken in the Simple Tree Model example.

In this section, we implement a simple model based on a list of strings, so the QAbstractListModel provides an ideal base class on which to build.

Whatever form the underlying data structure takes, it is usually a good idea to supplement the standard QAbstractItemModel API in specialised models with one that allows more natural access to the underlying data structure. This makes it easier to populate the model with data, yet still enables other general model/view components to interact with it using the standard API. The model described below provides a custom constructor for just this purpose.

A Read-only Example Model

The model implemented here is a simple, non-hierarchical, read-only data model based on the standard QStringListModel class. It has a QStringList as its internal data source, and implements only what is needed to make a functioning model. To make the implementation easier, we subclass QAbstractListModel because it defines sensible default behaviour for list models, and it exposes a simpler interface than the QAbstractItemModel class.

When implementing a model it is important to remember that QAbstractItemModel does not store any data itself, it merely presents an interface that the views use to access the data. For a minimal read-only model it is only necessary to implement a few functions as there are default implementations for most of the interface. The class declaration is as follows:

```
class StringListModel: public QAbstractListModel
{
    Q_OBJECT
public:
```

```
    StringListModel(const QStringList &strings, QObject
*parent = 0)
        :QAbstractListModel(parent),stringList(strings) {}
int rowCount(const QModelIndex &parent = QModelIndex())
const;
QVariant data(const QModelIndex &index, int role) const;
QVariant headerData(int section, Qt::Orientation
orientation,
                int role = Qt::DisplayRole) const;
private:
    QStringList stringList;
};
```

Apart from the model's constructor, we only need to implement two functions: rowCount() returns the number of rows in the model and data() returns an item of data corresponding to a specified model index.

Well behaved models also implement headerData() to give tree and table views something to display in their headers.

Note that this is a non-hierarchical model, so we don't have to worry about the parent-child relationships. If our model was hierarchical, we would also have to implement the index() and parent() functions.

The list of strings is stored internally in the stringList private member variable.

Dimensions of the Model

We want the number of rows in the model to be the same as the number of strings in the string list. We implement the rowCount() function with this in mind:

```
int StringListModel::rowCount(const QModelIndex &parent)
const
{
    return stringList.count();
}
```

Since, the model is non-hierarchical, we can safely ignore the model index corresponding to the parent item. By default, models derived from QAbstractListModel only contain one column, so we do not need to reimplement the columnCount() function.

Model Headers and Data

For items in the view, we want to return the strings in the string list. The data() function is responsible for returning the item of data that corresponds to the index argument:

```
QVariant StringListModel::data(const QModelIndex &index,
int role) const
```

```
{
    if (!index.isValid())
        return QVariant();
    if (index.row() >= stringList.size())
        return QVariant();
    if (role == Qt::DisplayRole)
        return stringList.at(index.row());
else
        return QVariant();
}
```

We only return a valid QVariant if the model index supplied is valid, the row number is within the range of items in the string list, and the requested role is one that we support.

Some views, such as QTreeView and QTableView, are able to display headers along with the item data. If our model is displayed in a view with headers, we want the headers to show the row and column numbers. We can provide information about the headers by subclassing the headerData() function:

```
QVariant StringListModel::headerData(int section,
Qt::Orientation orientation,
                                     int role) const
{
        if (role != Qt::DisplayRole)
            return QVariant();
        if (orientation == Qt::Horizontal)
            return QString("Column %1").arg(section);
        else
            return QString("Row %1").arg(section);
}
```

Again, we return a valid QVariant only if the role is one that we support. The orientation of the header is also taken into account when deciding the exact data to return. Not all views display headers with the item data, and those that do may be configured to hide them. Nonetheless, it is recommended that you implement the headerData() function to provide relevant information about the data provided by the model. An item can have several roles, giving out different data depending on the role specified. The items in our model only have one role, DisplayRole, so we return the data for items irrespective of the role specified. However, we could reuse the data we provide for the DisplayRole in other roles, such as the ToolTipRole that views can use to display information about items in a tooltip.

An Editable Model

The read-only model shows how simple choices could be presented to the user but, for many applications, an editable list model is much more useful. We can modify the read-only model to make the items editable by changing the data() function we implemented for read-only, and by implementing two extra functions: flags() and setData(). The following function declarations are added to the class definition:

```
Qt::ItemFlags flags(const QModelIndex &index) const;
bool setData(const QModelIndex &index, const QVariant &value,
             int role = Qt::EditRole);
```

Making the Model Editable

A delegate checks whether an item is editable before creating an editor. The model must let the delegate know that its items are editable. We do this by returning the correct flags for each item in the model; in this case, we enable all items and make them both selectable and editable:

```
Qt::ItemFlags  StringListModel::flags(const  QModelIndex
&index) const
{
    if (!index.isValid())
        return Qt::ItemIsEnabled;
    return QAbstractItemModel::flags(index)
                 |Qt::ItemIsEditable;
}
```

Note that we do not have to know how the delegate performs the actual editing process. We only have to provide a way for the delegate to set the data in the model. This is achieved through the setData() function:

```
bool StringListModel::setData(const QModelIndex &index,
            const QVariant &value, int role)
{
    if (index.isValid() && role == Qt::EditRole) {
            stringList.replace(index.row(),
value.toString());
            emit dataChanged(index, index);
            return true;
    }
    return false;
}
```

In this model, the item in the string list that corresponds to the model index is replaced by the value provided. However, before we can modify the string list, we must make sure that the index is valid, the item is of the correct type, and that the role is supported.

By convention, we insist that the role is the EditRole since, this is the role used by the standard item delegate. For boolean values, however, you can use Qt::CheckStateRole and set the Qt::ItemIsUserCheckable flag; a checkbox is then used for editing the value. The underlying data in this model is the same for all roles, so this detail just makes it easier to integrate the model with standard components.

When the data has been set, the model must let the views know that some data has changed. This is done by emitting the dataChanged() signal. Since, only one item of data has changed, the range of items specified in the signal is limited to just one model index. Also the data() function needs to be changed to add the Qt::EditRole test:

```
QVariant StringListModel::data(const QModelIndex &index,
int role) const
{
    if (!index.isValid())
        return QVariant();
    if (index.row() >= stringList.size())
        return QVariant();
    if (role == Qt::DisplayRole || role == Qt::EditRole)
        return stringList.at(index.row());
    else
        return QVariant();
}
```

Inserting and Removing Rows

It is possible to change the number of rows and columns in a model. In the string list model it only makes sense to change the number of rows, so we only reimplement the functions for inserting and removing rows.

These are declared in the class definition:

```
bool insertRows(int position, int rows, const QModelIndex
&index = QModelIndex());
bool removeRows(int position, int rows, const QModelIndex
&index = QModelIndex());
```

Since, rows in this model correspond to strings in a list, the insertRows() function inserts a number of empty strings into the string list before the specified position.

The number of strings inserted is equivalent to the number of rows specified.

The parent index is normally used to determine where in the model the rows should be added. In this case, we only have a single top-level list of strings, so we just insert empty strings into that list.

```
bool StringListModel::insertRows(int position, int rows,
const QModelIndex &parent)
{
    beginInsertRows(QModelIndex(), position, position+rows-
1);
```

```
    for (int row = 0; row < rows; ++row) {
        stringList.insert(position, "");
    }
    endInsertRows();
    return true;
}
```

The model first calls the beginInsertRows() function to inform other components that the number of rows is about to change. The function specifies the row numbers of the first and last new rows to be inserted, and the model index for their parent item. After changing the string list, it calls endInsertRows() to complete the operation and inform other components that the dimensions of the model have changed, returning true to indicate success.

The function to remove rows from the model is also simple to write. The rows to be removed from the model are specified by the position and the number of rows given. We ignore the parent index to simplify our implementation, and just remove the corresponding items from the string list.

```
bool StringListModel::removeRows(int position, int rows,
const QModelIndex &parent)
{
      beginRemoveRows(QModelIndex(),  position,
position+rows-1);
      for (int row = 0; row < rows; ++row) {
stringList.removeAt(position);
      }
      endRemoveRows();
      return true;
}
```

The beginRemoveRows() function is always called before any underlying data is removed, and specifies the first and last rows to be removed. This allows other components to access the data before it becomes unavailable. After the rows have been removed, the model emits endRemoveRows() to finish the operation and let other components know that the dimensions of the model have changed.

Next Steps

We can display the data provided by this model, or any other model, using the QListView class to present the model's items in the form of a vertical list. For the string list model, this view also provides a default editor so that the items can be manipulated. We examine the possibilities made available by the standard view classes in View Classes. The Model Subclassing Reference document discusses the requirements of QAbstractItemModel subclasses in more detail, and provides a guide to the virtual functions that must be implemented to enable various features in different types of models.

8

Distributed Database Administration

GLOBAL DATABASE NAMES AND GLOBAL OBJECT NAMES

In a distributed database system, each database should have a unique global name. Global database names identify each database in the system. A global database name consists of two components: a database name of eight characters or less (for example, SALES) and a domain name that contains the database.

The domain name component of a global database name must follow standard Internet conventions. Levels in domain names must be separated by dots and the order of domain names is from leaf to root, left to right. The database name and the domain name are determined by the initialisation parameters DB_NAME and DB_DOMAIN.

A database link should be given the same name as the global database name of the remote database it references. When you set the initialisation parameter GLOBAL_NAMES to TRUE, Oracle ensures that the name of the database link is the same as the global database name of the remote database.

Attention: If you set the initialisation parameter GLOBAL_NAMES to FALSE, you are not required to use global naming. However, Oracle Corporation highly recommends that you use global naming because many useful features, including Oracle Advanced Replication, require global naming be enforced.

Once you have enabled global naming, database links are essentially transparent to users of a distributed database because the name of a database link is the same as the global name of the database to which the link points. For example, the following statement creates a database link in the local database.

```
CREATE PUBLIC DATABASE LINK sales.division3.acme.com...;
```

Oracle uses the global database name to globally name the schema objects using the following naming scheme:

```
<schema>.<schema_object>@<global_database_name>
```

where

<schema>: A schema is a collection of logical structures of data, or schema

objects. A schema is owned by a database user and has the same name as that user. Each user owns a single schema.

<*schema_object*>: A schema object is a logical data structure like a table, view, synonym, procedure, package, or a database link.

<*global_database_name*>: The name that uniquely identifies a remote database. This name must be the same as the concatenation of the remote database's initialisation parameters DB_NAME and DB_DOMAIN.

For example, using the previously defined database link, a user or application can now reference remote data using the global object name:

SELECT * FROM scott.emp@sales.division3.acme.com.

TYPES OF DATABASE LINKS

To support application access to the data and schema objects throughout a distributed database system, administrators must create all necessary database links. The compares the various types of database links that Oracle provides.

Private, Public, and Global Database Links

Oracle allows you to create private, public, and global database links.

- *Private Database Link:* You can create a private database link in a specific schema of a database. Only the owner of a private database link or PL/SQL subprograms in the schema can use a private database link to access data and database objects in the corresponding remote database.
- *Public Database Link:* You can create a public database link for a database. All users and PL/SQL subprograms in the database can use a public database link to access data and database objects in the corresponding remote database.
- *Global Database Link:* When an Oracle network uses Oracle Names, the names servers in the system automatically create and manage global database links for every Oracle database in the network. All users and PL/SQL subprograms in any database can use a global database link to access data and database objects in the corresponding remote database.

Determining the type of database links to employ in a distributed database depends on the specific requirements of the applications using the system.

Consider some of the advantages and disadvantages for using each type of database link.

- A private database link is more secure than a public or global link, because only the owner of the private link, or subprograms within the same schema, can use the private link to access the specified remote database.
- When many users require an access path to a remote Oracle

database, an administrator can create a single public database link for all users in a database.

- When an Oracle network uses Oracle Names, an administrator can conveniently manage global database links for all databases in the system. Database link management is centralised and simple.

Creating a Private Database Link

To create a private database link, you specify:

```
CREATE DATABASE LINK...;
```

Creating a Public Database Link

To create a public database link, you use the keyword PUBLIC:

```
CREATE PUBLIC DATABASE LINK...;
```

Security Options for Database Links

A database link defines a communication path from one database to another. When an application uses a database link to access a remote database, Oracle establishes a database session in the remote database on behalf of the local application request.

When you create a private or public database link, you can determine which schema on the remote database the link will establish connections to by creating fixed user, current user, and connected user database links.

Fixed User Database Links

To create a fixed user database link, you embed the credentials (in this case, a username and password) required to access the remote database in the definition of the link:

```
CREATE DATABASE LINK... CONNECT TO username IDENTIFIED BY
password...;
```

When an application uses a fixed user database link, the local server always establishes a connection to a fixed remote schema in the remote database.

The local server also sends the user's credentials across the network when an application uses the link to access the remote database. If an unsecure network supports a distributed database that uses fixed user database links, consider encrypting login packets for server-to-server connections.

Connected User and Current User Database Links

Connected user and current user database links do not include any credentials in the definition of the link.

The credentials used to connect to the remote database can change depending on the user that references the database link and the operation being performed by the application. To understand the difference between the two types of database links, you must first understand the concepts of connected and current users.

- A connected user is a user that connects to a database using a database application. For example, when you start SQL*Plus and connect to an Oracle database as SCOTT, the connected user is SCOTT.
- A current user is determined by the security context in which a database operation executes. For example, when you connect to an Oracle database as the user SCOTT and execute the procedure SALES.DEL_EMP, the current user while executing the DEL_EMP procedure defaults to SALES because a stored procedure executes within the security context of its owner.

To understand the difference between connected user and current user database links, simply extend your understanding of the different types of users. With a connected user database link, an operation being performed in a remote database always occurs within the security context of the connected user at the local database. With a current user database link, an operation performed in a remote database always occurs within the security context of the current user at the local database.

For example, consider what happens when the user SCOTT calls a procedure SALES.DEL_EMP, and the procedure deletes an employee record from a remote database. If the procedure references a connected user database link to access the remote database, the deletion of the remote employee record happens as SCOTT, the connected user in the local database. However, if the procedure references a current user database link to access the remote database, the deletion of the remote employee record happens as SALES, the current user in the local database.

To create a connected user database link, you merely omit the CONNECT TO clause. The following example creates a connected user database link:

```
CREATE DATABASE LINK sales.division3.acme.com USING 'sales';
```

To create a current user database link, use the following syntax:

```
CREATE DATABASE LINK... CONNECT TO CURRENT_USER...;
```

To use a current user database link, the current user must be a global user that is authenticated by the Oracle Security Server.

Shared Database Links

Every application that references a remote server using a standard database link establishes a connection between the local database and the remote database. Many users running applications simultaneously can cause a high number of connections between the local and remote databases.

Shared database links enable you to limit the number of network connections required between the local server and the remote server. To use shared database links, the local server must run in multi-threaded server (MTS) mode. The remote server can either run in multi-threaded server mode, or can run in dedicated server mode.

Attention: Although shared database links can reduce the number of required connections between the local and remote server, you could cause more physical connections and processes to be required than simply using standard (not shared) database links, if you use this functionality incorrectly.

Properties of Shared Database Links

Shared database links differ from standard database links in two ways:

- Network connections made for shared database links can be shared among those that use the same database link schema object. When a user needs to establish a connection to a remote server from a particular shared server process, the shared process can reuse connections already established to the remote server (if that connection was established on the same shared server with the same database link).
- When you use a shared database link, a network connection is established directly out of the shared server in the local server. For a normal (non-shared) database link, if the local server was a multithreaded server, this connection would have been established through the local dispatcher, requiring context switches for the local dispatcher, and requiring data to go through the dispatcher.

Use Shared Database Links

You should look carefully at your application and your multi-threaded server configuration to determine whether to use shared links or not.

For example, if you have designed your application to use a standard public database link, and 100 users simultaneously require a connection, 100 network direct network connections will also be required.

However, if your application uses shared database links, and there are ten shared servers in the local MTS-mode database, the 100 users that use the same (shared public) database link will require only 10 network connections (or fewer) to the remote server. Each local shared server may only need one connection to the remote server.

Shared database links are not useful in all situations. Suppose there is only one user that accesses the remote server. If that user defines a shared database link, and there are ten shared servers in the local database, that one user can require up to 10 network connections to the remote server. Every shared server may have established a connection to the remote server, since, each shared server might have been used by that user.

Clearly, a standard database link would be preferable in this situation because it would require (and allow) only one network connection. The lesson: shared database links can lead to more network connections in single-user scenarios, therefore, they should be used only when you expect that many users will need to use the same database link. Typically, this is the case for public database links, but may also be true for private database links if you expect many clients to use the same local schema (and therefore the same private database link). A rule of thumb is to use shared database links when the number of users accessing a database link is expected to be much larger than the number of shared servers in the local database.

Setting Up Shared Database Links

To create a shared database link you use the keyword SHARED in the SQL CREATE DATABASE LINK command:

```
CREATE SHARED DATABASE LINK dblink_name
[CONNECT TO username IDENTIFIED BY password] | [CONNECT TO
CURRENT_USER]
AUTHENTICATED BY schema_name IDENTIFIED BY password
[USING 'service_name'];
```

Whenever the keyword SHARED is used, the clause AUTHENTICATED BY is also required. There must be an account on the remote database with the specified USERID/PASSWORD and with the CREATE SESSION privilege. No other privileges are required.

The schema specified in the AUTHENTICATED BY clause is only used for security reasons and could be considered a "dummy" schema. It is not affected when using shared database links, nor does it affect the users of the shared database link. The AUTHENTICATED BY clause is required to prevent unauthorised clients from masquerading as a database link user and gaining access to unauthorised information.

CONNECTION QUALIFIERS

In some situations, you may want to have several database links of the same type (*e.g.*, public) that point to the same remote database, yet establish connections to the remote database using different communication pathways. For example, if a remote database is using the Oracle Parallel Server, you might want to define several public database links at your local node so that connections can be established to specific instances of the remote database.

To facilitate such functionality, Oracle allows you to create a database link with an optional connection qualifier in the database link name. When creating a database link, a connection qualifier is specified as the trailing portion of the database link name, separated by an at sign ("@"). For example, assume that a remote database HQ.ACME.COM is managed by the Oracle Parallel Server. The HQ database has two instances, named HQ_1 and HQ_2. The local database can contain the following public database links to define pathways to the remote instances of the HQ database:

```
CREATE PUBLIC DATABASE LINK hq.acme.com@hq_1
          USING 'string_to_hq_1';
```

```
CREATE PUBLIC DATABASE LINK hq.acme.com@hq_2
          USING 'string_to_hq_2';
CREATE PUBLIC DATABASE LINK hq.acme.com
          USING 'string_to_hq';
```

Notice in the above examples that a connection qualifier is simply an extension to a database link name. The text of the connection qualifier does not necessarily indicate how a connection is to be established; this information is specified in the service name of the USING clause. Also notice that in the third example, a connection qualifier is not specified. In this case, just as when a connection qualifier is specified, the instance is determined by the USING string.

To use a connection qualifier to specify a particular instance, include the qualifier at the end of the global object name:

```
SELECT * FROM scott.emp@hq.acme.com@hq_1
```

Database Link Resolution

Whenever a SQL statement includes a reference to a global object name, Oracle searches for a database link with a name that matches the database name specified in the global object name. Oracle does this to determine the path to the specified remote database.

Oracle always searches for matching database links in the following order:

- Private database links in the schema of the user who issued the SQL statement.
- Public database links in the local database.
- Global database links (only if an Oracle Name Server is available).

If a SQL statement specifies a complete global database name; that is, both the database and domain components are specified, Oracle searches for private, public, and global database links that match only the explicitly specified global database name. If any portion of the domain is specified, Oracle assumes that a complete global database name is specified. However, if a SQL statement specifies a partial global database name; that is, only the database component is specified, Oracle appends the local database's network domain component to the database name to form a complete global database name. Then Oracle searches for private, public, and network database links that match only the constructed global database name. If a matching database link is not found, Oracle returns an error and the SQL statement cannot execute.

Optimisation: If a global object name references an object in the local database and a connection qualifier is not specified, Oracle automatically detects that the object is local and does not search for, or use, database links to resolve the object reference.

Oracle expands a global object reference, whether or not a connection qualifier is specified. Furthermore, if a connection qualifier is specified, only database links that match, including the connection qualifier, are used to resolve the object reference.

Oracle does not necessarily stop searching for matching database links when a first match is found. Oracle must search for matching private, public, and network database links until a complete path to the remote database (both a remote account and service name) is determined.

The first match determines the remote schema; that is, if no CONNECT clause is specified a connected user database link will be used, if the "CONNECT TO username IDENTIFIED BY password" clause is specified a fixed user database link will be used, and if a "CONNECT TO CURRENT_USER" clause is specified a current user database link.

If the first match does not specify a USING clause, the search continues until a link that specifies a database string is found. If matching database links are found and a database string is never identified, Oracle returns an error. Once a complete path is determined, Oracle creates a remote session, assuming an identical connection is not already open on behalf of the same local session.

Schema Object Name Resolution

Once the local Oracle database connects to the specified remote database on behalf of the local user that issued the SQL statement, object resolution continues as if the remote user had issued the associated SQL statement. That is, if a fixed user database link is used, object resolution proceeds in the specified schema; if a connected user database link is used, object resolution proceeds in the connected user's remote schema (including synonyms) and if a current user database link is used object resolution proceeds in the current user's remote schema. If the object is not found, public objects of the remote database are then checked.

VIEWS, SYNONYMS, PROCEDURES AND GLOBAL NAME RESOLUTION

A remote schema object can be referenced by its global object name in the definition of a view, synonym, or PL/SQL programme unit (*e.g.*, procedure, trigger). If a complete global object name is referenced in the definition of a view, synonym, or programme unit, Oracle stores the definition of the object as specified, without having to perform any expansion of the global object name being referenced. However, if a partial global object name (that is, only the database name and not the domain name) is referenced in the definition of a view, synonym, or programme unit, Oracle must expand the partial name using the domain component of the local database's global database name.

The following list explains when Oracle completes the expansion of a partial global object name for views, synonyms, and programme units:

- When a view is created, partial global object names in the defining query are not expanded; the data dictionary stores the exact text of the defining query. Instead, Oracle expands a partial global object name each time a statement that uses the view is parsed.

- When a synonym is created, partial global object names are expanded; the definition of the synonym stored in the data dictionary includes the expanded global object name.
- Each time a programme unit is compiled, partial global object names are expanded.

The above behaviour should be considered when creating views, synonyms, and procedures that reference remote data using partial global object names. If the global database name of the containing database is changed (which should rarely happen), views and procedures may try to reference a different database than they did before the global database name change; alternatively, synonyms do not expand database link names at runtime, so they do not change.

Depending on the situation, this behaviour may or may not be desired. For example, consider two databases named SALES.UK.ACME.COM and HQ.UK.ACME.COM. Also, assume that the SALES database contains the following view and synonym:

```
CREATE VIEW employee_names AS
            SELECT ename FROM scott.emp@hq;
CREATE SYNONYM employee FOR scott.emp@hq;
```

Oracle expands the EMPLOYEE synonym definition and stores it as:

```
"scott.emp@hq.uk.acme.com"
```

The company undergoes a reorganisation. First, consider the situation where both the Sales and Human Resources departments are moved to the United States. Consequently, the corresponding global database names are both changed to SALES.US.ACME.COM and HQ.US.ACME.COM. In this case, the defining query of the EMPLOYEE_NAMES view still expands to the correct database when the view is used:

```
"SELECT ename FROM scott.emp@hq.us.acme.com"
```

However, the definition of the EMPLOYEE synonym continues to reference the previous database name, HQ.UK.ACME.COM.

Now consider that only the Sales department is moved to the United States. Consequently, the corresponding new global database name is SALES.US.ACME.COM, while the Human Resources database is HQ.UK.ACME.COM. In this case, the defining query of the EMPLOYEE_NAMES view expands to a non-existent global database name when the view is used:

```
"SELECT ename FROM scott.emp@hq.us.acme.com"
```

Alternatively, the EMPLOYEE synonym continues to reference the correct database, HQ.UK.ACME.COM.

In summary, you should decide when you want to use partial and complete global object names in the definition of views, synonyms, and procedures. Keep in mind that database names should be stable and databases should not be unnecessarily moved within a network.

Dropping a Database Link

You can drop a database link just as you can drop a table or view. The command syntax is:

```
DROP DATABASE LINK dblink;
```

For example, to drop the database link NY_FIN, the command would be:

```
DROP DATABASE LINK ny_fin;
```

Listing Available Database Links

The data dictionary of each database stores the definitions of all the database links in that database. The USER/ALL/DBA_DB_LINKS data dictionary views show the database links that have been defined at the local database.

Any user can query the data dictionary to determine what database links are available to that user. For information on viewing the data dictionary.

Limiting the Number of Active Database Links

You can limit the number of connections from a user process to remote databases with the initialisation parameter OPEN_LINKS. This parameter controls the number of remote connections that a single user session can use concurrently within a single SQL statement per session.

TECHNIQUES FOR LOCATION TRANSPARENCY

Users of a distributed database system need not (and often should not) be aware of the location and functioning of the parts of the database with which they work. The DBA and network administrators can ensure that the distributed nature of the database remains transparent to users.

Synonyms and Privileges

A synonym is a reference to the actual object. A user who has access to a synonym for a particular schema object, must also have privileges on schema object itself. For example, if the user attempts to access a synonym but does not have privileges on the table it identifies, an error occurs indicating that the table or view does not exist.

Assume a local synonym is an alias for a remote object. The owner of the local synonym cannot grant any object privileges on the synonym to any other local user. This behaviour is different from privilege management for synonyms that are aliases for local tables or views. In the case where a synonym is an alias for a remote object, local privileges for the synonym cannot be granted, because this would amount to granting privileges for the remote object, which is not allowed. Therefore, no local privilege management can be performed when synonyms are used for location transparency; security for the base object is controlled entirely at the remote node. For example, the user ADMIN cannot grant any object privileges for the EMP_SYN synonym. Unlike a database link referenced in a view or procedure definition, a database link referenced in a synonym is resolved by first looking for a private link owned by the schema in effect at the time the reference to the synonym is parsed. Therefore, to ensure the desired object resolution, it is especially important to specify the underlying object's schema in the definition of a synonym.

Procedures and Location Transparency

PL/SQL programme units called procedures can also provide location transparency. There are two options:

- A local procedure references remote data
- A local synonym references a remote procedure.

The second option provides location transparency through synonyms.

Local Procedure Referencing Remote Data

Procedures or functions (either stand-alone or in packages) can contain SQL statements that reference remote data. For example, consider the procedure created by the following statement:

```
CREATE PROCEDURE fire_emp (enum NUMBER) AS
BEGIN
DELETE FROM emp@hq.acme.com
WHERE empno = enum;
END;
```

When a user or application calls the FIRE_EMP procedure, it is not apparent that a remote table is being modified. A second layer of location transparency is possible if the statements in a procedure indirectly reference remote data using local procedures, views, or synonyms. For example, the following statement defines a local synonym:

```
CREATE SYNONYM emp FOR emp@hq.acme.com;
```

Given this synonym, the FIRE_EMP procedure can be defined with the following statement:

```
CREATE PROCEDURE fire_emp (enum NUMBER) AS
BEGIN
DELETE FROM emp WHERE empno = enum;
END;
```

If the table EMP@HQ is renamed or moved, only the local synonym that references the table needs to be modified. None of the procedures and applications that call the procedure require modification.

Procedures and Privileges

Assume a local procedure includes a statement that references a remote table or view. The owner of the local procedure can grant the EXECUTE privilege to any user, thereby giving that user the ability to execute the procedure and, indirectly, access remote data.

In general, procedures aid in security. Privileges for objects referenced within a procedure do not need to be explicitly granted to the calling users.

STATEMENT TRANSPARENCY

Oracle allows the following standard DML statements to reference remote tables:

- SELECT (queries)
- INSERT
- UPDATE
- DELETE
- SELECT... FOR UPDATE
- LOCK TABLE.

Queries including joins, aggregates, subqueries, and SELECT... FOR UPDATE can reference any number of local and remote tables and views. For example, the following query joins information from two remote tables:

```
SELECT empno, ename, dname FROM scott.emp@sales.division3.
acme.com e,
jward.dept@hq.acme.com d
WHERE d.deptno = d.deptno;
```

UPDATE, INSERT, DELETE, and LOCK TABLE statements can reference both local and remote tables. No programming is necessary to update remote data.

For example, the following statement inserts new rows into the remote table EMP in the SCOTT.SALES schema by selecting rows from the EMP table in the JWARD schema in the local database:

```
INSERT INTO scott.emp@sales.division3.acme.com
    SELECT * FROM jward.emp;
```

RESTRICTIONS

Several restrictions apply to statement transparency:

- Within a single SQL statement, all referenced LONG and LONG RAW columns, sequences, updated tables, and locked tables must be located at the same node.
- Oracle does not allow remote data definition language (DDL) statements (for example, CREATE, ALTER, and DROP).

The LIST CHAINED ROWS clause of an ANALYSE statement cannot reference remote tables.

Values for Environmentally-Dependent SQL Functions

In a distributed database system, Oracle always evaluates environmentally-dependent SQL functions, such as SYSDATE, USER, UID, and USERENV with respect to the local server, no matter where the statement (or portion of a statement) executes.

Shared SQL for Remote and Distributed Statements

The mechanics of a remote or distributed statement using shared SQL are essentially the same as those of a local statement. The SQL text must match, the referenced objects must match, and the bind types of any bind variables must be the same. If available, shared SQL areas can be used for the local and remote handling of any statement (or decomposed query).

DISTRIBUTED RELATIONAL DATABASE ADMINISTRATION FOR THE SPIFFY CORPORATION

Spiffy Corporation requires that each dealership have one or more System i™ products and that those systems must be available to the network at certain times. However, each dealership manages its data processing resources and procedures as a stand-alone enterprise. The size of the system and the number of business processes that are automated on it are determined by each dealership's needs and the resources available to it. The Spiffy Corporation requires all dealerships to be active in the inventory distributed relational database. Because the corporation operates its own dealerships, it has a full complement of dealership software that might or might not access the distributed relational database environment. The Spiffy dealerships use the full set of software tools. Most of the private franchises also use them because they are tailored specifically to the Spiffy Corporation way of doing business.

The regional distribution centers manage the inventory for their region. They also function as the database administrator for all distributed database resources used in the region. The responsibilities involved vary depending on the level of data processing competency at each dealership. The regional centre is always the first contact for help for any dealership in the region.

The Minneapolis regional distribution centre has a staff of i5/OS® programmers with a wide range of experience and knowledge about the systems and the network. The dealership load is about one half that of other regional centers to allow this centre to focus on network-wide i5/OS support functions. These functions include application programme development, programme maintenance, and problem handling.

DATABASE ADMINISTRATION AND AUTOMATION

Database administration is the function of managing and maintaining database management systems (DBMS) software. Mainstream DBMS software such as Oracle, IBM DB2 and Microsoft SQL Server need ongoing management. As such, corporations that use DBMS software often hire specialised IT (Information Technology) personnel called Database Administrators or DBAs.

DBA RESPONSIBILITIES

- Installation, configuration and upgrading of Database server software and related products.
- Evaluate Database features and Database related products.
- Establish and maintain sound backup and recovery policies and procedures.
- Take care of the Database design and implementation.
- Implement and maintain database security (create and maintain users and roles, assign privileges).
- Database tuning and performance monitoring.
- Application tuning and performance monitoring.
- Setup and maintain documentation and standards.
- Plan growth and changes (capacity planning).
- Work as part of a team and provide 24 × 7 support when required.
- Do general technical troubleshooting and give cons.
- Database recovery.

TYPES OF DATABASE ADMINISTRATION

There are three types of DBAs:

- *Systems DBAs:* focus on the physical aspects of database administration such as DBMS installation, configuration, patching, upgrades, backups, restores, refreshes, performance optimisation, maintenance and disaster recovery.
- *Development DBAs*: focus on the logical and development aspects of database administration such as data model design and maintenance, DDL (data definition language) generation, SQL writing and tuning, coding stored procedures, collaborating with developers to help choose the most appropriate DBMS feature/ functionality and other pre-production activities.
- *Application DBAs*: usually found in organisations that have purchased 3rd party application software such as ERP (enterprise resource planning) and CRM (customer relationship management) systems. Examples of such application software includes Oracle Applications, Siebel and PeopleSoft (both now part of Oracle Corp.) and SAP. Application DBAs straddle the fence between the DBMS and the application software and are responsible for ensuring that the application is fully optimised for the database and vice versa. They usually manage all the application components that interact with the database and carry out activities such as application installation and patching, application upgrades, database cloning, building and running data cleanup routines, data load process management, etc.

While individuals usually specialise in one type of database administration, in smaller organisations, it is not uncommon to find a single individual or group performing more than one type of database administration.

NATURE OF DATABASE ADMINISTRATION

The degree to which the administration of a database is automated dictates the skills and personnel required to manage databases. On one end of the spectrum, a system with minimal automation will require significant experienced resources to manage; perhaps 5-10 databases per DBA. Alternatively an organisation might choose to automate a significant amount of the work that could be done manually therefore reducing the skills required to perform tasks. As automation increases, the personnel needs of the organisation splits into highly skilled workers to create and manage the automation and a group of lower skilled "line" DBAs who simply execute the automation.

Database administration work is complex, repetitive, time-consuming and requires significant training. Since, databases hold valuable and mission-critical data, companies usually look for candidates with multiple years of experience. Database administration often requires DBAs to put in work during off-hours (for example, for planned after hours downtime, in the event of a database-related outage or if performance has been severely degraded). DBAs are commonly well compensated for the long hours

One key skill required and often overlooked when selecting a DBA is database recovery (under disaster recovery). It is not a case of "if" but a case of "when" a database suffers a failure, ranging from a simple failure to a full catastrophic failure. The failure may be data corruption, media failure, or user induced errors. In either situation the DBA must have the skills to recover the database to a given point in time to prevent a loss of data. A highly skilled DBA can spend a few minutes or exceedingly long hours to get the database back to the operational point.

DATABASE ADMINISTRATION TOOLS

Often, the DBMS software comes with certain tools to help DBAs manage the DBMS. Such tools are called native tools. For example, Microsoft SQL Server comes with SQL Server Enterprise Manager and Oracle has tools such as SQL*Plus and Oracle Enterprise Manager/Grid Control. In addition, 3rd parties such as BMC, Quest Software, Embarcadero Technologies, EMS Database Management Solutions and SQL Maestro Group offer GUI tools to monitor the DBMS and help DBAs carry out certain functions inside the database more easily.

Another kind of database software exists to manage the provisioning of new databases and the management of existing databases and their related resources. The process of creating a new database can consist of hundreds or thousands of unique steps from satisfying prerequisites to configuring backups where each step must be successful before the next can start. A human cannot be expected to complete this procedure in the same exact way time after time - exactly the goal when multiple databases exist. As the number of DBAs grows, without automation the number of unique configurations frequently grows to be costly/difficult to support. All of these complicated procedures can be modelled by the best DBAs into database automation software and executed by the standard DBAs. Software has been created specifically to improve the reliability and repeatability of these procedures such as Stratavia's Data Palette and GridApp Systems Clarity.

THE IMPACT OF IT AUTOMATION ON DATABASE ADMINISTRATION

Recently, automation has begun to impact this area significantly. Newer technologies such as Stratavia's Data Palette suite and GridApp Systems Clarity have begun to increase the automation of databases causing the reduction of database related tasks. However at best this only reduces the amount of mundane, repetitive activities and does not eliminate the need for DBAs. The intention of DBA automation is to enable DBAs to focus on more proactive activities around database architecture, deployment, performance and service level management.

Learning Database Administration

There are several education institutes that offer professional courses, including late-night programmes, to allow candidates to learn database administration. Also, DBMS vendors such as Oracle, Microsoft and IBM offer certification programmes to help companies to hire qualified DBA practitioners. College degree in Computer Science or related field is helpful but not necessarily a prerequisite.

9

Standards for Creating Bibliographic Databases

DESIGN AND DEVELOPMENT OF WEB-ENABLED DATABASES

Application of computers certainly has improved the ways in which we acquire, process, store and disseminate information in libraries. As a result, we have automated house-keeping operations, catalogue and, user services in libraries. Moreover, with the advancement in the network technology during last decade, we have started providing user services through various online modes, *viz.*, e-mail, FTP, Telnet, etc. These static/interactive modes of data/information sharing over network have improved the library services and, their popularity among the users.

During 1994, libraries began to show their presence on the internet by setting up their web sites. In the beginning, libraries built their web pages by providing mainly static information. However, in the late 1997, libraries began re-engineering their web pages with the intention of providing information from databases in a dynamic manner. Today the advancements in web and database technology have enabled the libraries to share/publish the data/information directly from the databases over the internet. Now web has become a dynamic platform for information delivery over the internet and very useful for libraries to provide various user services.

This paper intends to provide an overview of the database tools available for designing in-house databases in the libraries as well as the web technology for publishing such databases over the web. Besides, the thesis discusses the need of developing in-house databases in libraries, advantages of web-enabled databases, and selection of database tools from RDBMS commonly available.

IN-HOUSE DATABASES IN LIBRARIES

There are a number of ready-made library automation software packages in the market which can be used to automate the library functions and user services. However, many of these packages lack web interface and, thus, do not provide library database access through web. Moreover, these commercial packages provide less flexibility to librarians for making desired changes to the existing databases and to publish the same on the web. An in-house designed database system provides full flexibility to the developer/administrator/librarian and is simpler to install, maintain and, use without having to rely on external support, and also is highly customisable and can be designed to meet local needs. Librarians can also participate in design/development process as now a days easy and user-friendly database tools are available with in-built web interface. As per the survey conducted in order to get a clear understanding of the current role of library web master, 100 percent of the respondents felt that librarians should have some role in web site design and maintenance.

BENEFITS OF WEB-ENABLED DATABASES

Web-enabled databases have certain advantages over other means of sharing/publishing information over internet. These advantages are common to bibliographic databases also where libraries can put their OPACs and other databases on web. *L.J.Haravu; Kristin Aantelman and; Chong Ho Yu, the benefits of web-enabled databases are as follows:*

- Global/wide access to data with a single user inter face.
- Format in dependent access of data.
- Up-to-minute up dated access of data in real time.
- Dynamic updating of data from many locations.
- Cost-effective way of data sharing.
- Instant feedback from users.
- Seamless links from resource to resource.
- Unlimited download/printing.
- Environmental friendly.

Besides, Ortiz-Repiso and Norm Medeiros have written excellent papers on differences between traditional v/s innovative means of library catalogs, while B. Ramesh Babu, *et al* have presented an overview of web OPACS with their advantages in libraries.

DATABASE TOOLS

In the early days of database development, it was the flat-file system to store data in a single file by using field separators and record separators. Later, such flat-file systems were facilitated by an index in which a single index file stored keywords and pointers to the records that were stored in main file. This made retrieval more efficient, still flat-file systems were seriously inefficient. It showed data-redundancy, poor data control, and did not supported complex data types.

After 1960s, two database models were developed in quick succession to solve the limitations of flat-file systems. These database models were Hierarchical Database Model and Network Database Model. The Hierarchical

Database composes of a root segment, parent segments and child segments. This model depicts a set of one-to-many relationships between a parent and its children. However, this model has number of limitations.

It does not include *ad hoc* querying capability and, a multi-parent relationship is difficult to implement, as in a many-to-many relationship. The Network Database Model attempted to deal with many of the hierarchical model's limitations. The network database structure easily accommodates the multiple child, although, its structural complexities often limit its effectiveness and efficiency. Both of these database models are obsolete now mainly because of their incompatibility with web environment and have been replaced by RDBMS. RDBMS is the current database implementation standard being used for publishing information on the web.

It includes the following features which make it suitable for web environment:

- Provide extremely useful tools for database administration;
- Adhere to powerful query language SQL developed by Microsoft Corporation;
- Compliant with ODBC/JDBC and other database interface tools;
- Work in client/server mode;
- Offer distributed database and distributed processing options; and
- Have referential integrity controls to ensure data consistency and, thus, suitable for web environment.

It is easier to design applications in RDBMS due to the following features:

- Requires less programming skill
- Availability of third party tools, and
- Inbuilt web interface.

These all features of RDBMS have made them ideal for library applications to setup bibliographic database solutions and publishing them over the web. In the early days of library systems development, vendors have designed library applications software by using pre-relational database technology. Still some library systems suppliers are continuing to maintain and develop such products. These proprietary library applications software have their own advantages and disadvantages.

However, in the library management systems marketplace, there is a growing trend towards the use of RDBMS as shown in the figures. Other points to be considered while selecting database tools for library applications are easiness, user-friendliness, flexibility and low cost. In most of the cases in libraries where bibliographic databases are dealt with, commonly available consumer database products such as *MS Access*, and *File Maker Pro* are sufficient. These products can support up to 1GB of data and provide cheaper solutions. However, these database tools are suitable for small databases and not useful for large databases, hence provide limitations in web environment. There are specific database solutions for large databases available from *MS SQL Server, DB2, Oracle, Informix, Sybase,* etc. These database tools support up to several terra byte of data; permit thousands of simultaneous users; work in client/server mode; show natural affinity towards web environment and, thus, suitable for large bibliographic, web-enabled databases in libraries. However, to design full-text databases in libraries where large files are to be stored and retrieved, these tools do not offer good solutions as most of these tools support 200-255-400 characters field length. Although, many of these tools allow unlimited entries in memo field, the data inside a memo field are not searchable and thus, offer limited utility.

In this respect, *MS SQL Server* has extended the searchable field length up to 8063 characters and thus, provide solutions for moderate full-text databases. As a common trend, a number of libraries have been using open source software available either free or on nominal prices. These database management systems include the most common *mySQL, mSQL* and, recently updated *PostgreSQL*. These database tools are easy to work and run on various platforms such as UNIX, Lynux, NT, etc. Besides, there are some library specific text retrieval database tools for management of full-text large files, generally known as 'Free Form Databases', provide powerful search engine. Although, in some ways they are at the opposite end of the RDBMS, little database structure imposed on the designer and, thus, provide an easy and readymade database structure. However, they provide some limitations in achieving integration in the modules other than searching such as cataloguing, classification, management module, etc. These software are *BRS/Search, Basis Plus, Status,* etc.

WEB TECHNOLOGY

World Wide Web or WWW or web, sometimes wrongly mentioned as synonymous to internet, is a sub-set of it and is a most promising mode of publishing/sharing of data/information. Now, the web has emerged as the dominant protocol over internet due to its special features like easy interfacing of diverse platforms/technologies; provision to incorporate text, graphics, audio and video, etc.; permitting to access data/information in a non-linear way and; jumping from one document/resource to another through hyperlinks. The superiority of www over other modes of online sharing, *viz.*, e-mail, FTP, Telnet, Gopher, etc., has been well explained by Paul Scully. In fact, web has provided a single user interface to facilitate the user interaction with the databases or systems resources.

The web uses unique URL (universal resource locator) address which facilitates the access of information seamlessly across the diverse platforms in a client-server mode. The actual data represented in a structured way reside in a powerful computers called server, while the latter is equipped with server tools/software to populate the information over web. The client/user equipped with web browser such as Microsoft Internet Explorer (MSIE) and Netscape Navigator, etc., which interact with the server through common communications protocol TCP/IP over high speed network/internet. In fact, the client/user sends its query to the server while the latter processes the request and gets the response/results from the database and sends it back to the client/user over the web.

COMPONENTS OF WEB-BASED SYSTEMS

Web Browser

It is a software that helps users to interact with the server for sending queries and getting results over the web. MSIE and Netscape are the most popular web browsers, both of these are available free.

Web Server

Web server is the software that helps in sharing the system resources/ files over the internet through web browsers. The latter communicate with a web server via the standard Hyper-Text Transfer Protocol (HTTP). In fact, web servers receive queries from the client, process it, get data from databases and send it back to the client over web. The popular web servers are Apache, Microsoft IIS, iPlanet from Sun-Netscape alliance, and newly developed *Zeus* from Zeus Technology Ltd. Although web servers are increasingly found as components within full-featured server operating systems, there are some basic selection points that should be highlighted. These points are scalability and performance; high availability and reliability; interoperability and open standards; system administration and; security.

In fact, there are not much choice in the web server segments as many of them come along with database tools, show natural affinity with the database tools from same vendor, and some other work better with certain platform/ operating systems. The widely followed Netcraft web survey, approximately 60 percent of web servers run Apache, with Microsoft's IIS and the Netscape/ iPlanet web server as its major competitors. However, Gartner studies have given Netscape/iPlanet a larger share of public web sites, followed by Apache and Microsoft/IIS. Apache is being used for the public sites of companies such as Merck, American Express, Texaco, Chrysler, and others.

However, it is easier to find both Microsoft/IIS and Netscape/iPlanet as the servers for large corporate public web sites when using the lookup facility offered by Netcraft. Also, for intranets, most counts credit Microsoft/IIS and Netscape/iPlanet as the leaders, followed by Apache, IBM's Lotus Domino Go server, and others. Among hot e-commerce sites, E*Trade runs the Netscape/iPlanet server, eBay runs Windows/IIS, and Amazon runs Apache.

WEB AUTHORING TOOLS

Basic web server software does nothing except it sends HTML data in response to a browser request. However, certain other web-authoring and scripting tools are required to extend the functionality of web server to extract the data from databases. These web-authoring tools and scripting tools are required to write web pages and scripts to interact with back-end databases. In early days of web-based applications, *CGI* (common gateway interface) programmes were used extensively to extend the server functionality by allowing web users to interact with the web server to request specific data from the databases. Although, writing *CGI* programme is difficult and requires programming skill, however, it works with high reliability. Now-a-day, number visual editors are available to generate the web pages and write scripts automatically.

The common editors are *Microsoft Front Page, Visual Interdev, Netscape Composer, Web Builder,* etc. Besides, other technologies have been introduced to communicate with the back-end databases. These technologies are Microsoft *Active Server Pages (ASP*) and *Java Server Pages (JSP)* from Sun Micro Systems. Both the technologies have combined the HTML codes with the scripts in a single page and thus, making it easier to interact with back-end databases. During last few years, object-oriented and component based solutions were added to further make it easier to interact with the back-end databases.

These solutions include:

- Microsoft COM/DCOM,
- ActiveX Data Objects (ADO);
- OMA and CORBA (Common Objects Request Broker Architecture) from Object Management Group;
- Sun's EJB (Enterprise Java Beans),
- Java Applets (for client) and
- Java Servlets (for server), etc.

Besides, some database connectivity tools such as ODBC and JDBC have also emerged as in-built features of operating systems, etc.

FREE WIZARDS AND THIRD PARTY TOOLS

Writing HTML codes and scripts for database interaction is the most difficult part, requires programming skill, systems logic and manipulation planning, especially for non-computer professionals. However, a number of free wizards and third party tools are available on internet which can generate hundred of lines of codes automatically with a single click, thus, making it easier for non-skilled users to set up web-enabled database solutions in libraries. Some of the free wizards are Rule Zero, Power ASP, Active Server Pages Tools and Components, etc. Besides, *Microsoft FrontPage* also provides database wizard to generate *ASP* pages/*VBScripts* automatically to interact with back-end databases, while *Visual InterDev* provides a visual interface to develop a web-enabled web site with minimum efforts.

DATABASE SEARCHING IN CENTRAL UNIVERSITY LIBRARIES IN INDIA

In consequence of the recommendation of the National Knowledge

Commission, each of the Indian states has at least one fully-funded central university. Now there are 39 central universities. Privately funded and owned statelegislated universities are also being established to cater to the increased demand for higher education. In between there are many universities that are not legislation-based but are authorised by the University Grant Commission to award degrees.

Central universities are better-equipped in terms of financial resources, faculty, and infrastructure, and thus have an edge over the usually fund-starved state universities. The libraries across the globe are challenged to integrate e-resources into their collection, services, and patrons' lives and academic libraries face obstacles when virtual learning environment (VLEs) become "the primary means of interaction between students and universities. Providing access to electronic journals and other e-resources is an important area of librarianship. The design of usable online interfaces is a crucial issue. Traditional library services and printed material are still more effective to researchers in Indian universities than web-based information and resources. Barriers to progress in this area in university libraries in India cannot be overlooked.

NETWORK INFRASTRUCTURE AND STRENGTH

Fast and effective information retrieval to support information sharing requires sound and wide network with adequate bandwidth. The UGC-sponsored Infonet is the mainstay of the academic info-network infrastructure. The UGC has constituted a national committee called the Central Monitoring Committee (CMC) for smooth implementation and execution of information infrastructure. The CMC has chosen ERNET India to establish information network in universities. The committee has recommended high bandwidth campus wide networks for Internet and external connectivity. So far 149 universities have been provided connectivity with raw bandwidth ranging from 512 KBPS to 20 MBPS. The Inflibnet is administering and funds its cost for all these universities.

ONLINE DATABASES

Retrieval Techniques

Net Server and CD-ROM mirror servers are very popular among the universities. The university libraries under study no longer provide CD-ROM services. Multimedia databases are available only in DU and JNU, while all the eight libraries own and provide access to full text and bibliographic databases. or academic libraries the two most important consortia are the UGC-Infonet and Indest. All the libraries have self-subscribed as well as consortia based databases, whereas the DU and JNU have also developed in-house databases. Being traditional and general universities under the preview of the UGC, all are members of the UGC-Infonet, while DU is also member of

AICTE Indest consortia. All the universities use commercial as well as open source databases while DU and JNU have also their home grown databases. Open source databases are also available there, but the study found that only DU, BHU, IGNOU and JNU host important open source online databases on their web sites. Other universities are not able to create this kind of facility for their users merely because the staff of these libraries are not conversant with open access sources on the Internet.

Databases can be accessed through login and password, but the misuse of these is a common complaint. Therefore, IP access is more suitable. Now most of the universities allow online access to databases either through their intranet or directly from the Web. Experienced librarians prefer a campus-wide facility for providing access to databases. AU, IGNOU, Jamia, JNU and Viswabharati allow access from limited and specified terminals within campuses.

Assam, IGNOU, Jamia, JNU and Viswabharati allow access through campus wide Intranet or Internet with identification and password. Many busy scholars and faculty have less time to visit the library. Therefore, access to online information must be provided on their desktops. This requires campus wide Internet accessibility. Further it was found that AU, BHU, DU, Jamia, JNU, PU and Viswabharati allow IP enabled access while IGNOU databases are password based.

Download Facility

Downloading of the required files is a critical issue. In case of commercial databases it is costly as the host library has to pay per download. But indeed it is an essential facility. It has been found that all the libraries provide downloading of PDF and HTML files, while image downloading facilities are available in all except at BHU and DU. RTF downloading is not permitted by BHU, DU and Jamia Millia Islamia, Whereas word file are not downloadable at BHU, DU and Jamia. DU and JNU provide DBMS software to download the data oriented information.

Data Retrieval Techniques

Some of the universities provide common databases linked through federated search. Only DU has the federated search engine GIST find. In this survey, only DU and PU revealed their online search techniques while the other libraries kept these confidential.

DU uses Boolean, Interactive, and Proximity searches, while PU uses quick search. Simple search Advanced/Boolean search in addition to menudriven searches are provided by their vendors. Both these libraries provide facilities for further refinement of large chunks of search output to make the search more precise and relevant. Nevertheless, none of the universities use data mining.

Complexity of Information Retrieval

Indeed information retrieval techniques vary from university to university system. It depends upon both internal and external factor of database.

User Orientation

For optimum use of all resources and services of a library, user orientation programmes, especially of new users, are a proven effective measure. User orientation is the most important component in the online databases for the users to gain knowledge and enhance usability of databases. All the university libraries in this study have positively voted for provision of such programmes to help users in the effective use of the retrieval system for information access. This survey found that orientation programme are conducted by all except AU, BHU, IGNOU, and Viswa Bharati. It is important to note that regular orientation programmes are required to make the users familiar with new feature of new databases.

DU conducted programmes as "How to search the online databases," while the Pondicherry library provides instructions in the use of library resources including eresources and effective online searching. BHU conducts programmes on Science Direct and Proquest. DU provides need-based instruction and PU provides general instruction in effective search and the publishers also conducted such programmes to faciliatets searching of their supplied databases. DU conducts such programmes throughout the years, while PU organises orientation of the users at the beginning of the academic years. PU also offers need based person to person training. It is clear that there is no uniform pattern of conducting user's orientation programmes. Indeed we need a dedicated library staff for online training of library users, especially in the electronic environment. here are posts of information scientist in universities funded initially by the by UGC. Those hired are mostly from computer science and not conversant with library philosophy and routine. There is an urgent need of a designated post for an online librarian who can provide assistance in using e-resources and may also take care of any aspect of user orientation for sharing and dissemination of library e-resources. The survey showed that none of the library staff has any formal education and training in online searching. Most have learned it on the job, and most have learned by trial and error.

XML AND RELATIONAL DATABASES: USES AND OPPORTUNITIES FOR LIBRARIES

Extensible Markup Language (XML) is becoming an indispensable tool for virtually every type of content that is digitally produced. The advantages of XML for libraries have been well described by others.

On a general level, XML has at least three key advantages:

- *XML is standard.* XML is a subset of Standard Generalised Markup

Language (SGML), a well established and highly regarded ISO standard. XML also offers mechanisms to encourage and enforce common definitions of the logical structure of a document so that standards for the documents themselves are easier to apply.

- *XML is extensible.* XML has no limits on the number of markup languages that can be defined using it, and each of these languages can consist of an unlimited number of tags. This flexibility is essential for fostering the widespread adoption of XML and helps explain why XML has been utilised for markup languages in every conceivable subject area, ranging from chess playing to mind reading.
- *XML is well supported.* It seems that almost every serious Web technology is now expected to define its relationship to XML, and XML has fostered an explosion of related technologies. The W3C has made many tools and toolkits freely available to Web developers, and utilities and applications for XML are being developed by a worldwide community of vendors, open source contributors, and other groups that seek to move information across the Web.

XML has been used extensively for authoring standalone documents, but database solutions for storing and managing large collections of materials in XML format are becoming more common. As Bourett, a researcher who tracks developments in XML databases, points out, choosing between an RDBMS and other database options for storing XML often comes down to whether you are working with data or documents. If the XML content is usually manipulated at the individual field level, needs to be accessed with standard query and reporting tools, and pulls together information from sources that are updated and maintained separately, then a Relational Database Management System (RDBMS) approach may make the most sense. xamples of this kind of "data-centric" content include purchase orders, flight schedules, and scientific data.

If the XML content is largely contained in individual documents, and the content will be edited and updated at the document level, then Object Orientated Databases (OODBMS), Object/ Relational Databases, and other solutions that can maintain XML documents as a more complete unit on the backend will be preferred. Data housed in an RDBMS are typically based on individual rows in tables, using "keys" or "ids" to pull together content dynamically.

Most RDBMS solutions for storing XML assemble XML representations of the data on the fly. Object relational databases and some RDBMS addons, such as Oracle's Internet File System (IFS), step slightly outside of the standard RDBMS tables to work with Binary Large Object (BLOB) or other mechanisms built into the database to store whole XML documents without parceling pieces of it to separate tables. his allows the document to be stored with all tags and ordering preserved. Of course, the data and document distinction is not absolute, and there are other factors that can influence the choice of a database. An organisation may have built up a high level of Oracle experience, for example, and that would have a huge impact on any data management decisions.

Libraries are also in a somewhat unique situation in that they house collections of both data-centric and document-centric materials that may require database solutions. or example, libraries with finding aids in Encoded Archival Description (EAD) format or full text materials marked up with Text Encoding Initiative (TEI) are more likely to favour "document-centric" solutions and require extensive full text searching capabilities that are more prevalent in OODBMS and Object/ Relational Databases. Libraries are even more likely to deal with content that is "data-centric", such as purchase orders and circulation records; they may already have RDBMSs in place to support the processing activities associated with this data.

MARC AND XML

The difficulty in separating data from document-based content can be seen in the Machine Readable Cataloguing (MARC) format, one of the library community's most successful and durable standards. Like many document-centric formats, MARC records can carry a lot of text-intensive information. Libraries may even choose to convert MARC records to standalone XML documents in order to take advantage of mainstream XML tools for indexing or for presentation purposes. On the other hand, MARC records are "data-centric" in the sense that they can often bring together data sources that are maintained outside of the bibliographic description of an item. Authority, holdings and item records, for example, play a key role in helping to define the bibliographic view of the physical and virtual objects in the library's collection, yet these records are often processed and updated separately. Libraries have begun to explore the use of XML for MARC.

Lane Medical Library at Stanford University has created a DTD and released conversion software for converting MARC records to XML documents in an initiative called XMLMARC. K.T. Lam has also proposed a DTD for MARC and suggests that the use of a decentralised authority repository may one day be possible with XML linking technologies. •This would allow libraries to "point" to established names and subjects that could be maintained remotely rather than replicated by each individual library. Clearly, there is interest on the part of libraries in bringing MARC fully into an XML environment.

The challenge is to define an XML infrastructure that can handle the amount of materials that libraries catalogue without isolating the content from the transactional processes that libraries use for acquiring and circulating the collection. ataloguing records are typically maintained by dozens of library staff and are linked to ordering and circulation processing procedures that involve many updates. Any application of XML that is tied directly to where cataloguing records are maintained and use XML as a means of updating content may need to be "transaction aware" and support a high level of multi-user access.

MIDDLEWARE ALTERNATIVES

A number of middleware mapping tools exist for layering XML representations of information that is housed in an RDBMS on top of individual tables, such as IBM's DatabaseDOM. The middleware typically uses Structured Query Language (SQL) to pull together the fields needed for the XML input/output. The advantages of this approach are that this greatly increases the number of database systems that a library can select from because all major RDBMSs support SQL, and that this allows great flexibility for moving from one database to another. For formats like MARC, these tools also offer the possibility of using XML technologies without losing the robustness of relational databases for maintaining content and linkages that are updated by multiple users. The disadvantages of this approach include the overhead required to assemble and disassemble XML documents as they move in and out of the database, and the extra groundwork to define an XML representation that takes full advantage of both the RDBMS and XML technologies.

A good example of an XML mapping tool for relational databases is Castor, an open source project from Exolabs. he mapping file in Castor determines how the XML will be produced from the contents of the RDBMS. In addition to defining whether a field in the RDBMS is to be rendered as a node or an attribute, an ID reference is provided that identifies the records in the appropriate table. Castor is very "Java-centric," which can be an advantage or disadvantage depending on how comfortable an organisation is with the Java platform. By working with Java, a developer can use Castor to render the records in an RDBMS accessible and updatable as XML documents. Databases that can be used with Castor include Oracle, MySQL, and PostgreSQL.

THE WEB AS THE WORLD'S BIGGEST RELATIONAL DATABASE

The way that an RDBMS references rows from multiple tables can be compared to Web links. A Web page is, in some ways, much like an RDBMS "view" of disparate data. From a user perspective, the content is brought together based on a predefined logic and a series of "keys" or "pointers" that identify relevant material. A dynamically generated Web page comes even closer to the conceptual model of an RDBMS, particularly if much of the content of the page is based on remote network resources retrieved through URLs. For example, a search of a library catalogue on the Web typically involves a cgi-bin programme that dynamically displays results using HTML. Each result record is usually linked to a fuller display via a URL that specifies from where the information is to be retrieved.

The linking mechanisms of the Web have recently been leveraged to support the OpenURL framework. he OpenURL framework has been proposed as an architecture for retrieving references to scholarly works by enabling third parties to provide links for a referenced item. Although OpenURLs have typically been deployed to provide links to the full text of scholarly works, the framework can also be utilised to identify a catalogued item in an ILS. Ex Libris' ALEPH500 System, for example, directly supports OpenURL, and exploratory work has been carried out to generalise the OpenURL framework beyond reference linking scholarly environments. f the Web can be thought of as an ever-growing RDBMS, and OpenURLs can be utilised to provide "RDBMS-like" standard and precise links between specific items in information systems, then there are possibilities for providing extensive distributed search and retrieval functions in Web-based library services.

For example, a remote database consisting of Library of Congress names and subject headings could be searched within a browser environment, and the results could provide links to items in the local catalogue. Web-based union catalogues support standardised indexing and searching at a central location. With OpenURLs, links can be made to point to holdings and other localised information within the member library's Integrated Library System. ll of this fits within the RDBMS notion of creating and maintaining data with as little duplication as possible, and linking it together to provide a logical view of the content itself. XML plays a role by greatly enhancing the linking mechanisms of the Web. XML technologies such as Xinclude, Xpath, and Xlink, provide sophisticated methods for drawing on network resources. Xinclude allows the contents of a separate XML resource to be inserted into an XML document based on a link. path will be familiar to anyone who has worked with XSTL and other XML stylesheet tools.

It allows the creation of expressions for specifying every visual and interface portion of a document. Xlink is the XML linking language and offers much more sophisticated types of linking than currently offered by the familiar HREF and NAME elements found in HTML. Xlink's extended element can name one or more linked resources. The arc element in this example tells an application about the behaviour expected when moving through the linked resources.

The role and title attributes are used to describe the function of the linked resource in the context of the local resource. Role is meant to be descriptive to the application and title is meant to be descriptive to the user. n this case, the roles are meant to identify an author's works and biographies. The *acutate* element describes how the resources should appear. The value "onRequest" specifies that the resource should appear when the link is selected, and the value "embed" for the *show* attribute tells the application to insert the specified resource inline within the current document. Finally, an *item* element is used to represent where this particular resource can be found in physical form in the library. If an XML representation of an RDBMS-based library catalogue or other library database is made available, the library can make use of XML linking technologies and other XML tools for manipulating database contents. OpenURL lays the groundwork for using links as virtual keys to content that goes far beyond individual tables, and the content can be as broad as the diversity of the Web itself.

STANDARDS FOR CREATING BIBLIOGRAPHIC DATABASES INDIAN ACADEMIC LIBRARIES UNDER INFLIBNET UMBRELLA

The concept of "standard" in the field of library and information science is interpreted as codes of cataloguing rules, classification schemes, subject headings and various other documents contained recommendations for good library practice, all of which are subject to varying interpretation. But, for another professionals, standards are extremely precise technical specifications for communication between software and machines in an automated information-processing environment. For example, Operating Systems, TCP/IP, etc. Standards are documented agreements containing technical specifications or other precise criteria to be used consistently as rules, guidelines, or definitions of characteristics, to ensure that materials, products, processes and services are fit for their purpose Field of bibliographic standards are not limited to the rules only but spread up to the authority files such as person names, corporate names, subject headings, classification schemes, series names, institution names, software and standardisation form and format, etc. In beginning, during the initiation of automation to library professionals, there was not much focus on bibliographic standards and were creating databases in any formats.

That affected to the automation of their libraries, which forced them to think over the issue. Now, gradually, the libraries and information centres are realising the importance of bibliographic standards. Centres like Information and Library Network (INFLIBNET), Ahmedabad is playing important role in bringing all libraries together to work on a single platform of standards with linking under one huge national network, *i.e.* UGC-Infonet. INFLIBNET Centre is an Inter-University Centre of University Grants Commission (UGC), working on Academic library system in India. In 1990, UGC launched it as a programme for five years on pilot basis. On June 1996, the programme was recognised as a full-fledged Centre. UGC-Infonet is a project of UGC being implemented by INFLIBNET Centre in collaboration with ERNET (Education and Research Network), New Delhi. It is an Intra-Network of Indian universities and colleges across the country based on the

Open IP platform, employing state-of-the-art technologies like IP or TV, enabling online response to queries. The network facilitates Intranet and Internet access to its users on high data rates.

STANDARDS FOR BIBLIOGRAPHIC DATABASE

Well-known simple definition of database is a set of records and record is a set of fields, where, field is a combination of different pieces of information. Bibliographic database is a database of resources available at libraries in print format. With the revolution of information technology in the field of libraries, bibliographic catalogue has come up into the form of bibliographic database. For making compatible with these changes, there, many library institutions have come up with different standards and formats such as CCF, AUSMARC, CANMARC, UKMARC, USMARC, UNIMARC, MARC21, AACR2, ISBD, LCSH, MeSH, etc. Some of the Internationally recognised standards and formats being used by many libraries of different countries for creating databases. As per the INFLIBNET's guidelines following standards are recommended for use:

Standardised Bibliographic Formats

During the inception of the Programme, The Task Group on "Union Catalogue, Data Capturing and Standardisation" was constituted by UGC. The Task Group was assisted by a Sub-Committee on implementation of Common Communication Format (CCF) for data capturing and data exchange. Later on, the Sub-Committee formalised some fields based on CCF and named it as "Guidelines for Data Capturing: a user manual". During the initial stage of automation, Micro CDS/ISIS software (developed by Unesco) were suggested to use for creating bibliographic databases based on the format recommended by the Centre.

Simultaneously, other DBMS such as DBase, FoxPro, FoxBase, etc., were also being used by different libraries for creating the databases. In addition, the Centre had also the library house keeping software called "ILMS – Integrated Library Management System" developed on COBOL language on Unix platform, and was distributed freely to the member libraries of the Centre. Later in February 2000, Centre developed another library house keeping software called "SOUL – Software for University Libraries" on Power Builder language on Windows platform by using the client-server architecture to keep in mind the shortcomings being faced in ILMS software. The software is developed based on the format formalised by Sub-Committee of the Task Force.

Later, early 2001, The Ministry of Human Resource Development (MHRD), Govt. of India visualises building up a national database of library holdings in the country based on the MARC21 format. Further, after approval the committee directed INFLIBNET Centre to implement the MARC21 format in all libraries of the country. In this regards, the Centre formed the MARC21 Core Group during December 2001, which formalised the fields for implementing it with the SOUL library house keeping software. The main reason for preferring MARC21 over CCF and other formats was that most of the countries in the world use MARC and it is comprehensive having number of fields.

STANDARD FOR RENDERING INFORMATION/ BIBLIOGRAPHIC DESCRIPTIONS

AACR2R, ISBD and CCC are standards for bibliographic descriptions. But, INFLIBNET Centre suggests their participating libraries to follow the Anglo American Cataloging Rules-II (AACRII) Revised version for rendering bibliographic information.

STANDARDISED SUBJECT HEADINGS

Different subject headings list are available, developed by different institutions such as LCSH, Sear's List of Subject Headings, MeSH, Thesaurus, etc. But INFLIBNET suggests to its member library to use LCSH (for generalised subject headings) and Engineering Index, MeSH and thesaurus (for specialised Subject Headings).

STANDARD FOR CLASSIFICATION SCHEMES

There are various classification schemes have been developed by different organisations for classifying the books on different subjects. Functionally, most of the libraries are using the Dewey Decimal Classification (DDC) for assigning the Classification Number to the documents. But, under INFLIBNET umbrella, all the libraries are free to use any classification scheme for classifying the document, as it is very difficult for any library to reclassify the entire collection based on any new scheme. As per the library practice any classification scheme can be used as MARC21 has capability to adopt any kind of classification schemes.

ISO–2709 INFORMATION EXCHANGE FORMAT

This standard specifies the requirements for generalised interchange format that will accommodate data describing all forms of material. It describes a generalised structure designed specifically for exchange of data between processing systems and not necessarily for use as a processing format within systems. The format may be used for the interchange of records using various communication media. INFLIBNET Centre recommends to follow this Exchange Format for contributing records to the Centre. The exchange format has implemented too with the in-house developed software SOUL for exchanging records. Physical structure of the implemented information exchange format is given below:

Physical Structure

Leader

Each record begins with a leader of fixed length of 24 character positions and is the first instance of the ISO 2709 format of a record. It contains:

- *Record length (5 characters):* The length of the record includes the leader, directory, data fields and record separator.
- *Record Status Code:* Always '0' for output files, ignored on input files.
- *Implementation Codes:* These codes are defined for each specific implementation of the ISO 2709 format. Second character position represents Bibliographic level codes and rest of the character positioned not used. Here, Bibliographic level is defined here as per the INFLIBNET's use. For the MARC21 based records, it follows the description defined for bibliographic level in MARC21 bibliographic format.
- *Indicator length:* This is always '0', because here at INFLIBNET database indicator is not being used. But the value is '2', when we export records from SOUL to MARC21 in ISO 2709 format.
- *Subfield identifier length:* '2' The subfield identifier length. This shows the number of characters being used for the subfield identifier.
- *Base address of data:* A decimal number indicating the number of control characters which precede the variable data fields. This number, when added to the starting address of the record, gives the address of the first character of the variable fields.
- *For user systems:* These character positions are not used. Always '000' in output files.
- *Length of "Length of Datafield" field:* '4' the length of "Length of Datafield" in the directory.
- *Length of "Starting character" position:* '5' the length is "Starting character position" in the directory.
- *Rest:* These character positions are not used. Always sets on '00'.

Directory

A directory entry in this bibliographic record is made up of a tag, length-of-field, and field starting position. It is of variable length and consists of a series of fixed fields, referred to as "entries". One directory entry is associated with each datafield present in the record. Each directory entry is 12 characters in length and is divided into three parts:

- *Tag:* A three numeric ASCII character code identifying the datafield, which corresponds to the directory entry. In software, names of the fields are being used in alphabetical name, but during the export in ISO 2709 format and display on screen, it converts in three-numeric digit ASCII character code.

- *Length of datafield:* A four digit number showing how many characters are occupied by the datafield, including datafield separator but excluding the record separator code if the datafield is the last field in the record.
- *Starting character position:* A five-digit number giving the position of the first character of the datafield relative to the base address of data, *i.e.*, the first character of the first of the datafields.

Datafields

A datafield consists of subfield and datafield separator:

- Subflield: A subfield consists of a subfield identifier followed by a data string, which is terminated by either another subfield identifier or a field separator. A subfield identifier consists of a subfield identifier flag, *i.e.*, cap (^) sign followed by one another character, that can be alphabet a to z (small or capital) and numeric 1 to 9, INFLIBNET Centre uses here small alphabets. For MARC21 based records "$" graphical sign is used as a subfield identifier.
- Datafield Separator: The datafield separator, *i.e.*, hash (#) sign constitutes the final character of every datafield. ASCII value 30 (character 1/14 of ISO 646) is being used as a field separator in MARC21 based data.

Record Terminator/ Separator

The record terminator is the final character of the record, *i.e.*, hash (#) sign. It follows the field separator of the final datafield of the record. ASCII 29 (character 1/13 of ISO 646) is being used as record separator in MARC21 based data.

OTHER STANDARDS RELATED TO BIBLIOGRAPHIC DATABASE

There are some other standards related to the bibliographic databases, are given below:

Z39.50 Retrieval protocol

Z39.50 refers to the International Standard, ISO 23950: "Information Retrieval (Z39.50): Application Service Definition and Protocol Specification", and to ANSI/NISO Z39.50. The standard specifies a client/serverbased protocol for searching and retrieving information from remote databases.

OAI (Open Archive Initiative)

The Open Archive Initiative (OAI) for metadata harvesting is a new protocol dedicated to solving problems of digital library interoperability by defining simple protocols, most recently for the exchange of metadata. Although, Z39.50 Information Retrieval Protocol is also one of the harvesting protocols. Some digital library systems are using for retrieving and searching the records for example Maxwell System. It is crucial to explain, discuss, and disambiguate the concepts and terminology used among OAI implementers to harvesting approach to interoperability. The harvesting protocol defined by the OAI is a request/ response protocol with 6 request types, *viz. Identity, ListMetadataFormats, ListSets, GetRecords ListRecord, and ListIdentifiers.* It has defined in such a way to support a common set of principles and a technical framework to achieve interoperability. Although, both the standards are not being used with the INFLIBNET database right now, but being explored to implement it in near future.

PURPOSE OF THE BIBLIOGRAPHIC STANDARDS

Mostly, purpose of using these standards for creating bibliographic databases or suggesting using it at libraries of India, has following reasons behind it:

- Pursuing Universal Bibliographic Control
- Exchange of information among union databases for the purpose of global resource sharing
- Cooperation at the local level, transferring data from one system to another

IMPORTANCE OF THE BIBLIOGRAPHIC STANDARDS

Following bibliographic standards for creating the databases produces following importance:

- It makes uniformity in records;
- It provides better resource sharing between different resource centres.
- It helps in exchanging of records and facilitates it without data loss.
- It helps in creating national/ International bibliographic union database.
- It helps to adopt any system and provides platform interoperability.

10

Knowledge Organization as a Tool of Library Database Management

KNOWLEDGE ORGANIZATION SYSTEMS: AN OVERVIEW

The term *knowledge organization systems* are intended to encompass all types of schemes for organizing information and promoting knowledge management. Knowledge organization systems include classification schemes that organize materials at a general level, subject headings that provide more detailed access and authority files that control variant versions of key information. They also include less-traditional schemes, such as semantic networks and ontologies. Because knowledge organization systems are mechanisms for organizing information, they are at the heart of every library, museum, and archive.

Knowledge organization systems are used to organize materials for the purpose of retrieval and to manage a collection. A KOS serves as a bridge between the user's information need and the material in the collection. With it, the user should be able to identify an object of interest without prior knowledge of its existence. Whether through browsing or direct searching, whether through themes on a Web page or a site search engine, the KOS guides the user through a discovery process. In addition, KOSs allow the organizers to answer questions regarding the scope of a collection and what is needed to round it out.

All digital libraries use one or more KOS. Just as in a physical library, the KOS in a digital library provides an overview of the content of the collection and supports retrieval. The scheme may be a traditional KOS relevant to the scope of the material and the expected audience for the digital library, a commercially developed scheme such as the Yahoo or Excite categories, or a locally developed scheme for a corporate intranet.

The decision of what knowledge organization system to use is central to the development of any digital library. The KOS must be applicable, either automatically or by human catalogers, to the resources included in the digital library. Once the material is included in the collection, the KOS must be meaningful to its users. This section outlines the characteristics of KOSs, describes the common types, and discusses their origins and traditional uses.

COMMON CHARACTERISTICS OF KNOWLEDGE ORGANIZATION SYSTEMS

It is often said that humans are inherent organizers. From an early age, children play sorting and matching games. We cope with our ever-changing world by comparing new objects or experiences with those with which we are familiar, identifying patterns and categorizing what is new into our existing frame of reference. The emphasis on developing comprehensive KOS's can be seen in the writings of our earliest philosophers, many of whom continue to influence our view of the world. For example, Aristotle's effort to categorize knowledge into groups is reflected in our language, our education, and our science.

The original classification scheme of the Library of Congress, used between 1800 and 1814, was based on the philosophical works of Sir Francis Bacon and inherited from the English tradition. Beginning in 1814, the influence of Thomas Jefferson can be seen on the Library of Congress collection. Jefferson, who reclassified the library, reflected a more humanist philosophy. There is no single knowledge classification scheme on which everyone agrees.

Michael Lesk speculates that while a single KOS would be advantageous, it is unlikely that such a system will ever be developed. Culture may constrain the knowledge classification scheme so that what is meaningful to one culture is not necessarily meaningful to another. Therefore, we live in a world of multiple, variant ways to organize knowledge.

Despite their diversity, KOSs have the following common characteristics that are critical to their use in organizing digital libraries:

- The KOS imposes a particular view of the world on a collection and the items in it.
- The same entity can be characterized in different ways, depending on the KOS that is used.
- There must be sufficient commonality between the concept expressed in a KOS and the real-world object to which that concept refers that a knowledgeable person could apply the system with reasonable reliability. Likewise, a person seeking relevant material by using a KOS must be able to connect his or her concept with its representation in the system.

TYPES OF KNOWLEDGE ORGANIZATION SYSTEMS

A review of some typical knowledge organization systems shows their scope and applicability to a variety of digital library settings. While there are specific definitions for many of these KOSs in the computer science and information science literature, and even in standards documents, there is debate over these definitions. Terms are often used, particularly in the popular press and in the book trade, in nonstandard ways. Reflecting the scope of this practice, a recent *National Information Standards Organization* (NISO) work shop on electronic thesauri emphasized the need to improve the definitions of "terminology relating to terminology".

The descriptions given here provide an overview of possible systems for organizing digital libraries. The descriptions are based on characteristics such as structure and complexity, relationships among terms, and historical function. The list is not comprehensive; nor are the definitions of these terms contained in specific standards documents. They are grouped into three general categories: term lists, which emphasize lists of terms often with definitions; classifications and categories, which emphasize the creation of subject sets; and relationship lists, which emphasize the connections between terms and concepts.

Term Lists

Authority Files

Authority files are lists of terms that are used to control the variant names for an entity or the domain value for a particular field. Examples include names for countries, individuals, and organizations. Nonpreferred terms may be linked to the preferred versions. This type of KOS generally does not include a deep organization or complex structure. The presentation may be alphabetical or organized by a shallow classification scheme. A limited hierarchy may be applied to allow for simple navigation, particularly when the authority file is being accessed manually or is extremely large. Examples of authority files include the Library of Congress Name Authority File and the Getty Geographic Authority File.

Glossaries

A glossary is a list of terms, usually with definitions. The terms may be from a specific subject field or from a particular work. The terms are defined within a specific environment and rarely include variant meanings. Examples include the *Environmental Protection Agency* (EPA) Terms of the Environment.

Dictionaries

Dictionaries are alphabetical lists of words and their definitions. Variant senses are provided where applicable. Dictionaries are more general in scope than are glossaries. They may also provide information about the origin of a word, variants and multiple meanings across disciplines. While a dictionary may also provide synonyms and through the definitions, related words, there is no explicit hierarchical structure or attempt to group them by concept.

Gazetteers

A gazetteer is a list of place names. Traditional gazetteers have been published as books or have appeared as indexes to atlases. Each entry may also be identified by feature type, such as river, city, or school. An example is the U.S. Code of Geo-graphic Names. Geospatially referenced gazetteers provide coordinates for locating the place on the earth's surface. The term *gazetteer* has several other meanings, including an announcement publication such as a patent or legal gazetteer. These gazetteers are often organized using classification schemes or subject categories.

Classifications and Categories

Subject Headings

This scheme type provides a set of controlled terms to represent the subjects of items in a collection. Subject heading lists can be extensive and cover a broad range of subjects; however, the subject heading list's structure is generally very shallow, with a limited hierarchical structure. In use, subject headings tend to be coordinated, with rules for how they can be joined to provide concepts that are more specific.

Examples include:

- The Medical Subject Headings (MeSH); and
- The Library of Congress Subject Headings (LCSH).

Classification Schemes, Taxonomies, and Categorization Schemes

These terms are often used interchangeably. Although there may be subtle differences from example to example, these types of KOSs all provide ways to separate entities into "buckets" or broad topic levels. Some examples provide a hierarchical arrangement of numeric or alphabetic notation to represent broad topics.

These types of KOSs may not follow the rules for hierarchy required in the ANSI NISO Thesaurus Standard and they lack the explicit relationships presented in a thesaurus.

Examples of classification schemes include:

- The Library of Congress Classification Schedules,
- The Dewey Decimal Classification, and
- The Universal Decimal Classification.

Subject categories are often used to group thesaurus terms in broad topic sets that lie outside the hierarchical scheme of the thesaurus. Taxonomies are increasingly being used in object-oriented design and knowledge management systems to indicate any grouping of objects based on a particular characteristic.

Relationship Lists

Thesauri

Thesauri are based on concepts and they show relation-ships among terms. Relationships commonly expressed in a thesaurus include hierarchy, equivalence and association or relatedness.

These relationships are generally represented by the notation:

- BT (broader term),
- NT (narrower term),
- SY (synonym), and
- RT (associative or related term).

Associative relationships may be more detailed in some schemes. For example, the *Unified Medical Language System* (UMLS) from the National Library of Medicine has defined more than 40 relationships, many of which are associative. Preferred terms for indexing and retrieval are identified. Entry terms point to the preferred terms to be used for each concept. There are standards for the development of monolingual thesauri and multilingual thesauri. In these standards, the definition of a thesaurus is fairly narrow.

Standard relationships are assumed, as is the identification of preferred terms, and there are rules for creating relation-ships among terms. The definition of a thesaurus in these standards is often at variance with schemes that are tradi-tionally called thesauri. Many thesauri do not follow all the rules of the standard but are still generally thought of as thesauri. Another type of thesaurus, such as the *Roget's Thesaurus,* represents only equivalence. Many thesauri are large; they may include more than 50,000 terms. Most were developed for a specific discipline or a specific product or family of products. Examples include the Food and Agricultural Organization's *Aquatic Sciences and Fisheries Thesaurus* and the *National Aeronautic and Space Administration (NASA) Thesaurus* for aeronautics and aerospace-related topics.

Semantic Networks

With the advent of natural language processing, there have been significant developments in semantic networks. These KOSs structure concepts and terms not as hierarchies but as a network or a web. Concepts are thought of as nodes, and relationships branch out from them. The relationships generally go beyond the standard BT, NT, and RT. They may include specific whole-part, cause-effect, or parent-child relationships. The most noted semantic network is Princeton University's WordNet, which is now used in a variety of search engines.

Ontologies

Ontology is the newest label to be attached to some knowledge organization systems. The knowledge-management community is developing ontologies as specific concept models. They can represent complex relationships among objects, and include the rules and axioms missing from semantic networks. Ontologies that describe knowledge in a specific area are often connected with systems for data mining and knowledge management. All of these examples of knowledge organization systems, which vary in complexity, structure, and function, can provide organization and increased access to digital libraries.

THE ORIGIN AND USE OF KNOWLEDGE ORGANIZATION SYSTEMS

In the physical library, classification schemes such as *Library of Congress* (LC), Dewey Decimal System, and the Universal Decimal Classification reflect, among other things, the need to store a single item at a single location on a shelf. To provide multiple access points beyond the limits of a single physical location, subject headings are applied. Libraries use subject heading schemes such as LCSH, Sears, or other specialized schemes developed for specific content or specific collections.

At the level of specific content, libraries have used authority files to control variant forms of personal, organizational, and geographic names. However, KOSs can be found in settings other than libraries. An awareness of the KOSs available from alternative sources is valuable when considering the development of digital libraries for a specific audience.

Abstracting and Indexing Services

Abstracting and indexing (A&I) services developed as an outgrowth of traditional bibliographies and the explosion of journal literature. In the sciences, the development of A&I services was spurred by the post-World War I concerns about inadequate access to scientific information. In the 1950s, investment in A&I services was fueled by the Cold War and Sputnik. Abstracting and indexing services in the humanities, such as the Bibliography of the History of Art or the *Modern Languages Association* (MLA) Bibliography, generally took a different growth path than did their scientific and technical counterparts, but they also quickly became important resources for scholarship in the online environment.

The scope of A&I services varies from broad discipline-oriented services to narrowly defined aspects of the literature and subdisciplines. Special KOSs, such as thesauri and subject categories, were developed to support A&I services and their specific products and audiences. These organizations applied increasingly complex schemes to provide subject access to the literature in a variety of subjects.

By the 1960s, A&I services were moving from the provision of printonly products to print and online services through large online vendors such as Dialog. Later, the products were distributed on CDROM and now, increasingly, on the Web. In many cases, the KOSs migrated from print to electronic media following the products they supported. While increased computing power, more sophisticated search engines, and more independent end-user searching have led to changes in some KOSs, most have retained their importance, even in the Web environment.

For many years, the KOSs related to A&I services were applied only by catalogers and indexers trained in using the KOS indexing for a particular product or products. The primary users of KOSs were librarians and other professional searchers. However, the proliferation of electronic data, the explosion of electronic publishing, and increasing concerns about the difficulty of locating information have led to a renewed interest in these KOSs for use not only by professionals but also by end users.

Publishers

As publishers have migrated to electronic composition systems, they have become increasingly involved in the production of A&I products. Large journal publishers such as Academic Press and Elsevier have developed their own systems to provide bibliographic records linked to the full text of documents. As the content of online journals has grown, it has become necessary to move from systems that provide browsing by table of contents and journal issue to systems that support searching by both free text and by KOS. Electronic journals have resulted in additional KOSs, particularly classification and categorization schemes. For example, Elsevier's Web site has a subject categorization scheme to provide access to individual Web sites of its more than 2000 titles.

Trade, Professional, and Governmental Organizations

A variety of authority files and classification schemes are used to support business and commerce. They range from the *Standard Industrial Classification* (SIC) code and the *North American Industrial Classification System* (NAICS), used in procurement and government statistics, to disease codes used to communicate patient illnesses and treatments among physicians, hospitals, and insurance companies. As more organizations develop Web sites, additional KOSs are being developed to support them.

Internal Projects

Organizations are among the most prolific creators and users of KOSs. Developers of corporate intranets and knowledge management systems have discovered hundreds of specific classification schemes, glossaries, categorization schemes, and other vocabularies in use within organizations. Many of these are geared towards specific tasks and are, therefore, very narrow both in subject scope and target audience. However, for these audiences, they can also be rich sources of information. For example, the *Department of Energy* (DOE), *Environmental Management Science Programme* (EMSP) and the Office of Scientific and Technical Information are developing a digital library to support EMSP programme managers. Programme managers and researchers have developed "needs categories" and "science categories" to organize the *Environmental Science Network* (ESN).

The categories are used primarily to support the process of grant submission and award; however, the ESN also uses them to provide access to related material from within DOE and from other distributed databases from the EPA, the Department of Defence, and NASA. Vocabulary is currently being organized around these categories for use with a Web mining tool that will provide highly relevant Web resources for project managers in specific areas.

LINKING DIGITAL LIBRARY RESOURCES TO RELATED RESOURCES

This section emphasizes the ability of knowledge organization systems to link digital library resources to other related resources. The basis for this linking is the identification of information within a digital resource that can be extracted and used to search and locate information within a KOS. The KOS may then be used to expand codes to more explanatory full text, to provide more descriptive records, or to link entity names to resources of physical specimens.

EXPANDING CODES TO FULL TEXT

Practitioners of a discipline use coding schemes to facilitate communication within that discipline. It is often helpful to connect these coding schemes to the full names for which the code stands. The examples provided here include links between databank registration codes and the biological sequence data, and between industrial codes and the full name that the code represents.

Linking Sequence Numbers to Biosequence Databanks

The lengthy biochemical and genetic sequences that molecular biologists, biotechnologists, and geneticists identify each day are kept in databanks. Several databanks have been developed, for example, to cover protein sequences, nucleotides, and cell lines. One of the largest databanks contains information on the mapping of the human genome. As molecular biologists began to discover these sequences, they reported them in scientific journals. Difficulties in composing, proofreading, and printing the text soon arose.

Through an ad hoc standards process, major biomedical publishers agreed to require the inclusion of codes or databank numbers for these sequences in articles when they are published. In addition, the sequence itself must be registered in a databank before the paper can be published. Some of the most frequently referenced databanks are listed on the Web site of the National Center for Biotechnology Information. They include GenBank and the Research Collaboratory for Structural Bioinformatics Protein Data Bank.

Each sequence number is different, but all begin with a persistent code identifying the databank. How can the link be made between the literature and the databank? Through a search profile, a text analysis programme, or keyword indexing, the text can be analysed and the sequence databank numbers identified. An active link can be embedded. The active link consists of a search strategy to locate that sequence number in the databank where the actual sequence is stored. When the user clicks on the active link, the script is generated and launched from the user's browser.

The Web-enabled database is searched, and the sequence record is returned to the user. Depending on the services provided by the databank site, the user can analyse the sequence using a number of tools provided by the databank or download the sequence for local manipulation. This type of connection exists between the *National Library of Medicine's* (NLM) search service, PubMed, and GenBank at the National Center for Biotechnology Information. If a search in PubMed yields records that have GenBank numbers, the user can automatically search and display the sequence records from GenBank.

Linking Individual Industrial Codes to the Full Scheme

In business, classification schemes serve to communicate important facts about a company or product. These codes are generally controlled by a government, professional, trade, or international standards organization. They often serve as shorthand for users interested in material in a particular area of industry or a specific business sector. Perhaps the most familiar scheme is the SIC code, which was last updated in 1987. The SIC codes have been used by the U.S. government, economists, financial markets, regulators, and procurement offices to identify manufacturing, agriculture, and service sectors of the economy.

In 1997, a new scheme was approved for use within the United States. The North American Industrial Classification System was developed with Canada and Mexico as a means of providing an agreed-upon scheme for the collection, reporting, and analysis of information about the economy by sector, both within and across borders. Information about NAICS is available from the Web site of the U.S. Census Bureau. The digital library can provide related information by using the authority files for the coding schemes as a linked authority file.

If a company or economic sector mentioned in the digital library's collection can be linked to an SIC or NAICS code, the code can be searched against the official tables of definitions maintained by the U.S. Census Bureau. These files provide definitions of the codes and place each code in the classification scheme with other economic sectors. The digital library's content can be further enhanced by making a link between the SIC and NAICS codes.

LINKING TO DESCRIPTIVE RECORDS

Linking the name of an entity, such as a personal name, organization, or location, to additional information about that entity was one of the first uses of hyperlinking. Knowledge organization systems such as dictionaries, glossaries, and classification schemes can be used to link the entities in one resource to richer descriptions of that entity in another resource. This is particularly helpful for users who are new to a topic and in cases where the additional information can make the user's task more efficient. The examples that follow are from three disciplines. The first example links organism names to records that not only describe the species more fully but also put it in the context of the overall classification scheme for living organisms. The second example links chemical names to descriptive records and molecular structures. In the third example, proper names are linked to the biographies for the person.

Linking Organism Names to Taxonomic Records

Genus-species names are the Latin names for organisms—*e.g.*, plants, animals, and microorganisms. Taxonomists, who study and classify living organisms, create records for each of these organisms. Generally, these records are linked relationally to the other organisms in a hierarchy. Beyond the organism name and the information that it and its placement in the hierarchy convey, taxonomic records use other elements to describe the organism. These may include distribution patterns, the authority for naming and classification, and the date the organism was identified.

Scientists base the information on specimens that are retained because they serve as the physical evidence of the description. Natural history museums, private collections, and individual scientists number, or code, the specimens in their collections. Sometimes specimens are supported by photographs or line drawings, which may be digitized. By using a taxonomic authority file as an intermediate authority file, one can link a text or an image file containing a name or picture of an organism to additional related information.

By automatically processing the text or embedding a link from the organism name in the text or from the image to the taxonomic authority record, one can extend the knowledge conveyed by the text. The text can include the descriptive and historical information in the taxonomic record and, ultimately, link to a photograph, a drawing, or appropriate video or audio segments. Because of the ambiguity in organism names, many examples of this type are now created manually. However, depending on the extent of the files involved, the ambiguity of the Latin and common names for organisms can be overcome.

An example of a taxonomic intermediate file is the *Integrated Taxonomic Information System* (ITIS). ITIS is a partnership of U.S., Canadian, and Mexican government agencies, private organizations, and taxonomic specialists cooperating to develop an online, scientifically credible list of biological names of North American plants and animals. It is used by many U.S. govern-ment agencies for consistent naming of plants and animals for regulatory and monitoring purposes. To link textual material in a digital library to the ITIS record, the organism name can be identified manually or automatically in the text and submitted as a query to the ITIS database. When a match is found, ITIS presents the ITIS record, which provides essential information about the organism. The information includes synonymous names, including some common names, and an indication of the placement of the organism in the larger taxonomic classification scheme.

Linking Chemical Names to Molecular Structures

The unique identification for a chemical substance is not its name but its molecular structure. However, chemical names are commonly used in research documents, project plans, catalogs, and directories, all of which may be resources in a digital library. There are competing systems of nomenclature as well as common and commercial synonyms. The ambiguity is resolved by providing links between the chemical names in the text and the molecular structure. This is done through a chemical registry number or code that is connected to a particular chemical name and an authority record that provides additional information about the chemical. This information includes the chemical's synonyms and some of its chemical and physical properties.

Most important in today's research environment is the link from this authority file to a chemical structure file. Structure files, used with the appropriate software, graphically depict the molecular structure. This sophisticated software allows for three-dimensional visualization, rotation, and substitution of the chemical bonds. An example of the use of the chemical registry number to link chemical names with molecular structures can be seen in the work of BIOSIS, the world's largest not-for-profit producer of biological and biomedical databases.

In 1993, BIOSIS began processing its bibliographic citations to automatically identify chemical names. BIOSIS assigns CAS *Registry Numbers* (RNs) to the chemical names identified in this process. In the STN International online system, hosted in the United States by CAS, a user of BIOSIS can select one or more of the records resulting from a search and extract the RN. The extracted RN can be applied against the CAS Registry File, which contains more than 21 million substances, including organics, inorganics, biosequences, metals, and alloys.

The registry file record for the chemical name, including the link to the synonyms for the chemical name and the structure file itself, can then be accessed. With special tools developed by CAS, the structure can be viewed and manipulated. It can be imported into modeling tools that allow the chemist to manipulate the structure and thereby envision new chemicals. Alternatively, the user can start with any database that contains CAS RNs and extract the resulting RNs to perform a search for complementary bibliographic records in the BIOSIS database. Linking chemical names to structures using RNs on a large scale is neither inexpensive nor easy. There are two approaches to identifying chemical names in text.

Some journal articles include the CAS RN for the major chemicals discussed. In this case, an analysis of the text for the terms "RN", "CAS RN", and variations preceding numerics can identify RNs that can be used as a link. Alter-natively, a programme to identify chemical names in text, similar to that developed by BIOSIS, could be devised.

Developing the identification programme, as well as searching chemical databases, is costly; however, if the digital library has license agreements for chemistry databases, this type of linkage may be possible. In addition, many organizations have small chemical files of their own that may include RNs and other information of particular relevance to the organization's research. It may be possible to link to these local databases using methods that are more direct.

Linking Personal Names to Biographical Information

A common type of authority file is the personal name authority, which controls variants of personal names. For example, the *Library of Congress Name Authority File* (LCNAF) is used to control variant personal names for authors, editors, artists, and others. The *Union List of Artist Names* (ULAN), developed by the Getty Vocabulary Programme, is another example. Name authorities serve as tools for catalogers and indexers. They ensure that the proper form of the name, rather than an unapproved variant, is used and bring together all works by or about the person.

A name authority file can also be used to link a biblio-graphic record or document containing the person's name to a variety of other related materials. If the digital library's resource has a standardized form of the name, it can be identified and searched against the authority file to locate variants. The standardized and variant forms can be joined in a search against a variety of other resources that can provide related information. For example, in the case of a digital library of images of artists' works or biographical or critical text, a name authority file such as the ULAN or the LCNAF can act as an intermediate file to provide additional information.

The file, which contains integrated variant names, can be searched by the name appearing in the digital library collection. When the record is found, the information about the artist can be displayed, providing a wide range of contextual material for the user. Citations to significant biographical or critical works about the artist, some of which may also be available on the Web, may also be provided in the name authority file.

The variant names from a name authority can also be used to locate and provide automatic links from the personal name in the text to a biography, without requiring that the name be presented in the same fashion in the two resources. One such resource that could be linked to for biographical information is Gale's Biography Resource, which contains more than 142,000 biographies and related citations from more than 1,000 periodicals. However, to produce this kind of link, there must be a mechanism for locating personal names in text. Several programs can do this type of text analysis; among those that have been developed commercially are NameFinder from the Carnegie Group and the Intelligent Agent from IBM. In addition, variant names can be extracted from the name authority itself, grouped, and run as a search against the text to locate name occurrences.

LINKING ENTITY NAMES TO PHYSICAL SPECIMENS

In some cases, it is possible to go another step and connect entity names in the digital library resources to physical specimens. The curation of physical specimens or artifacts is critical to the advancement of many disciplines. Exhibition catalogs describe the art objects in a particular exhibition. Museum catalogs provide inventories of the art, natural history, or cultural objects held by a particular museum.

These catalogs, increasingly available as computerized databases, are knowledge organization systems that not only provide descriptive records but also point to the location of the object in a museum, an archive, or another collection. For example, in biology, a physical specimen is particularly important when it is the result of the discovery and description of a new organism or of the reclassification of a known organism.

A type specimen is the example collected from the field by a taxonomist to serve as the prime example for the description of the organism and the validation of its taxonomic classification and naming. These specimens are held by natural history collections, and their deposit is required by the rules of various taxonomic societies. As part of the curatorial activity, the collections assign identification codes. While the primary use of identification codes has been to organize the physical collections, numerous projects are under way in the natural history community to digitize photographs of specimens and create database records for the specimens, including their identifiers, and thereby make them more rea dily accessible.

The degree of digitization varies from specialty to specialty. For example, in botany, virtually all significant research herbaria are digitally cataloging their type collections instead of maintaining paper records. Many are also making digital photographs of the type specimens available over the Web. The publication of identification codes in the journal literature is also changing. Historically, identification codes have been presented in the "Materials Used" sections of journal articles.

The level of specificity of the identification code has varied, depending on the biological discipline. For example, botanical journals tend to list only the institution and the catalog, while vertebrate journals provide the code to the specimen level.

The current trend is to require lists of specimens that are more detailed. As the lists become longer and the printing costs increase, journal publishers are beginning to request links to independent Web sites maintained by the researchers or their organizations that carry all the specimens used in the study and provide some level of identification.

If the digital library collection contains resources that include the identification codes, these codes can be extracted and matched against the Web-based catalogs or databases. This link can provide users with location and contact information to allow them to access the physical object mentioned in the digital library resource. Curators or registrars of artistic, archaeological, and cultural history collections also assign inventory or accession numbers to items in their collections. Identification numbers may also be found in scholarly catalogues raisonnés. Links similar to those described for natural history can be made between text related to works of art and the physical work in a particular collection. An article about a work of art can be linked to additional information about the physical specimen by linking the identification number in the text with an online catalog containing the number and additional information about the work. As museums digitize their collections to establish a presence on the Web or to reduce the handling of the physical objects, KOSs that can link the digital library resources to the physical object are being developed. If there is a museum with a collection that complements that of the digital library, it is worthwhile to discuss ways in which the digital library and digital museum collections may "co-evolve."

MAKING RESOURCES ACCESSIBLE TO OTHER COMMUNITIES

Someone recently compared the Web with a large room filled with books that were scattered all over the floor. The Web is the world's largest mass of bits and bytes. It is a meeting place that brings together disparate communities. The "Internet Commons," as this meeting place has been called, requires connections between and among disparate communities in order for an "economy" to develop. This economy will provide the framework within which both commercial and noncommercial transactions can occur. KOSs are one means of connecting these disparate communities.

Knowledge organization systems can be used to:

- Provide alternate subject access,
- Add modes of understanding to digital library resources,
- Support multilingual access, and
- Supply terms for expansion of free-text searches in domains that are relatively unknown to the user.

PROVIDING ALTERNATE SUBJECT ACCESS

Alternate subject access refers to the provision of one or more additional subject orientations that make the resources of the digital library accessible to different audiences. This approach is particularly valuable when the digital library resources appeal to groups that do not share a common terminology. It can be a system of subject headings, a classification scheme, or any other subject-oriented system.

Alternate subject access can be provided by:

- Indexing or classifying the resources using multiple schemes,
- Retaining original schemes from organizations that contribute to the digital library, or
- Mapping between the primary scheme and an alternate scheme.

Indexing the Material with Multiple Schemes

The most direct method for providing alternate subject access to a collection is by classifying or indexing the resources with multiple schemes, but it may also be the most costly. This approach requires redundant cataloging or catalogers who are knowledgeable in both schemes. It may also require modifications to the cataloging tools and procedures. However, if the cataloging is at a high level or if the schemes are not difficult or detailed, it may be a reasonable approach.

Retaining Alternate Indexing from Contributors

If the digital library is being built through contributions from a variety of sources, the originating organization may have applied an alternate scheme that could be used. For example, the NASA database on aeronautics and astronautics receives relevant bibliographic records from other U.S. agencies, such as the Department of Defence and the Depart-ment of Energy.

The controlled vocabulary terms assigned by the contributing organization are processed through a machine-aided indexing process to create candidate indexing terms from the *NASA Thesaurus* for review by NASA's indexers. However, the final records contain both the *NASA Thesaurus* terms and the controlled vocabulary terms from the contributing organization, with the alternate indexing terms retained in a separate data element in the bibliographic record. The terms collected from other organizations can be viewed as an alternate access point, so that at least part of the collection is accessible through another discipline's terminology.

Mapping Multiple Schemes

The third method for providing alternate subject access is the most indirect, that of mapping one or more schemes. Several examples of this approach can be found among A&I services. Both BIOSIS, the world's largest private sector A&I service in the life sciences, and the NLM apply MeSH to BIOSIS documents. The records that BIOSIS contributes to NLM's TOXLINE database are processed automatically to have appropriate MeSH terms added.

This is based on a mapping of the natural language terms that occur in the toxicology literature and BIOSIS' normalized natural language keyword indexing with the MeSH terminology.

In the new BIOSIS relational indexing structure, BIOSIS builds and maintains authority files that connect natural language disease names to the MeSH-controlled disease terms. When the BIOSIS indexer assigns the free text keyword for the disease name, the appropriate MeSH term is also added to the record as an alternate access point. The assignment is based on the development over time of a mapping between the terminology used by BIOSIS and the MeSH-controlled terms. In addition to providing alternate access points to BIOSIS products, the inclusion of the MeSH terms makes it possible to perform cross database searching on the indexing field with MEDLINE and other databases that include MeSH terms. From 1999 forward, users can search BIOSIS databases using MeSH disease terms. The disease terms can be extracted from the MeSH authority file or from a MEDLINE record and then used in a search against the BIOSIS files, or *vice versa*. This helps users find relevant records that are unique to either BIOSIS or MEDLINE. The inclusion of terms from an alternate KOS, such as MeSH, therefore supports the use of BIOSIS by medical librarians and practitioners who are familiar with MeSH terminology. A more extensive example of mapping variant schemes is the metathesaurus developed by the NLM's *Unified Medical Language System* (UMLS). This system has linked more than 40 separate KOSs from various medical specialties. They range from MeSH to coding and classification schemes used by insurance companies and physicians to describe treatments and diseases on patient records.

The UMLS is licensed by many other organizations for inclusion in applications that can bridge various health care communities. How can digital libraries use alternate indexing? While many digital libraries do not have the A&I resources of large database producers such as NLM and BIOSIS, the concept of applying alternate indexing can be scaled to fit. While the systems described deal with item-level bibliographic records, alternate indexing can be applied at several levels. Alternate subject access can be applied only at the resource level, for the database, electronic book, electronic journal, or image collection, so that other communities can identify resources of interest that must then by searched or browsed individually. This concept is conducive to use with portals that provide access to the same resources with different views for different audiences. Alternatively, if the digital library has bibliographic records or metadata records at a very detailed level, it may be possible to develop switching programs that will translate concepts from the original organization of the digital library or resource to that of the alternate scheme.

ADDING NEW MODES OF UNDERSTANDING TO THE DIGITAL LIBRARY

People perceive the world through many modes, including textual and graphical. Some people comprehend information more easily in one mode than another. Most people benefit from a variety of modes that reinforce one another or that can be used when appropriate to the context. Many digital library projects remain text-based; however, this text-only dimension is changing as digital libraries become oriented more to multimedia and as other modes of information presentation become viable on the Internet. KOSs can be used to bring new dimensions to an information resource or a collection in a digital library.

In the digital library environment, these dimensions can be viewed as layers that can be added on top of one or more objects. Various tools and services can be developed that are geared to a particular mode. For example, the results of a text search can be presented in graphical or visual form, based on the number of occurrences of a term or concept or on the occurrences of documents from a particular country, journal title, or author. A more complex dimension that can be added is the geospatial dimension, which emphasizes access by place.

A "geolibrary" is defined as a digital library consisting of "geoinformation", or material that can be accessed by place. This so-called geo-referencing can be either direct or indirect. Georeferencing of textual objects is facilitated by a gazetteer, which brings together the place name and the spatial footprint for its location. Many gazetteers also include feature types for each footprint. The vocabulary used for the feature types varies among gazetteers, but may include terms such as "airport", "harbor", and "railroad station".

Although many organizations, including federal and state agencies, are currently required to provide geospatial referencing as part of the National Spatial Data Infrastructure Programme, the geospatial referencing is not readily available for older works. How can the data sets of today be integrated with the textual information of yesterday? The answer is by adding geospatial referencing to the text resource. Geospatial referencing requires that the text name for a place have an associated spatial footprint. This can be achieved by using a georeferenced, digital gazetteer that provides geospatial footprints for place names.

Through this type of knowledge organization system, place names in a library catalog or bibliographic database can have footprints assigned. If one or more of the library's resources have latitude or longitude coordinates in the catalog record or in the full text but no place name, the coordinates can be extracted and submitted to the gazetteer service. The service will return the place name for the footprint.

Alternatively, the resource may have a textual place name. This place name can be extracted and searched against the gazetteer, and the footprint can be provided to a mapping application. The latter search may result in more than one footprint, since place names may be ambiguous. Therefore, it is important that the user interface be designed to allow the user to distinguish the locations.

Once the footprint has been determined, a user can access the text resource through a geographic mapping tool. Alternatively, a user of the text resource can find a set of results and have the place names displayed as footprints on a map.

In disciplines such as ecology, environmental science, and even public health and epidemiology, it would be beneficial to build a digital library with access to such a digital gazetteer service. Users could then access the system through the text mode or the geographic mode, depending on their comfort level and the type of information needed. Presenting the results on a map allows users to make new associations and analyse the results more easily. Through a geospatial KOS, they can see connections between disparate data, because the data are presented in an alternate mode.

PROVIDING MULTILINGUAL ACCESS

A third way that KOSs can support the use of digital libraries by disparate communities is to provide multilingual access. A variety of sources, including multilingual dictionaries and multilingual thesauri, can support this type of access. One of the most extensive multilingual thesaurus efforts is the *Generalized Multilingual Environmental Thesaurus* (GEMET) from the *European Environment Agency* (EEA), produced by Italy's research council, the *Consiglio Nazionale delle Ricerche* (CNR).

The GEMET is available in 12 languages, and plans for a global environmental thesaurus in many more languages were recently announced. GEMET is available by agreement with the EEA. The European Topic Centre on Catalogue of Data Sources in Germany is developing a system that will link data sources and metadata information in a virtual library. GEMET will be used to convert a search in one language into searches for the same concepts in other languages. Users will retrieve documents not only in their native language but also in other languages. This will allow data systems from throughout the EEA and beyond to be accessed as a virtual library collection with both controlled vocabulary and free-text term searching in multiple languages.

EXPANDING FREE-TEXT SEARCH TERMS

Free-text searching is the main method of searching on the Web. Only a small percentage of Web resources have metadata, and an even smaller percentage have controlled vocabulary assigned. However, variations in natural language make free-text searching problematic. Even a knowledgeable user may not know all the terminology that can be used in the literature to express a concept. The problem is exacerbated when the user is unfamiliar with the topic or is interested in an interdisciplinary area. How can the user expand his or her search to overcome these terminology differences? One possibility is to use KOSs as aids to the selection of free-text keywords. The

Getty Vocabulary Project emphasizes support for searching as a significant application of its vocabularies. Harpring reports that the vocabularies are increasingly being used in search engines to look for different terms that refer to the same concept.

The Getty vocabularies are particularly rich in equivalence relationships. "When these equivalence relationships are exploited in search engines, there are typically two possible scenarios: the user may be allowed to first query the vocabulary database, locating appropriate terms, and then applying those chosen terms in a query across target databases; or there may be little or no user interaction with the vocabulary, when the vocabularies are used behind the scenes..." Getty developed a prototype called *a.k.a.* to experiment with the use of equivalence terms to broaden or narrow searches across databases on the Web. In addition to expanding routine search queries, KOSs can be used in Web mining tools. Northern Light has developed a Web mining tool that reportedly returns a high degree of relevant hits. The KOS that supports the Northern Light site was built by ingesting large existing vocabularies and thesauri.

The result was then organized under an extensive classification scheme developed by Northern Light. The terms can be used to extend a user's search or to distinguish between multiple meanings of the terms supplied by the user. The results of a search are organized into "folders" based on the classification scheme. These high-level categories, represented by the folders, help distinguish multiple meanings of the same term. For example, an ambiguous word such as "pitcher" might result in two folders being presented to the user. One folder would be titled "Sports", the second "Decorative Arts". The user who chooses only the Sports folder will be presented with only those Web resources that use "pitcher" in the baseball sense.

The user who selects the folder called "Decorative Arts" will be presented only with those resources that are related to water pitchers. KOSs can be very powerful in supporting free-text searching within digital libraries and in integrating Web resources into existing digital libraries. However, these systems must be used with caution. KOSs have generally been developed for a specific discipline, task, or function, or for the indexing of a specific collection or database. Therefore, depending on the domain in which the KOS is being used and the complexity of the system, it may or may not suggest relevant free-text terms. Expanding a search with related terms, rather than pure synonyms, may return hits that are only peripherally relevant to the user.

PLANNING AND IMPLEMENTING KNOWLEDGE ORGANIZATION SYSTEMS IN DIGITAL LIBRARIES

This section provides general guidelines that may be useful for an organization that wants to use knowledge organization systems to organize a digital library. The framework described is applicable for KOSs of any type or subject.

PLANNING KNOWLEDGE ORGANIZATION SYSTEMS

Analysing User Needs

Of primary importance to any digital library project is an analysis of its users' needs, in terms of content and functionality. Many volumes have already been written about needs assessment, and providing detailed guidance on this subject is beyond the scope of this paper. However, when analysing how a KOS might be used with a particular digital library, it is essential to thoroughly understand the environment of the user.

One must look not only at the needs for organizing the digital library materials but also at possible links between content within and outside the digital library walls. This is particularly important for KOSs that are acting as intermediate authority files, because in such cases the links may not be readily apparent. It is important to consider other views that might be valuable for users and peripheral communities that might benefit from the digital library's content were it accessible to them through a KOS.

Locating Knowledge Organization Systems

Once the user's needs have been analysed, it is necessary to locate KOSs to meet the need. While an alternate system can be built locally, it is preferable to find an existing KOS for several reasons. First, it is costly and time-consuming to build a KOS. Second, KOSs often benefit by having been built over time. Many of the systems described in this report have been built over decades; some existed in paper before digitization. The value of a KOS comes from its acceptance by the user community; sources built by noted authorities such as learned societies, trade associations, or standards groups will be viewed as more trustworthy than those built internally.

Finally, the networked environment has resulted in both an explosion of primary materials, including documents, electronic journals, and Web-based databases, and in an equivalent explosion of KOSs on the Web. There are several ways to identify KOSs that may be of interest. Many users are already aware of KOSs on the Web within their discipline. Developers may also turn to directories, librarians in the field, and reference sources, or they may perform a general search of the Internet.

Planning the Infrastructure

It is necessary to make decisions about the architecture of the KOS in the context of the digital library setting. The physical location of the KOS is important. Will the system be held externally or internally? There are pros and cons to either approach. If the system is available on the Web, it is possible to consider linking to the KOS as an external system. This architecture requires a script or some search query to locate the resource. One must then launch a query against the resource to obtain the piece of information that will serve as the key between the two files. This key could be a *universal resource locator* (URL) or input to another search query.

A query may be necessary if the KOS is stored in a database. The script may transfer log-on information from the digital library system to the external KOS, in order to provide access to the Web-enabled database. In the case of a more direct link, the access may be by URL. However, the use of a URL as the link has the same problem with persistence as does direct access via a URL from a browser. The organization may move the KOS, thereby changing the URL that is being used as the key. It is important to determine how often the URLs in the KOS change, whether there is a means of notification of these changes, and whether it is possible to consider an alternative that would be more persistent.

Schemes such as the Digital Object Identifier and the Persistent URL have been devised to enable resources to be physically moved among servers without having their names changed. Another alternative is the use of other Uniform Resource Identification (URI) schemes and the *Uniform Resource Name* (URN), which can be sent from the newer Web browsers. The benefit of linking to a remote resource is that the resource will always be upto-date. The maintenance of the KOS is in the hands of the owner, not the digital librarian. It may also be more apparent to users that the KOS is not owned by the digital library.

Linking to a remote KOS also has disadvantages. Persistence and unexpected changes in the organization and content of the system may cause problems. The software or telecommunications route between the digital library server and the KOS may be unreliable. In systems requiring fast response time or large amounts of data transfer, and, therefore, high bandwidth, the fact that a connection must be made between the digital library and the external KOS may make the system unacceptable to the user. Alter-natively, the KOS may be obtained from the owner and loaded locally.

In many cases, this requires licensing that may not be required when the KOS is accessed remotely, because a copy of the whole resource is being provided to the digital library. Loading a KOS locally also requires that one consider issues such as maintenance, local system administration, and disk storage. If the KOS uses special software, such as a database management system, loading the KOS locally will require a copy of that software, which may require additional purchase or licensing. Other considerations are the need for firewalls and interface design.

On the positive side, the KOS is under more local control. Therefore, it may be possible to improve the response time by not accessing the KOS over the Internet. If the KOS is to be used behind the scenes, concerns of speed and integration become more important. If additional modifications need to be made to the KOS to integrate it with the digital library, it will also be necessary to load the KOS locally. If the digital library intends to incorporate numerous secondary KOSs, it is important to consider the degree to which the architecture is scaleable.

The National Library of Medicine's UMLS incorporates more than 40 different sources. While its main purpose has been to develop a metathesaurus for moving among these vocabularies, the management of the systems, regardless of the mapping issues, has been a major consideration. Ingest has been a major concern, with the need to develop a system that can handle a variety of input formats-from ASCII text files to highly structured database output.

The architecture must also accommodate the character sets of the incoming sources. This is particularly important if a mark-up language has been used to represent special characters and diacritical marks. Systems that have been developed in Unicode, which extends ASCII to accommodate diacritical marks and non-Roman character sets, cannot be handled by systems that deal only with ASCII or extended ASCII sets. Since many digital library systems are being built as extensions or applications of existing *integrated library systems* (ILS), it is important to consider how the KOSs will integrate with the library system.

Unfortunately, many ILS vendors have not considered links to external files or databases in their system designs. In some cases, the vendor may require that the information be stored in the proprietary format of the ILS. The system may require that the files be on the same directory or server as the accessing ILS. The fields that can be linked to the Web or searched may be limited. Outside communi-cations may require Z39.50 client-server connections. With relatively closed systems, ILSs may be a difficult environ-ment in which to implement alternative and nontraditional KOSs.

Digital libraries that are interested in using KOSs should consider this integration when developing requirements for the procurement of a system to support them. Vendors should be encouraged to support relatively open architectures and to consider the extension of traditional library systems to support broader digital library functionality.

In addition to these immediate concerns, it is important to consider the incorporation of future KOSs. Initial success may spur the desire for integration of additional KOSs or enhanced functionality for the existing KOS. Success may breed additional requirements and increase the strain on hardware, software, and network architectures.

Maintaining the Knowledge Organization System

For a digital library, an outdated KOS can be more of a hindrance than a benefit. Maintenance, both of content and of the system, should be considered when planning a KOS. This is particularly important if the digital library is to be self-supporting or revenue generating. Version control of the KOS is extremely important. Reloading a new version from the system provider is one way to accommodate changes; however, this may not be acceptable if the locally held version differs substantially from that held by the system's provider. If there has been significant transformation or processing of the original KOS, it may be difficult, or impossible, to reload the original and recreate the changes that have been made.

A transaction-based approach, whereby only changes are transferred between the KOS provider and the library, is also possible; however, this requires that the system provider have the infrastructure, both machine and human, to produce these transactions. It also requires that the changes to the original KOS be identifiable in order to create change transactions. For example, Stuart Nelson of the NLM's UMLS Project recently reported that many systems can create annual transaction records to inform the UMLS about the changes that have occurred to the original system.

However, the changes are often not indicated with enough detail to support automatic change transactions in the UMLS. If a change date, for example, is recorded only at the level of the concept record, it is impossible to tell whether the term has changed or if the relationship between this concept and another concept has changed. Since the UMLS splits the incoming terminology and its relationships into a variety of files, it is often difficult to tell how the UMLS files must be change based on the changes made during the maintenance of the original KOS.

Presenting the Knowledge Organization System to the User

In addition to deciding which KOS should be used and what functions it should serve, the digital library will need to determine how to present the KOS to its users. A KOS may be exposed to the user or made relatively transparent. The KOS can be exposed to the user in different ways. Material can be grouped into KOS-related themes or categories on the digital library's Web site.

The KOS may be used at a higher level to identify specific portals for different uses or users. If the content of the digital library includes metadata records, the KOS may be displayed as index terms on the records or in its entirety as a navigation aid to searching. In other cases, the KOS may be transparent. For example, a thesaurus can be used behind the scenes to extend the user's search to include synonyms, to connect the digital library's resources to other information and resources, or to filter or rank the information obtained.

IMPLEMENTING KNOWLEDGE ORGANIZATION SYSTEMS

Acquisition and Intellectual Property Issues

It is critical to properly handle the acquisition of knowledge organization systems. The first question is whether the KOS is under copyright. If so, the copyright holder should be contacted concerning the KOS. It is important to ensure that the apparent contact is the official one. Many references have been reprinted or put on the Web without proper acknowled-gment of the real owner.

Once the contact has been made, there are several points for discussion:

- If the provider maintains the KOS, how will the digital library find out about any changes that may be made in it? Is there a notification mechanism in place? How frequently must the information be updated to be of benefit to the digital library's users? Will the maintenance be self-evident, or must the agreement include notification requirements? What will the owner do if the maintenance can no longer be performed?
- What will happen if the provider discontinues the product or sells or transfers it to someone else?
- What uses can the digital library make of the KOS under the proposed agreement? As with other licensing, it is advisable to aim for the broadest permissions and the longest term possible. At a minimum, the library should be able to renegotiate the terms of the agreement relatively easily.
- In a networked environment, it is beneficial to develop mechanisms for linking to online versions rather than to maintain a local copy of the resource. This ensures that what is presented is up-todate, and acknowledges more clearly the ownership of the KOS. However, there are numerous factors to consider. Will the KOS be used on an intranet or behind a firewall, where access to the outside or information coming into the organization might be prohibited? Does the KOS service use "cookies" or require knowledge of the user's Internet provider address? Does it require a user ID and password?
- If the KOS is to be accessed remotely, are there service issues? Is it likely to be accessed with bandwidth, model, and computer speeds that are adequate for outside connections of this type? Is the use of such a critical nature that unreliable service on the part of the KOS or the Internet connection will cause the digital library itself to be viewed as less useful? Does the KOS require a specialized search engine or search query formulation? Can the digital library system properly display the results, or would the results be better displayed through the KOS system? Will the resulting information be used in its native form or must it be extracted or transformed? If the KOS is to be loaded locally, in what formats can the content be received?
- If the KOS is not available electronically, can it be digitized? Is the owner interested in a cooperative venture, and are the human and financial resources for such an effort available?

Making the Link

There are two parts to establishing the link between the digital library and the KOS. The first is locating the key anchor information in the digital library's resource. The second involves the look up against the target file. The creation of this link may be more or less automatic, depending on the particular situation. The characterization of this activity is meant to be general and to allow both "on-thefly" links and embedded links.

Regardless of what function the KOS is going to serve in the digital library, the essential information contained in the digital library resource from which the link is to be made must be identified. The mechanism for doing this depends on the type of object from which the link is being made and on the information that is expected to be identified in the digital library's resource. The first step is to review any metadata related to the digital library resource. Do the metadata carry the term that is needed to make the link? If this information is included, the level at which the metadata are assigned should be reviewed.

If the metadata indicate the subject matter of the specific resource in which the user will be interested, the metadata can be used to make the links. However, in some cases, the terms that appear in the title or description at the resource level may not be indicative of the subject at the individual item level. Automatically making a link on the basis of the content description for an entire book may misrepresent the content of a chapter. Whether or not the metadata can be used will depend on the amount and type of information given in the metadata and the level at which the metadata are assigned.

If a text resource in the digital library provides no appropriate metadata, the procedure for identifying the key information may involve text analysis. A programme to perform simple string searching or a search engine that can preserve hit locations can be used if the text string has distinguishing characteristics, such as a database acronym, or a specific structure, such as a latitude and longitude coordinate. If the text string has no such cues, text mining or more complex textanalysis tools may be necessary. These tools use a variety of semantic and syntactic algorithms to locate key information.

There have been significant advances in commercially available text-mining tools, such as IBM's Intelligent Agent, which includes specific algorithms for identification of names of places and persons. The second step of the linking activity is to make the connection to the KOS. The methods for doing this vary, depending on whether the system is being loaded locally or is referenced remotely. If the system is loaded locally, it is possible to perform a significant amount of processing to match the two files, assuming that computer resources of this type are available to the digital library organization. If the system is only available remotely over the Web, the interaction will require knowledge of scripting and various Web-based access techniques. Scripting should be considered in both local and remote approaches, since the more integrated the linking is with the resource, the more maintenance may be required if there are changes in either the resource or the KOS. Regardless of the approach that is taken, making the link requires an analysis of both the information in the original digital library material and the corresponding information in the KOS. If the KOS is being used as an intermediate file to bridge between the digital library's resource and another resource, it is also important to understand the data and the process whereby the search is performed and information returned from the target resource. If the KOS must return a value to the original digital library resource, the data and process must be evaluated in a bidirectional sense.

Choosing the linking mechanism is equally important. The link may be fixed or "on-the-fly." In the case of a fixed link, a specific URL is embedded at the link point in the digital library material. However, as stated before, problems of persistence are inherent in this approach. Alternatively, a URN can be used. The URN requires the creation of a namespace on the point of the target file, and the search is to this namespace rather than to a specific URL. Persistent locators and *digital object identifiers* (DOIs) can also solve this problem. These schemes are sufficient if the material is an HTML document. Content in databases is more difficult to retrieve.

The National Library of Medicine now supports the searching of a variety of its databases through its *Internet Grateful Med* (IGM) URL function. IGM users can create URLs that will actually perform searches against the databases. Information on the syntax for creating such a URL is provided on the NLM Web site. While the intent is that the search URL will be bookmarked by an individual user, the same concept can be used for creating an active link at the anchor point for the link. With additional scripting, the creation of the term *pneumonia* can be automatically replaced with an active link that picks up the term where the link has been made.

THE FUTURE OF KNOWLEDGE ORGANIZATION SYSTEMS ON THE WEB

As online databases moved to the Web, they began to provide their products, including vocabulary aids, in this environment. *Portable document format* (PDF) versions of printed vocabulary aids are common, since PDF can be easily produced from a Postscript file and it retains the look of the printed product. With Adobe's tools for indexing and searching, the PDF file can provide some level of support for linking. Many of these aids, however, remain in the form of HTML files only—there is no database structure to easily support the linking and searching.

In some cases, the full structure of the KOS is not made available on the Web; the only format for a Web-based thesaurus may be an alphabetical list of terms that does not enable the user to navigate easily the hierarchical structure. As unique ways of using these resources are developed, it is hoped that more KOS providers will be encouraged to provide their systems in formats that are conducive to such networked uses. Some of the requirements for such electronic KOSs were identified at a workshop entitled "Electronic Thesauri: Planning for a Standard" and sponsored by NISO. While the focus of this meeting was digital thesauri, consideration was also given to other KOSs in digital form.

The identified requirements include persistent identifi-cation at the concept level, the need for a simple protocol for the distributed querying and response from a KOS, and the development of a standard set of metadata attributes for describing a remote KOS. To facilitate the search and display of information from a previously unknown KOS, the system must have unique and persistent identifiers for each of the concepts in the system. For example, the California Environmental Resources Evaluation System and the U.S. Geological Survey have developed a system for remote querying and response. It requires that each concept in the thesaurus have a unique identifier.

In the case of the previously described ITIS, which is accessed remotely by the CERES system, the ITIS record number is used as the identifier. Other unique identifiers could include the DOI, or a classification notation that has been made unique by appending the scheme name or the URL to the notation. The second requirement is a protocol for the distributed querying and response of KOSs. This is particularly critical for highly structured systems such as thesauri, semantic networks, and ontologies. Work has been done in this area within the Z39.50 community.

A profile has been proposed by the Zthes Working Group to tailor the Z39.50 protocol to operate on thesauri that follow the Z39.19 standard. A similar effort is under way at the CERES Project. Instead of a Z39.50-based protocol, CERES has developed a structure that is based on the *Resource Description Framework* (RDF) and the HTTP protocol of standard browsers.

The RDF's concept of containers is a natural for managing the hierarchical structure of complex systems such as thesauri. The structure proposed by CERES is likely to be encoded using XML, a mark-up format that lends itself to structured information. This protocol for linking distributed vocabularies will support both searching and cataloging.

The user will be presented with remote vocabularies that can be displayed and navigated by a local client. The third major finding from the NISO workshop was the need for a metadata content standard for the description of KOSs. Such a standard is key to provision of knowledge organization services over the Internet. The metadata identify the Web resource as a KOS and provide important information to allow an application to use it remotely without prior knowledge of its content or structure.

A draft set of attributes for describing KOSs available in a networked environment has been developed by a task group of the *Network Knowledge Organization Systems* (NKOS) Working Group, an ad hoc group of terminology experts from organizations that are interested in issues related to the use and interoperability of KOSs over the Internet. The draft attributes are based on work originally done by Linda Hill and Michael Raugh.

The attributes describe the KOS so that content from the system can be transferred over the Internet and handled by a remote browser or client application. The attributes include the depth of hierarchy, the types of relationships included, the subject, storage format, copyright and rights management, and contact information.

To facilitate the transfer of information, the attribute set also includes information on character set and file size. To facilitate the acquisition and licensing of the KOSs, the draft content description includes point of contact information. During discussions about the metadata content standard, workshop attendees identified three methods for storing the metadata for a KOS. First, the metadata could be stored with the KOS, as metadata elements for that resource. Second, the metadata could be stored in a physically separate knowledge organization registry.

The third possibility is a hybrid approach, where a minimal set of metadata elements is contained in a central registry. The more detailed information would be stored with the KOS itself. There is significant interest in the use of KOSs to organize and search material on the Internet. It is hoped that this interest will result in knowledge organization services that will make these sources more readily accessible to a variety of software applications and to a variety of users. As services and enabled software proliferate, it will be easier to integrate these KOSs into digital libraries.

CONCLUSION

Given that the digital library field is still quite new, it seems strange to be talking already about enhancing digital libraries. However, in this fast-moving environment, the initial digital libraries resulting from digitization projects, or even virtual collections, are being enhanced as user expectations and technology capabilities allow. In the midst of this furious activity, it is valuable to analyse users' needs and interests and then to identify KOSs that can be used to enhance the digital library. Knowledge organization systems refer to a range of traditional and nontraditional systems for the organization of knowledge.

The systems have been developed in numerous environments outside the traditional library environment, including those of A&I services, publishers and professional organizations, and corporations. Examples exist in many disciplines and for many target audiences. Knowledge organization systems can enhance the digital library in a number of ways. They can be used to connect a digital library resource to a related resource. The related information may reside within the KOS itself or the KOS may be used as an intermediary file to retrieve the key needed to access it in another resource. A KOS can make digital library materials accessible to disparate communities. This may be done by providing alternate subject access, by adding access by different modes, by providing multilingual access, and by using the KOS to support free text searching. A well-planned infrastructure for KOSs is required. This includes the resources, processes, and policies for analysing user needs; locating KOSs to answer these needs; and acquiring, implementing, and maintaining the KOS. Traditional and nontraditional KOSs provide an opportunity to extend the boundaries of the digital library. By going beyond the initial organization of the digital library, digital librarians can use the network environment to provide additional value to its users.

11

Library Catalogue

A library catalogue (or library catalogue) is a register of all bibliographic items found in a library or group of libraries, such as a network of libraries at several locations. A bibliographic item can be any information entity (*e.g.*, books, computer files, graphics, realia, cartographic materials, etc.) that is considered library material (*e.g.*, a single novel in an anthology), or a group of library materials (*e.g.*, a trilogy), or linked from the catalogue (*e.g.*, a webpage) as far as it is relevant to the catalogue and to the users (patrons) of the library.

The card catalogue was a familiar sight to library users for generations, but it has been effectively replaced by the online public access catalogue (OPAC). Some still refer to the online catalogue as a "card catalogue". Some libraries with OPAC access still have card catalogues on site, but these are now strictly a secondary resource and are seldom updated.

Many of the libraries that have retained their physical card catalogue post a sign advising the last year that the card catalogue was updated. Some libraries have eliminated their card catalogue in favour of the OPAC for the purpose of saving space for other use, such as additional shelving.

GOAL

Charles Ammi Cutter made the first explicit statement regarding the objectives of a bibliographic system in his *Rules for a Printed Dictionary Catalogue* in 1876.

Those objectives were:

- To enable a person to find a book of which either (Identifying objective)
  - The author
  - The title
  - The subject
  - The category
- To show what the library has (Collocating objective)
  - By a given author

  - On a given subject
  - In a given kind of literature
- To assist in the choice of a book (Evaluating objective)
  - As to its edition (bibliographically)
  - As to its character (literary or topical)

These objectives can still be recognized in more modern definitions formulated throughout the 20th century. 1960/61 Cutter's objectives were revised by Lubetzky and the Conference on Cataloguing Principles (CCP) in Paris. The latest attempt to describe a library catalogue's goals and functions was made in 1998 with Functional Requirements for Bibliographic Records (FRBR) which defines four user tasks: find, identify, select, and obtain.

TYPES

Traditionally, there are the following types of catalogue:

- *Author Catalogue:* A formal catalogue, sorted alphabe-tically according to the authors' or editors' names of the entries.
- *Title Catalogue:* A formal catalogue, sorted alphabe-tically according to the title of the entries.
- *Dictionary Catalogue*: A catalogue in which all entries (author, title, subject, series) are interfiled in a single alphabetical order. This was the primary form of card catalogue in North American libraries just prior to the introduction of the computer-based catalogue.
- *Keyword Catalogue:* A subject catalogue, sorted alphabetically according to some system of keywords.
- *Mixed Alphabetic Catalogue Forms:* Sometimes, one finds a mixed author/ title, or an author/title/keyword catalogue.
- *Systematic Catalogue:* A subject catalogue, sorted according to some systematic subdivision of subjects. Also called a *Classified* catalogue.
- *Shelf List Catalogue:* A formal catalogue with entries sorted in the same order as bibliographic items are shelved. This catalogue may also serve as the primary inventory for the library.

HISTORY

Library catalogues originated as manuscript lists, arranged by format (folio, quarto, etc.) or in a rough alphabetical arrangement by author. Printed catalogues, sometimes called *dictionary catalogues*, began to be published in the early modern period and enabled scholars outside a library to gain an idea of its contents. Copies of these in the library itself would sometimes be interleaved with blank leaves on which additions could be recorded, or bound as *guardbooks* in which slips of paper were bound in for new entries.

Slips could also be kept loose in cardboard or tin boxes, stored on shelves. The first card catalogues appeared in the late 19th century after the standardization of the 5 in. x 3 in. card for personal filing systems, enabling much more flexibility, and towards the end of the 20th century the Online public access catalogue was developed.

These gradually became more common as some libraries progressively abandoned such other catalogue formats as paper slips (either loose or in sheaf catalogue form), and guardbooks. The beginning of the Library of Congress's catalogue card service in 1911 led to the use of these cards in the majority of American libraries. An equivalent scheme in the United Kingdom was operated by the British National Bibliography from 1956 and was subscribed to by many public and other libraries.

- *C. 245 BC:* Callimachus is considered the first bibliographer and is the one that organized the library by authors and subjects. The *Pinakes* was the first ever library catalogue. Variations on this system were used in libraries until the late 1800s when Melvil Dewey developed the Dewey Decimal Classification in 1876, which is still in use today.
- *C. 800:* Library catalogues are introduced in the House of Wisdom and other medieval Islamic libraries where books are organized into specific genres and categories.
- *1595: Nomenclator* of Leiden University Library appears, the first printed catalogue of an institutional library.
- *1674:* Thomas Hyde's catalogue for the Bodleian Library.
- *1791:* The French Cataloguing Code of 1791

More about the early history of library catalogues has been collected in 1956 by Strout.

SORTING

In a title catalogue, one can distinguish two sort orders:

1. In the *grammatical* sort order (used mainly in older catalogues), the most important word of the title is the first sort term. The importance of a word is measured by grammatical rules. for example, the first noun may be defined to be the most important word.
2. In the *mechanical* sort order, the first word of the title is the first sort term. Most new catalogues use this scheme, but still include a trace of the grammatical sort order: they neglect an article (The, A, etc.) at the beginning of the title.

The grammatical sort order has the advantage that often, the most important word of the title is also a good keyword, and it is the word most users remember first when their memory is incomplete. However, it has the disadvantage that many elaborate grammatical rules are needed, so that only expert users may be able to search the catalogue without help from a librarian.

In some catalogues, person's names are standardized, i. e., the name of the person is always sorted in a standard form, even if it appears differently in the library material. This standardization is achieved by a process called authority control. An advantage of the authority control is that it is easier to answer question (which works of some author does the library have?). On the other hand, it may be more difficult to answer question (does the library have some specific material?) if the material spells the author in a peculiar variant. For the cataloguer, it may incur (too) much work to check whether *Smith, J.* is *Smith, John* or *Smith, Jack.*

For some works, even the title can be standardized. The technical term for this is *uniform title*. For example, translations and re-editions are sometimes sorted under their original title. In many catalogues, parts of the Bible are sorted under the standard name of the book(s) they contain. The plays of William Shake-speare are another frequently cited example of the role played by a *uniform title* in the library catalogue. Many complica-tions about alphabetic sorting of entries arise.

Some examples:

- Some languages know sorting conventions that differ from the language of the catalogue. For example, some Dutch catalogues sort *IJ* as *Y*. Should an English catalogue follow this suit? And should a Dutch catalogue sort non-Dutch words the same way?
- *Some Titles Contain Numbers, For Example 2001:* A Space Odyssey. Should they be sorted as numbers, or spelled out as *Two thousand and one*?
- *De Balzac, Honouré* or *Balzac, Honouré de*? *Ortega y Gasset, José* or *Gasset, José Ortega y*?

In a subject catalogue, one has to decide on which classification system to use. The cataloguer will select appropriate subject headings for the bibliographic item and a unique classification number (sometimes known as a "call number") which is used not only for identification but also for the purposes of shelving, placing items with similar subjects near one another, which aids in browsing by library users, who are thus often able to take advantage of serendipity in their search process.

ONLINE CATALOGUES

Online cataloguing has greatly enhanced the usability of catalogues, thanks to the rise of MAchine Readable Cataloguing = MARC standards in the 1960s. Rules governing the creation of catalogue MARC records include not only formal cataloguing rules like AACR2 but also special rules specific to MARC, available from the Library of Congress and also OCLC. MARC was originally used to automate the creation of physical catalogue cards. Now the MARC computer files are accessed directly in the search process.

OPACs have enhanced usability over traditional card formats because:

- The online catalogue does not need to be sorted statically. The user can choose author, title, keyword, or systematic order dynamically.

- Most online catalogues offer a search facility for any word of the title. The goal of the grammatic word order (provide an entry on the word that most users would look for) is reached even better.
- Many online catalogues allow links between several variants of an author name. So, authors can be found both under the original and the standardised name (if entered properly by the cataloguer).
- The elimination of paper cards has made the information more accessible to many people with disabilities, such as the visually impaired, wheelchair users, and those who suffer from mold allergies.

WHAT IS WRONG WITH THE LIBRARY CATALOGUE

Problems for the online library catalogue did not begin with the advent, quick development or broad adoption of the web. For more than 20 years, the library catalogue has been criticised for its difficult use and poor functionality. Despite a number of studies and papers suggesting ideas for improving library catalogues, changes have been slow and many of the ideas have not been implemented.

Most of the changes have been made on surface rather than in the core functionality, leaving library catalogues hard to use. Studies show that besides falling behind the trends on the web, the most problematic area is the catalogue's interface, lacking in functionality, intuitivity, and content.

Traditional library catalogues are poorly designed for the tasks of finding, discovering and selecting resources available in libraries. They are best at locating and obtaining known items, so the user must know precisely what he/she wants. But this emphasis on know-item searching does not follow the actual user behaviour and mental models in information retrieval.

Information retrieval process often begins with only a vague idea, which is then gradually formulated sufficiently to begin searching. Besides that, query formulation is difficult as the user needs to have the conceptual knowledge of how the terms can be combined and is required to use the terms that match those in the catalogue.

Boolean logic in query formulation is hard for the user to comprehend and research shows that there is in fact only minimal usage of Boolean operators. Due to the common use of the web, users are accustomed to naturallanguage searching and simply type multiple search terms (keywords) on a single line without connecting them with Boolean operators. They also build queries using only terms they have in mind, without consulting the controlled vocabulary the library uses, all leading to poor results.

That is why many think that a better alternative to query formulation would be searching by browsing, recognition and discovery. Browsing is recognized as a natural and effective way of searching that requires less effort and knowledge. It is also easier for the user to recognize than recall information. As Bates points out "information seeking is, after all, about finding out things that one does not know before the search begins". These are all reasons for turning the traditional paradigm "query-first-then browse" upside down, making the exploration and discovery by browsing the primary search interface, supported by secondary query method.

The second problematic area in library catalogues is the results list and navigation between results. Queries often return hundreds or thousands of hits, but users are willing to look at only a very limited number. Web search engines have therefore developed very sophisticated systems for relevance ranking of results.

Accustomed to get the most relevant results first, users are confused when in library catalogues irrelevant records appear before items they were looking for. With a large number of search results it is also very time-consuming to look at every hit in order to decide whether it is relevant or not. To enable easier and faster selection, result clustering and faceted navigation should be applied to quickly narrow and filter the results to a manageable number.

One possibility for meaningful clustering of results is also the use of Functional Requirements for Bibliographic Records (FRBR). The third most frequent reproach against the library catalogue is the lack of information presented to the user. Most records in the library catalogue display only basic textual bibliographic data.

To improve the user experience, the library catalogue needs to be enriched with cover art images, tables of contents, summaries, reviews, excerpts, popularity ranks, recommen-dation lists and features such as "find similar" or "users who borrowed this book also borrowed...". These are all things already available on some other web destinations, especially online bookshops. They offer users all this additional information in order to promote their collection and to help users choose the items they need.

THE STATE OF CURRENT LIBRARY CATALOGUES

To estimate the state of current library catalogues an expert study was carried out in January 2008, based on the framework from a study performed in July 2007. Following the examined literature, six main areas of research were formed, within each a number of features were observed, analysing their presence and realization in the library catalogues.

For the purpose of the expert study, six library catalogues were chosen:

- *One Traditional:* The Slovene union catalogue COBISS and
- *Five More Modern and Innovative ones:*
  - Ann Arbor District Library catalogue,
  - Hennepin County Library catalogue,
  - Queens Library catalogue,
  - Phoenix Public Library catalogue, and
  - WorldCat.

With the exception of WorldCat and COBISS, library catalogues have provided their users with additional information about the collection, offering enriched content such as cover art images, summaries, tables of content, and various recommen-dation lists. But there is still room for improvement, especially in the way this additional content is integrated in the catalogue. Libraries should also offer more multimedia content and recommendations on similar books. Taking a small lead in more social features are Ann Arbor and Hennepin library catalogues, followed by the Phoenix library catalogue.

From reference point of view it is important to stress the potential of user participation and personalization. Personalization enables the system to adapt the interface to the end-user's wishes and recommend materials from the library collection according to the users' recent searches, favourite titles, or areas of interest. Another way to offer reading recommen-dations is also by using user participation features.

Tags and user created lists can be embedded in the library catalogue, pointing users to similar items chosen by other users. Ratings, reviews, comments, and forums bring to the library the wisdom of crowds that helps the user form an opinion on the material.

The expert study showed three different groups of library catalogues:

- Library catalogues that have not yet begun with this kind of modernization,
- Library catalogues that have focused more on improving functional features, and
- Library catalogues that devoted their attention to Web 2.0 trends.

Interestingly, catalogues focused on functional improve-ments offer less user participation and personalization while catalogues with more enhanced 2.0 features have not modernized their search and navigation. Using and testing all catalogues in the expert study we found that the latter catalogues are much harder to use and are not user friendly despite offering users to participate.

The new features are shaded by poorly designed interfaces that can frustrate web-savvy users. On the other hand, catalogues that focused on modernizing functional aspects of catalogues are easy and fun to use, supporting discovery and serendipity. With many interesting features that encourage users to research the catalogue, the lack of direct user participation and personali-zation is not really problematic.

PURPOSE OF CATALOGUING LIBRARY MATERIALS

Library collections house a wide variety of materials on many different topics and in many different formats. The challenge in making these things available for the use of library patrons is letting those patrons know what is in the library collection. This is the reason for having a library catalogue, and for taking the time to correctly catalogue library materials. The library catalogue might be compared to the index for a book. The index provides the reader with a way to find information in the book without having to read every page. The index tells the reader the page on which the information about a specific subject can be found.

The library catalogue does the same thing. It tells the library user exactly where materials meeting their specific needs can be found, with the call number of the book corresponding to the page number in an index. The information contained in the cataloguing record provides the many access points needed by the patron looking for information in the library. Traditionally, the library card catalogue provided access by the author's name, the title of an item, and the subject(s) covered in the item. Other points of access were additional authors, names of series, illustrators, and sometimes the titles of contents.

Computer catalogs can, in theory, provide access to any part of the information contained in the record for an item in the library. The development of MARC (Machine Readable Cataloguing) in the 1960's made it possible to encode all areas of a cataloguing record to be searchable. In MARC cataloguing, each piece of information in a catalogue record is given a numerical code, or field, and sometimes an alphabetical or numerical sub field. This coding makes it possible for a computer programme to be written that looks for particular numbered fields when a particular type of search, such as a subject or title, is requested. Because all of the information in the cataloguing record is encoded, searches could optionally be done by ISBN number, by series, by publisher, by date or by any of the pieces of information stored in the cataloguing record. MARC has set the standard for all computer catalogs used in libraries today, and if the records contained in the catalogue comply with MARC requirements, the only controls on areas to be searched are the limits of the particular cataloguing programme.

When library materials are catalogued in a careful and complete manner, access is provided for the library patrons and staff to all sources of information on a particular topic, by a particular author, or in a particular format, that the library possesses. The better the access, the more use the collection receives, and the more satisfied the patron is in his or her search for information in the library.

12

Cataloguing and Processing: A Resource for Library

A.L.A. CATALOGUE

The A.L.A. Catalogue is the first general book selection guide cooperatively prepared for use by American public libraries. In the early stage of public libraries' development, book selection is the job of library committee composed of library director and trustees rather than librarians.

However, there might be problems for the committee to reach an agreement on which book should be include/exclude for their libraries due to the following two reasons:

- Firstly, the committee members might be different in terms of education background and personal interests, therefore, they might come up with "different theories of what the library shall be".
- Secondly, even without the disagreement of theories, it is impossible for committee members to have an adequate knowledge of "books, editions, and prices, outside of their own line of reading."

Thus they need the assistance from experts to revise and complete their booklist for libraries.

DEWEY AND THE CATALOGUE

The A.L.A. Catalogue, also known as the Catalogue of A.L.A. Library, as one of the most popular booklists developed by experts, is the "first general book selection guide cooperatively prepared for use by American public libraries." Before the development of the catalogue, Melvil Dewey first promoted the idea of a universal library collection guide in an article "The Coming Catalogue" in Library Journal in 1877.

He suggested a co-operative way for creating the collection guide among library committee, field specialist, as well as authors, for the reason that "no one person living unites in himself the wisdom necessary to make the best notes on all the books of the library", and "not one but many minds must contribute to the work." Dewey also suggested American Library Association (A.L.A) appoints a committee to take "entire charge" of the "coming catalogue". The primary usage of such catalogue would be "as a guide in the purchase of books for either private or public collection. as the main catalogue of many of these libraries."

Based on Dewey's article, A.L.A. began to take steps of creating such catalogue. In November 1878, A.L.A. appointed five people as the committee in charge of the catalogue. They decided to adopt a classified arrangement of the catalogue. The catalogue was planned to be about 250 pages with a fixed price of $2.50.

After years' cession of catalogue development, Dewey attempted to re-start his plan for A.L.A. catalogue when he worked at Columbia College as the "Librarian in Chief" in 1883. He tried to obtain suggestion from Columbia faculty members through their lectures on "bibliography and literature in their areas of expertise" when the School of Library Economy was established in 1887, and later Dewey moved to University of the State of New York in 1888, where he continued his work on catalogue by asking his library employees and students in Albany to compile the catalogue through scholarly journals.

The Catalogue was finally published and promoted in the A.L.A. annual conference in 1893 at the Chicago World's Fair. The 1893 Catalogue of A.L.A. library provides a list of 5000 "best reading selections" that were "approved by distinguished specialists in various lines and organized by librarians into two separate classification schemes".

EARLY ADOPTION IN LIBRARIES

After the Catalogue had been developed, more and more libraries began to adopt it as the guide for book selection. For instance, Mrs. Horace M. Towner, one of the trustee members of Iowa Library Commission in Corning, published a short paper "Trustees' Problems" in *Iowa Library Quarterly* in 1908 discussing the budget problem related to book purchasing.

Towner states that the general rules for books purchasing is depending on the specific situation within each library. In other words, there is no fixed rule for book purchasing. However, Towner discussed a lot about the "right" evaluation of fiction. In order to avoid unsuitable and vicious fiction in a library, trustees should rely on "best" book reviews, in addition to "Booklist" from ALA. Towner pointed out trustee members should read report from professional journals, like Library Journal and Public Libraries, to obtain knowledge from other library about the budget issue.

ANGLO-AMERICAN CATALOGUING RULES

The Anglo-American Cataloguing Rules (AACR) were first published in 1967. AACR2 stands for the *Anglo-American Cataloguing Rules, Second Edition*. It is published jointly by the American Library Association, the Canadian Library Association, and the Chartered Institute of Library and Information

Professionals in the UK. The editor is Michael Gorman, a British-born librarian living in the Chicago area and honoured by both the ALA and CILIP. AACR2 is designed for use in the construction of catalogues and other lists in general libraries of all sizes. The rules cover the description of, and the provision of access points for, all library materials commonly collected at the present time.

Despite the claim to be 'Anglo-American', the first edition of AACR was published in 1967 in somewhat distinct North American and British texts. The second edition of 1978 unified the two sets of rules (adopting the British spelling 'cataloguing') and brought them in line with the International Standard Bibliographic Description. Libraries wishing to migrate from the previous North American text were obliged to implement 'desuperimposition', a substantial change in the form of headings for corporate bodies.

AACR2 exists in several print versions, as well as an online version. Gorman has edited several revisions of AACR2 including a concise edition. Print versions are available from the publishers. The online version is available only via Cataloger's Desktop from the Library of Congress. Various translations are also available from other sources.

Principles of AACR include cataloguing from the item 'in hand' rather than inferring information from external sources and the concept of the 'chief source of information' which is preferred where conflicts exist.

Over the years AACR2 has been updated by occasional amendments, and was significantly revised in 1988 and 2002. The 2002 revision included substantial changes to parts for non-book materials. A schedule of annual updates began in 2003 and ceased with 2005.

AACR2 has been succeeded by Resource Description and Access (commonly referred to as RDA), which was released in June 2010. This new code is informed by the Functional Requirements for Bibliographic Records and was conceived to be a framework more flexible and suitable for use in a digital environment.

In the fall of 2010, the Library of Congress, National Library of Medicine, National Agricultural Library, and several other institutions and national libraries of other English-speaking countries performed a formal test of RDA, the results of which were released in June 2011.

ACCESSION NUMBER (LIBRARY SCIENCE)

An accession number is a sequential number given to each new book, magazine subscription, or recording as it is entered in the catalogue of a library. If an item is removed from the collection, its number is usually not reused for new items. This numbering system is usually in addition to the library classification number (or alphanumeric code) and to the ISBN or International Standard Book Number assigned by publishers.

Accession numbers are also used by an arboretum, botanic garden, greenhouse, or museums to identify objects or plants by the order in which they entered the museum's collection. Typically, the accession number consists of the year acquired and a sequential number separated by a period.

In addition, departments or art classifications within the collection or museum may reserve parts of numbers. For example, objects identified by the numbers 11.000 through 11.999 may indicate objects obtained by the museum in 1911. the first 300 numbers may be used to indicate American art, while the next fifty (11.301-350) may be used for African art.

AgMES

The AgMES (Agricultural Metadata Element set) initiative was developed by the Food and Agriculture Organization (FAO) of the United Nations and aims to encompass issues of semantic standards in the domain of agriculture with respect to descri-ption, resource discovery, interoperability and data exchange for different types of information resources.

There are numerous other metadata schemas for different types of information resources.

The following list contains a list of a few examples:

- *Document-like Information Objects (DLIOs):* Dublin Core, Agricultural Metadata Element Set (AgMES)
- *Events:* VCalendar
- *Geographic and Regional Information:* Geographic information—Metadata ISO/IEC 11179 Standards
- *Persons:* Friend-of-a-friend (FOAF), vCard
- *Plant Production and Protection:* Darwin Core (1.0 and 2.0) (DwC)

AgMES as a namespace is designed to include agriculture specific extensions for terms and refinements from established standard metadata namespaces like Dublin Core, AGLS etc. Thus to be used for Document-like Information Objects, for example like publications, articles, books, web sites, papers, etc., it will have to be used in conjunction with the standard namespaces mentioned before. The AgMES initiative strives to achieve improved interoperability between information resources in agricultural domain by enabling means for exchange of information.

Describing a DLIO with AgMES means exposing its major characteristics and contents in a standard way that can be reused easily in any information system. The more institutions and organizations in the agricultural domain that use AgMES to describe their DLIOs, the easier it will be to interchange data in between information systems like digital libraries and other repositories of agricultural information.

USE OF AgMES

Metadata on agricultural Document-like Information Objects (DLIOs) can be created and stored in various formats:

- Embedded in a web site (in the manor as with the HTML meta tag)

- In a separate metadata database
- In an XML file
- In an RDF file

AgMES defines elements that can be used to describe a DLIO that can be used together with other metadata standards such as the Dublin Core, the Australian Government Locator Service. A complete list of all elements, refinements and schemes endorsed by AgMES is available from the AgMES website.

Creating Application Profiles

Application profiles are defined as schemas which consist of data elements drawn from one or more namespaces, combined by implementers, and optimized for a particular local application.

Application profiles share the following four characteristics:

- They draw upon existing pool of metadata definition standards to extract suitable application-or requirement oriented elements.
- An application profile cannot create new elements.
- Application profiles specify the application specific details such as the schemes or controlled vocabularies. An application profile also contains information such as the format for the element value, cardinality or data type.
- Lastly, an application profile can refine standardized definitions as long as it is "semantically narrower or more specific". This capability of application profiles caters to situations where a domain specific termino-logy is needed to replace a more general one.

Sample Application Profiles Using AgMES

- The AGRIS Application Profile is a standard created specifically to enhance the description, exchange and subsequent retrieval of agricultural Document-like Information Objects (DLIOs). It is a format that allows sharing of information across dispersed bibliographic systems and is based on well-known and accepted metadata standards.
- The Event Application Profile is a standard created to allow members of the Agricultural community to 'know' about an upcoming event and guide them to the event Web site where they can find further information. The information communicated is thus minimum yet interoperable across domains and organizations.

AgMES AND THE SEMANTIC WEB

One of the advantages of the AgMES metadata schema is the ability to link between the metadata element and controlled vocabularies. The use of controlled vocabulary provides a "known" set of options to the indexer (and the search programmer) as to how the field can be filled out. Often the values may come from a specific thesaurus (*e.g.* AGROVOC) or classification schemes (*e.g.* the AGRIS/CARIS classification scheme)etc. Thanks to the possibility to use controlled vocabularies for metadata elements, the user is provided with the most precise information. In this context, work is also being carried out on exploiting the power of controlled vocabularies expressed as using URIs and machine-understandable semantics.

In this context, FAO is promoting the Agricultural Ontology Service (AOS) initiative with the objective of expressing more semantics within the traditional thesaurus AGROVOC and build a Concept Server as a repository from which it will be always possible to extract traditional KOS.

ALA-LC ROMANIZATION

ALA-LC is a set of standards for romanization, or the representation of text in other writing systems using the Latin alphabet. The initials stand for American Library Association-Library of Congress. This system is used to represent bibliographic information by North American libraries and the British Library (for acquisitions since 1975), and in publications throughout the English-speaking world.

AUTHORITY CONTROL

Authority control is the practice of creating and maintaining index terms for bibliographic material in a catalogue in library and information science. Authority control fulfills two important functions. First, it enables catalogers to disambiguate items with similar or identical headings.

For example, two authors who happen to have published under the same name can be distinguished from each other by adding middle initials, birth and/or death (or flourished, if these are unknown) dates, or a descriptive epithet to the heading of one (or both) authors.

Second, authority control is used by catalogers to collocate materials that logically belong together, although they present themselves differently. For example, authority records are used to establish uniform titles, which can collocate all versions of a given work together even when they are issued under different titles.

Although theoretically any piece of information on a given book is amenable to authority control, catalogers typically focus on authors and titles. Subject headings fulfill a function similar to authority records, although they are usually considered separately.

AUTHORITY RECORDS

The most common way of enforcing authority control in a bibliographic catalogue is to set up a separate index of authority records, which relates to and governs the headings used in the main catalogue. This separate index is often referred to as an "authority file." It contains an indexable record of all decisions made by catalogers in a given library (or—as is increasingly the case—cataloguing consortium), which catalogers consult when making, or revising, decisions about headings.

It is to be remembered that the function of authority files is essentially organizational, rather than informational. That is to say, they (ideally) contain a sufficient amount of information to establish a given author or title as unique, while excluding information that, while perhaps interesting to a reader, does not contribute to this goal.

Although practices certainly vary internationally, in the English-speaking world, it is generally the case that a valid authority record must contain:

- Heading refers to the form of name (or title) that the cataloguer has chosen as the authorized form.
- Cross references are other forms of the name (or title) that might appear in the catalogue. There are two types of cross-references: *see* references, which reference forms of the name (or title) that have been deprecated in favour of the authorized form. and *see also* references, which point to other forms of the name (or title) that are authorized.
- Statement(s) of justification: In addition to providing a heading and applicable references, a valid authority record should also contain a reference to whatever sources of information the cataloguer used to determine both the authorized and any deprecated forms of the name. This is usually done by citing the title and publication date of the source, the location of the name (or title) on that source, and the form in which it appears on that source.

ACCESS CONTROL

The act of choosing a single authorized heading to represent all forms of a name is often difficult, sometimes arbitrary and on occasion politically sensitive. An alternative is the idea of *access control*, where variant forms of a name are related without the endorsement of one particular form.

AUTHORITY CONTROL AND COOPERATIVE CATALOGUING

Before the advent of digital OPACs and the Internet, the work of creating and maintaining a library's authority files was generally carried out (if at all) by individual cataloguing departments. This meant that there could be a fair amount of disagreement among libraries over which form of a given name was considered authoritative. so long as a library's catalogue was internally consistent, differences between catalogs didn't much matter.

However, even before the Internet revolutionized the way libraries go about cataloguing their materials, catalogers began moving towards the establishment of cooperative consortia, such as OCLC and RLIN in the United

States, in which cataloguing departments from libraries all over the world contributed their records to, and took their records from, a shared database. This development gave rise to the need for national standards for authority work. In the United States, the primary organization for maintaining cataloguing standards with respect to authority work operates under the aegis of the Library of Congress, and is known as the Name Authority Cooperative Programme, or NACO Authority.

STANDARDS

- *ISAAR (CPF)*: International Standard Archival Authority Record for Corporate Bodies, Persons, and Families. Published by the International Council on Archives
- *MARC standards* for authority records in machine-readable format.
- *Metadata Authority Description Schema* (*MADS*), an XML schema for an authority element set that may be used to provide metadata about agents (people, organizations), events, and terms (topics, geographics, genres, etc.).
- *Encoded Archival Context*, an XML schema for authority records conforming to ISAAR(CPF)

BCM CLASSIFICATION

The British Catalogue of Music Classification (BCM Classification) is a faceted classification that was commissioned from E.J. Coates by the Council of the British National Bibliography to organize the content of the British Catalogue of Music. The published schedule (1960) was considerably expanded by Patrick Mills of the British Library up until its use was abandoned in 1998.

Entries in the catalogue were organized by BCM classmark from the catalogue's inception in 1957 until 1982. From that year the British Catalogue of Music was organized instead by Dewey Decimal Classification number, though BCM classmarks continued to be added to entries up to the 1998 annual cumulation.

The schedule is divided into two main parts: A-B representing Musical literature and C-Z representing Music—Scores and Parts. There are also seven auxiliary tables dealing with various sub-arrangements, sets of ethnic/locality subdivisions and chronological reference points.

The notation is retroactive using uppercase alphabetic characters omitting I and O, with the addition of slash/and parentheses which have specific anteriorizing functions. Retroactive notation requires that the classifier combines terms in reverse schedule order. This has the benefit of producing a compact notation by removing the need for facet indicators.

The schedule at A (Music Literature) parallels that from the Scores and Parts schedules thus Choral Music is at D while books about Choral Music are at AD. Harp Music is at TQ so books on harp music are at ATQ. The schedule at B accommodates books about specific composers and music in non-European traditions.

As a fully faceted scheme after the ideas of S.R. Rangan-athan, BCM class numbers are capable of being chain-indexed, allowing index access to each step of the hierarchy. BCM classification had a strong influence on Russell Sweeney's so-called Phoenix Dewey 780 schedule which in turn influenced the 780 Music schedule in the 20th edition of Dewey Decimal Classification. The music schedule of the second edition of the Bliss Classification is also strongly influenced by BCM.

BIBLIOGRAPHIC CONTROL

In library and information science, bibliographic control (also known as information organization or bibliographic organization) is the process by which information resources are described so that users are able to find and select that information resource. An information resource could be a book, a movie, or an image, among other things.

By providing a name, title, and subject access to the description, a bibliographic record is created. This bibliographic record, which is essentially metadata, is indexed by an information retrieval tool (such as a database or a search engine) so that a user can find out whether or not the information resource is relevant to them.

SIX FUNCTIONS OF BIBLIOGRAPHIC CONTROL

Ronald Hagler identified six functions of bibliographic control:

- "Identifying the existence of all types of information resources as they are made available." The existence and identity of an information resource must be known before it can be found.
- "Identifying the works contained within those information resources or as parts of them." Depending on the level of granularity required, multiple works may be contained in a single package, or one work may span multiple packages. For example, is a single photo considered an information resource? Or can a collection of photos be considered an information resource?
- "Systematically pulling together these information resources into collections in libraries, archives, museums, and Internet communication files, and other such depositories." Essentially, acquiring these items into collections so that they can be of use to the user.
- "Producing lists of these information resources prepared according to standard rules for citation." Examples of such retrieval aids include library catalogs, indexes, archival finding aids, etc.
- "Providing name, title, subject, and other useful access to these

information resources." Ideally, there should be many ways to find an item so there should be multiple access points. There must be enough metadata in the surrogate record so users can successfully find the information resource they are looking for. These access points should be consistent, which can be achieved through authority control.

- "Providing the means of locating each information resource or a copy of it." In libraries, the online public access catalogue (OPAC) can give the user location information (a call number for example) and indicate whether the item is available.

HISTORY OF BIBLIOGRAPHIC CONTROL

While the organization of information has been going on since antiquity, bibliographic control as we know it today is a more recent invention. Ancient civilizations recorded lists of books onto tablets and libraries in the Middle Ages kept records of their holdings. With the invention of the printing press in the 15th century, multiple copies of a single book could be produced quickly.

Johann Tritheim, a German librarian, was the first to create a bibliography in chronological order with an alphabetical author index. Konrad Gesner followed in his footsteps in the next century as he published an author bibliography and subject index. He added to his bibliography an alphabetical list of authors with inverted names, which was a new practice. He also included references to variant spellings of author's names, a precursor to authority control.

Andrew Maunsell further revolutionized bibliographic control by suggesting that a book should be findable based on the author's last name, the subject of the book, and the translator. In the 17th century Sir Thomas Bodley was interested in a catalogue arranged alphabetically by author's last name as well as subject entries.

In 1697 Frederic Rostgaard called for subject arrangement that was subdivided by both chronology and by size (whereas in the past titles were arranged by their size only), as well as an index of subjects and authors by last name and for word order to in titles to be preserved based on the title page.

After the French Revolution, France's government was the first to put out a national code containing instructions for cataloguing library collections. At the British Museum Library Anthony Panizzi created his "Ninety-One Cataloguing Rules" (1841), which essentially served as the basis for cataloguing rules of the 19th and 20th centuries.

Panizzi's "91 Rules" are also the origins of ISBD and Dublin Core. Charles C. Jewett took Panizzi's "91 Rules" and used them at the Smithsonian Institution, thus bringing Americans into the mix of cataloguing, a domain where Europeans had traditionally had more influence.

‡BIBLIOS.NET

‡biblios.net is a free browser-based cataloguing service with a data store containing over thirty-million records. Records are licensed under the Open Data Commons Public Domain Dedication and License, making the service the world's largest repository of freely-licensed library records. The service was created and is maintained by LibLime.

FEATURES

‡biblios.net (pronounced 'biblios dot net') features a metadata editor with templates, macros, authority auto-completion and embedded context-sensitive help. The central record repository contains 25-million bibliographic records and just under eight-million authority records.

The data is maintained by ‡biblios.net users similar to the Wikipedia model. Catalogers can use and contribute to the database without restrictions because records in ‡biblios.net are freely-licensed under the Open Data Commons Public Domain Dedication and License.

‡biblios.net also includes a built-in federated search system allowing catalogers to find records from any Z39.50 target. Additionally, there is a central Search Target Registry, seeded with over 2,000 Z39.50 servers, for catalogers to find, create and share Z39.50 targets.

In addition to offering a traditional cataloguing interface, ‡biblios.net offers social cataloguing features. Built-in forums and private messaging make finding help and communicating with others possible within the software.

BLISS BIBLIOGRAPHIC CLASSIFICATION

The Bliss bibliographic classification (BC) is a library classification system that was created by Henry E. Bliss (1870–1955), published in four volumes between 1940 and 1953. Although originally devised in the United States, it was more commonly adopted by British libraries than by American ones. A second edition of the system (BC2) has been developed in Britain since 1977.

Bliss was born in New York in 1870 and in 1891 began work in the library of the College of the City of New York (now City College of the City University of New York).

Bliss had a lifelong interest in the organization, structure and philosophy of knowledge and was very critical of the library classification systems that were available to him. He believed that because the popular Library of Congress system had been designed for a specific library (the Library of Congress) it had no use as a standard system outside that library. He also greatly disliked the Dewey Decimal system.

Bliss wanted a classification system that would provide distinct rules yet still be adaptable to whatever kind of collection a library might have, as different libraries have different needs. His solution was the concept of "alternative location," in which a particular subject could be put in more than one place, as long as the library made a specific choice and used it consistently. In 1908 Bliss reclassified 60,000 of his library's books, and in 1910 he published an article with a rough scheme of his general ideas. But as he continued to develop his system he realised that it was going to be a much larger project than he had anticipated. The first of his four volumes appeared in 1940 (the year he retired) and the last in 1953, two years before his death.

Some of the underlying policies of the BC system were:

- Alternative location
- Brief, concise notation
- Organizing knowledge according to academic expertise
- Subjects moving gradually from topic to topic as they naturally related to one another.

ADOPTION AND CHANGE

BC was not used by many North American libraries. The system was not without its flaws (the result of being largely a one-person project), and the layout of Bliss's text was difficult to read. A few library schools sometimes taught the BC system to their students, but only in a minor way. The failure of the system to catch on in North America was partly because of its internal deficiencies but also because the Dewey Decimal and Library of Congress systems were already well established.

The City College library continued to use Bliss's system until 1967, when it reluctantly switched to the Library of Congress system. It had become too expensive to train new staff members to use BC, and too expensive to maintain in general. Much of the Bliss stacks remain, however, as no-one has recatalogued the books. The case was different, however, in Britain. BC proved more popular there and also spread to other English-speaking countries. Part of the reason for its success was that libraries in teachers' colleges liked the way Bliss had organized the subject areas on teaching and education. By the mid-1950s the system was being used in at least sixty British libraries and in a hundred by the 1970s.

In 1967 the Bliss Classification Association was formed. Its first publication was the *Abridged Bliss Classification* (ABC), intended for school libraries. In 1977 it began to publish and maintain a much-improved, revised version of Bliss's system, the Bliss Bibliographic Classification or BC2. This retains only the broad outlines of Bliss's scheme, replacing most of the detailed notation with a new scheme based on the principles of faceted classification. Fifteen of approximately 28 volumes of schedules have so far been published.

The top level organisation is:

- 2/9-Generalia, Phenomena, Knowledge, Information science and technology
- A/AL-Philosophy and Logic
- AM/AX-Mathematics, Probability, Statistics

- AY/B-General science, Physics
- C-Chemistry
- D-Astronomy and earth sciences
  - DG/DY-Earth sciences
- E/GQ-Biological sciences
- GR/GZ-Applied biological sciences: agriculture and ecology
- H-Physical Anthropology, Human biology, Health sciences
- I-Psychology and Psychiatry
- J-Education
- K-Society (includes Social sciences, sociology and social anthropology)
- L/O-History (including area studies, travel and topography, and biography)
  - LA-Archaeology
- P-Religion, Occult, Morals and ethics
- Q-Social welfare and Criminology
- R-Politics and Public administration
- S-Law
- T-Economics and Management of economic enterprises
- U/V-Technology and useful arts (including household management and services)
- W-The Arts
  - WV/WX-Music
- X/Y-Language and literature
- ZA/ZW-Museology

BRINKLER CLASSIFICATION

Brinkler Classification is the library classification system of Bartol Brinkler described in his article *"The Geographical Approach to Materials in the Library of Congress Subject Headings"*. The geographical aspect of a subject may be conveyed through three types of headings labelled A, B, and C. Heading A uses a primary topical description with geographical subdivisions (*e.g.* Art—Paris). Type B uses a place-name for the main heading with a topical subdivision (*e.g.* Paris—Description). While with C headings use a geographical description of a phrase (*e.g.* Paris Literature).

Brinkler explores what type of heading is more useful to a patron, and he finds that it depends on the level of familiarity a patron has with a topic and what approach they take when searching for resources on their topic. Ideally readers will either be looking for everything on a particular topic, or everything regarding a particular place.

Bartol Brinkler investigates a system of classification that will best serve these two ideal types of patrons. He finds working with Type A headings will best assist a patron who is more topic oriented, while using Type B headings is preferable for those who are primarily interested in one place. However this is problematic in practice. One possibility is to assign Type A and Type B headings to every resource, but the cataloguing cost would be high. A system that aids readers regardless of their approach to a topic involves using cross-references. Admitting that see and see also references would require more work on the part of librarians, Bartol Brinkler notes that librarians must keep in mind "... readers do not have the same knowledge and do need all the help they can get... "

CANADIAN SUBJECT HEADINGS

Canadian Subject Headings (CSH) is a list of subject headings in the English language, using controlled vocabulary, to access and express the topic content of documents on Canada and Canadian topics. Library and Archives Canada publishes and maintains CSH on the Web. Prior to the merger of the National Library of Canada and the National Archives of Canada, the National Library of Canada published a print version of CSH. The headings are compatible with the United States Library of Congress Subject Headings, with modifications to include specifically Canadian content or to reflect a Canadian perspective. Library and Archives Canada also publishes Répertoire de vedettes-matière (RVM), a list intended to provide access to Canadian subject headings in the French language.

CATALOGUING IN PUBLICATION

In publishing and library science, Cataloguing in Publication (CIP, or Cataloguing in Publication) is basic cataloguing data for a work, prepared in advance of publication by the national library of the country where the work is principally published or by the library of a publishing organisation such as a government department. The name reflects the usual practice of including that information in the corresponding publication-—in the case of books, near the bottom of the copyright page, and can be very useful for less experienced cataloguers when adding such items to their collections. The national libraries' CIP staffs restrict the range of publications that CIP will be prepared for, for instance requiring access to assistance from the publisher's staff.

An all too frequent problem with CIP is when publishers change bibliographic details, such as the wording of a title, after receiving the CIP data. The CIP data as published in the item will be incorrect and not able to be used by subsequent catalogue-uing agencies without manual amendment and if a pre-publica-tion record has been entered onto a database it can be difficult to locate and edit to match the details on the item itself. Each national library maintains a database of the entries it writes.

COBISS

COBISS (abbreviation for *Co-operative Online Bibliographic System and*

Services) is an organisational model used to join libraries in a uniform library information system with shared cataloguing. It has many functions of the so-called virtual library. It is currently in use in Slovenia (COBISS.SI), Bosnia and Herzegovina (COBISS.BH), Republic of Macedonia (COBISS.MK), Serbia (COBISS.SR) and Montenegro (COBISS.CG).

These information systems are autonomous, but share the platform. Over 350 libraries use COBISS software for the automation of their operations. COBISS.Net is the name of the network connecting the COBISS co-operative bibliographic systems of different countries. COBISS has been developed by the Institute of Information Science (Slovene: *Institut informacijskih znanosti, IZUM*) from Maribor. In March 2011, all the management of IZUM decided to step down from their positions, the stated reason being the dismissive attitude of the Slovenian Ministry of Higher Education, Science and Technology (led by Gregor Golobiè) towards IZUM.

COLLABORATIVE CATALOGUING

Collaborative Cataloguing is shared action of a group making bibliographic records available to its participants in order to prevent duplication of bibliographic records. Thusly, cooperative cataloguing has benefits such as cost effectiveness and availability of a ready cataloguing model

A notable example of collaborative cataloguing takes place at the National Transportation Library or NTL, which is administered by the U.S. Department of Transportation. NTL participates in a consortium called the National Transportation Knowledge Network (TKN), "which was establishe[d]...to help facilitate access to information in support of transportation development". Pursuing that goal, the TKN engages in cooperative cataloguing with other transportation libraries. For example, in early summer 2011, the TKN held a meeting on cataloguing standards that are used by transportation libraries nationwide.

More specifically, NTL uses cooperative cataloguing to examine subject headings that are used in transportation literature. NTL is a key player in the organization of subject headings and has made significant contributions to the Transportation Research Thesaurus. The Transportation Research Thesaurus, or TRT, is a controlled vocabulary that was developed to improve the indexing and retrieval of transpor-tation information. The TRT is used by indexers, content managers and librarians in the transportation community and is an internationally recognized standard.

COLON CLASSIFICATION

Colon classification (CC) is a system of library classification developed by S. R. Ranganathan. It was the first ever faceted (or analytico-synthetic) classification. The first edition was published in 1933. Since then six more editions have been published. It is especially used in libraries in India.

Its name "colon classification" comes from the use of colons to separate facets in class numbers. However, many other classification schemes, some of which are completely unrelated, also use colons and other punctuation in various functions. They should not be confused with colon classification.

As an example, the subject "research in the cure of tuberculosis of lungs by x-ray conducted in India in 1950" results in a call number:

- L,45.421:6.253:f.44'N5

The components of this call number represent:

- *Medicine,Lungs.Tuberculosis:*Treatment.X-ray: Research.India'1950

ORGANIZATION

The colon classification uses 42 main classes that are combined with other letters, numbers and marks in a manner resembling the Library of Congress Classification to sort a publication.

Facets

CC uses five primary categories, or facets, to further specify the sorting of a publication.

Collectively, they are called PMEST:

- Personality
- Matter or property
- Energy
- Space
- Time

CONTROLLED VOCABULARY

Controlled vocabularies provide a way to organize knowledge for subsequent retrieval. They are used in subject indexing schemes, subject headings, thesauri, taxonomies and other form of knowledge organization systems. Controlled vocabulary schemes mandate the use of predefined, authorised terms that have been preselected by the designer of the vocabulary, in contrast to natural language vocabularies, where there is no restriction on the vocabulary.

IN LIBRARY AND INFORMATION SCIENCE

In library and information science controlled vocabulary is a carefully selected list of words and phrases, which are used to tag units of information (document or work) so that they may be more easily retrieved by a search. Controlled vocabularies solve the problems of homographs, synonyms and polysemes by a bijection between concepts and authorized terms. In short, controlled vocabularies reduce ambiguity inherent in normal human languages where the same concept can be given different names and ensure consistency.

For example, in the Library of Congress Subject Headings (a subject heading system that uses a controlled vocabulary), authorized terms—subject headings in this case—have to be chosen to handle choices between variant spellings of the same concept (American versus British), choice among scientific and popular terms (Cockroaches versus Periplaneta americana), and choices between synonyms (automobile versus cars), among other difficult issues.

Choices of authorized terms are based on the principles of user warrant (what terms users are likely to use), literary warrant (what terms are generally used in the literature and documents), and structural warrant (terms chosen by considering the structure, scope of the controlled vocabulary).

Controlled vocabularies also typically handle the problem of homographs, with qualifiers. For example, the term "pool" has to be qualified to refer to either swimming pool, or the game pool to ensure that each authorized term or heading refers to only one concept.

There are two main kinds of controlled vocabulary tools used in libraries: subject headings and thesauri. While the differences between the two are diminishing, there are still some minor differences.

Historically subject headings were designed to describe books in library catalogs by catalogers while thesauri were used by indexers to apply index terms to documents and articles. Subject headings tend to be broader in scope describing whole books, while thesauri tend to be more specialized covering very specific disciplines.

Also because of the card catalogue system, subject headings tend to have terms that are in indirect order (though with the rise of automated systems this is being removed), while thesaurus terms are always in direct order.

Subject headings also tend to use more pre-coordination of terms such that the designer of the controlled vocabulary will combine various concepts together to form one authorized subject heading. (*e.g.*, children and terrorism) while thesauri tend to use singular direct terms. Lastly thesauri list not only equivalent terms but also narrower, broader terms and related terms among various authorized and non-authorized terms, while historically most subject headings did not.

For example, the Library of Congress Subject Heading itself did not have much syndetic structure until 1943, and it was not until 1985 when it began to adopt the thesauri type term "Broader term" and "Narrow term".

The terms are chosen and organized by trained professionals (including librarians and information scientists) who possess expertise in the subject area. Controlled vocabulary terms can accurately describe what a given document is actually about, even if the terms themselves do not occur within the document's text. Well known subject heading systems include the Library of Congress system, MeSH, and Sears. Well known thesauri include the Art and Architecture Thesaurus and the ERIC Thesaurus.

Choosing authorized terms to be used is a tricky business, the designer has to consider the specificity of the term chosen, whether to use direct entry, inter consistency and stability of the language. Lastly the amount of pre-co-ordinate (in which case the degree of enumeration versus synthesis becomes an issue) and post co-ordinate in the system is another important issue. Controlled vocabulary elements (terms/phrases) employed as tags, to aid in the content identification process of documents, or other information system entities (*e.g.* DBMS, Web Services) qualifies as metadata.

INDEXING LANGUAGES

There are three main types of indexing languages:

- Controlled indexing language-Only approved terms can be used by the indexer to describe the document
- Natural language indexing language-Any term from the document in question can be used to describe the document.
- Free indexing language-Any term (not only from the document) can be used to describe the document.

When indexing a document, the indexer also has to choose the level of indexing exhaustivity, the level of detail in which the document is described. For example using low indexing exhaustivity, minor aspects of the work will not be described with index terms. In general the higher the indexing exhaustivity, the more terms indexed for each document.

In recent years free text search as a means of access to documents has become popular. This involves using natural language indexing with an indexing exhaustively set to maximum (every word in the text is *indexed*). Many studies have been done to compare the efficiency and effectiveness of free text searches against documents that have been indexed by experts using a few well chosen controlled vocabulary descriptors.

Controlled vocabularies are often claimed to improve the accuracy of free text searching, such as to reduce irrelevant items in the retrieval list. These irrelevant items (false positives) are often caused by the inherent ambiguity of natural language. Take the English word *football* for example.

Football is the name given to a number of different team sports. Worldwide the most popular of these team sports is Association football, which also happens to be called *soccer* in several countries. The English language word football is also applied to Rugby football (Rugby union and rugby league), American football, Australian rules football, Gaelic football, and Canadian football.

A search for *football* therefore will retrieve documents that are about several completely different sports. Controlled vocabulary solves this problem by tagging the documents in such a way that the ambiguities are eliminated.

Compared to free text searching, the use of a controlled vocabulary can dramatically increase the performance of an information retrieval system, if performance is measured by precision (the percentage of documents in the retrieval list that are actually relevant to the search topic).

In some cases controlled vocabulary can enhance recall as well, because unlike natural language schemes, once the correct authorized term is searched, you don't need to worry about searching for other terms that might be synonyms of that term. However, a controlled vocabulary search may also lead to unsatisfactory recall, in that it will fail to retrieve some documents that are actually relevant to the search question.

This is particularly problematic when the search question involves terms that are sufficiently tangential to the subject area such that the indexer might have decided to tag it using a different term (but the searcher might consider the same). Essentially, this can be avoided only by an experienced user of controlled vocabulary whose understanding of the vocabulary coincides with the way it is used by the indexer.

Another possibility is that the article is just not tagged by the indexer because indexing exhaustivity is low. For example an article might mention football as a secondary focus, and the indexer might decide not to tag it with "football" because it is not important enough compared to the main focus. But it turns out that for the searcher that article is relevant and hence recall fails. A free text search would automatically pick up that article regardless. On the other hand free text searches have high exhaustivity (you search on every word) so it has potential for high recall (assuming you solve the problems of synonyms by entering every combination) but will have much lower precision.

Controlled vocabularies are also quickly out-dated and in fast developing fields of knowledge, the authorized terms available might not be available if they are not updated regularly. Even in the best case scenario, controlled language is often not as specific as using the words of the text itself. Indexers trying to choose the appropriate index terms might misinterpret the author, while a free text search is in no danger of doing so, because it uses the author's own words.

The use of controlled vocabularies can be costly compared to free text searches because human experts or expensive automated systems are necessary to index each entry. Furthermore, the user has to be familiar with the controlled vocabulary scheme to make best use of the system. But, the control of synonyms, homographs can help increase precision.

Numerous methodologies have been developed to assist in the creation of controlled vocabularies, including faceted classification, which enables a given data record or document to be described in multiple ways.

APPLICATIONS

Controlled vocabularies, such as the Library of Congress Subject Headings, are an essential component of bibliography, the study and classification of books. They were initially developed in library and information science. In the 1950s, government agencies began to develop controlled vocabularies for the burgeoning journal literature in specialized fields. An example is the Medical Subject Headings (MeSH) developed by the U.S. National Library of Medicine. Subsequently, for-profit firms (called Abstracting and indexing services) emerged to index the fast-growing literature in every field of knowledge. In the 1960s, an online bibliographic database industry developed based on dialup X.25 networking.

These services were seldom made available to the public because they were difficult to use. specialist librarians called search intermediaries handled the searching job. In the 1980s, the first full text databases appeared. these databases contain the full text of the index articles as well as the bibliographic information.

Online bibliographic databases have migrated to the Internet and are now publicly available. however, most are proprietary and can be expensive to use. Students enrolled in colleges and universities may be able to access some of these services without charge. some of these services may be accessible without charge at a public library.

In large organizations, controlled vocabularies may be introduced to improve technical communication. The use of controlled vocabulary ensures that everyone is using the same word to mean the same thing. This consistency of terms is one of the most important concepts in technical writing and knowledge management, where effort is expended to use the same word throughout a document or organization instead of slightly different ones to refer to the same thing. Web searching could be dramatically improved by the development of a controlled vocabulary for describing Web pages. the use of such a vocabulary could culminate in a Semantic Web, in which the content of Web pages is described using a machine-readable metadata scheme. One of the first proposals for such a scheme is the Dublin Core Initiative. An example of a controlled vocabulary which is usable for indexing web pages is PSH.

It is unlikely that a single metadata scheme will ever succeed in describing the content of the entire Web. To create a Semantic Web, it may be necessary to draw from two or more metadata systems to describe a Web page's contents. The eXchangeable Faceted Metadata Language (XFML) is designed to enable controlled vocabulary creators to publish and share metadata systems. XFML is designed on faceted classification principles.

CONTROVERSIAL LITERATURE (LIBRARY OF CONGRESS SUBJECT HEADINGS)

Controversial literature is a subdivision of the Library of Congress Subject Headings, used in the description of religious books. In this context, it has the following narrow use:

- "Under names of individual religious and monastic orders,

individual religions, individual Christian denominations, and uniform titles of sacred works for works that argue against or express opposition to those groups or works".

Prior to 1998 the subdivision was permitted for 'general religious and philosophical topics'.

CUTTER EXPANSIVE CLASSIFICATION

The Cutter Expansive Classification system is a library classification system devised by Charles Ammi Cutter. The system was the basis for the top categories of the Library of Congress Classification.

HISTORY OF THE EXPANSIVE CLASSIFICATION

Charles Ammi Cutter, inspired by the decimal classification of his contemporary Melvil Dewey, and with Dewey's initial encouragement, developed his own classification scheme for the Winchester Town Library and then the Boston Athenaeum, at which he served as librarian for twenty-four years. He began work on it around the year 1880, publishing an overview of the new system in 1882. The same classification would later be used, but with a different notation, also devised by Cutter, at the Cary Library in Lexington. Many libraries found this system too detailed and complex for their needs, and Cutter received many requests from librarians at small libraries who wanted the classification adapted for their collections. He devised the Expansive Classification in response, to meet the needs of growing libraries, and to address some of the complaints of his critics. Cutter completed and published an introduction and schedules for the first six classifications of his new system (*Expansive Classification: Part I: The First Six Classifications*), but his work on the seventh was interrupted by his death in 1903.

The Cutter Expansive Classification, although adopted by comparatively few libraries, mostly in New England, has been called one of the most logical and scholarly of American classifications.

Library historian Leo E. LaMontagne writes:

- "Cutter produced the best classification of the nineteenth century. While his system was less "scientific" than that of J.P. Lesley, it's other key features – notation, specificity, and versatility – make it deserving of the praise it has received".

Its top level divisions served as a basis for the Library of Congress classification, which also took over some of its features. It did not catch on as did Dewey's system because Cutter died before it was completely finished, making no provision for the kind of development necessary as the bounds of knowledge expanded and scholarly emphases changed throughout the 20th century.

STRUCTURE OF THE EXPANSIVE CLASSIFICATION

The Expansive Classification uses seven separate schedules, each designed to be used by libraries of different sizes. After the first, each schedule was an expansion of the previous one, and Cutter provided instructions for how a library might change from one expansion to another as it grows.

SUMMARY OF THE EXPANSIVE CLASSIFICATION SCHEDULES

First Classification

The first classification is meant for only the very smallest libraries. The first classification has only seven top level classes, and only eight classes in all.

- A Works of reference and general works which include several of the following parts, and so could not go in any one.
- B Philosophy and Religion
- E Biography
- F History and Geography and Travels
- H Social sciences
- L Natural sciences and Arts
- Y Language and Literature
- YF Fiction

Further Classifications

Further expansions add more top level classes and subdivisions. Many subclasses arranged systematically, with common divisions, such as those by geography and language, following a consistent system throughout.

By the fifth classification all the letters of the alphabet are in use for top level classes, these are:

- A General Works
- B Philosophy
- C Christianity and Judaism
- D Ecclesiastical History
- E Biography
- F History, Universal History
- G Geography and Travels
- H Social Sciences
- I Demotics, Sociology
- J Civics, Government, Political Science
- K Legislation
- L Science and Arts together
- M Natural History
- N Botany
- O Zoölogy
- P Anthropology and Ethnology
- Q Medicine
- R Useful arts, Technology

- S Constructive arts (Engineering and Building)
- T Manufactures and Handicrafts
- U Art of War
- V Recreative arts, Sports, Games, Festivals
- W Art
- X English Language
- Y English and American literature
- Z Book arts

These schedules were not meant to be fixed, but were to be adapted to meet the needs of each library. For example, books on the English language may be put in X, and books on language in general in a subclass of X, or this can be reversed. The first option is less logical, but results in shorter marks for most English language libraries.

HOW EXPANSIVE CLASSIFICATION CALL NUMBERS ARE CONSTRUCTED

Most call numbers in the Expansive Classification follow conventions offering clues to the book's subject. The first line represents the subject, the second the author (and perhaps title), the third and fourth dates of editions, indications of translations, and critical works on particular books or authors. All numbers in the Expansive Classification are (or should be) shelved as if in decimal order.

Size of volumes is indicated by points (.), pluses (+), or slashes (/or//). For some subjects a numerical geographical subdivision follows the classification letters on the first line. The number 83 stands for the United States—hence, F83 is U.S. history, G83 U.S. travel, JU83 U.S. politics, WP83 U.S. painting. Geographical numbers are often further expanded decimally to represent more specific areas, sometimes followed by a capital letter indicating a particular city. The second line usually represents the author's name by a capital letter plus one or more numbers arranged decimally. This may be followed by the first letter or letters of the title in lower-case, and/or sometimes the letters a, b, c indicating other printings of the same title. When appropriate, the second line may begin with a 'form' number—*e.g.*, 1 stands for history and criticism of a subject, 2 for a bibliography, 5 for a dictionary, 6 for an atlas or maps, 7 for a periodical, 8 for a society or university publication, 9 for a collection of works by different authors. On the third line a capital Y indicates a work about the author or book represented by the first two lines, and a capital E (for English—other letters are used for other languages) indicates a translation into English. If both criticism and translation apply to a single title, the number expands into four lines.

Cutter Numbers

One of the features adopted by other systems, including Library of

Congress, is the Cutter number. It is an alphanumeric device to code text so that it can be arranged in alphabetical order using the fewest characters. It contains one or two initial letters and Arabic numbers, treated as a decimal. To construct a Cutter number, a cataloguer consults a Cutter table as required by the classification rules. Although Cutter numbers are mostly used for coding the names of authors, the system can be used for titles, subjects, geographic areas, and more.

DEWEY DECIMAL CLASSIFICATION (DDC)

Dewey Decimal Classification (also called the Dewey Decimal System) is a proprietary system of library classification developed by Melvil Dewey in 1876. It has been greatly modified and expanded through 23 major revisions, the most recent in 2011. This highly organized system categorizes books on library shelves in an efficient, specific and repeatable order that makes it easy to find any book and return it to its proper place on the library shelves. The system is used in 200,000 libraries in at least 135 countries. A designation such as *Dewey 16* refers to the 16th edition of the DDC.

DESIGN

The DDC attempts to organize all knowledge into ten main classes. The ten main classes are each further subdivided into ten divisions, and each division into ten parts, giving ten main classes, 100 divisions and 1000 parts. DDC's advantage in using decimals for its categories allows it to be purely numerical, while the drawback is that the codes are much longer and more difficult to remember as compared to an alphanumeric system.

Just as an alphanumeric system, it is infinitely hierarchical. It also uses some aspects of a faceted classification scheme, combining elements from different parts of the structure to construct a number representing the subject content (often combining two subject elements with linking numbers and geographical and temporal elements) and form of an item rather than drawing upon a list containing each class and its meaning.

Except for general works and fiction, works are classified principally by subject, with extensions for subject relationships, place, time or type of material, producing classification numbers of at least three digits but otherwise of indeterminate length with a decimal point before the fourth digit, where present (for example, 330 for economics +.9 for geographic treatment +.04 for Europe = 330.94 European economy. 973 for United States +.05 form division for periodicals = 973.05 periodicals concerning the United States generally).

Books are placed on the shelf in increasing numerical order of the decimal number, for example, 050, 220, 330, 330.973, 331. When two books have the same classification number the second line of the call number (usually the first letter or letters of the author's last name, the title if there is no identifiable author) is placed in alphabetical order.

The DDC has a number for all books, including fiction: American fiction is classified in 813. Most libraries create a separate fiction part to allow shelving in a more generalized fashion than Dewey provides for, or to avoid the space that would be taken up in the 800s, or simply to allow readers to find preferred authors by alphabetical order of surname.

Some parts of the classification offer options to accommodate different kinds of libraries. An important feature of the scheme is the ability to assign multiple class numbers to a bibliographical item and only use one of them for shelving. The added numbers appear in the classified subject catalogue (though this is not the usual practice in North America).

For the full benefit of the scheme the relative index and the tables that form part of every edition must be understood and consulted when required. The structure of the schedules is such that subjects close to each other in a dictionary catalogue are dispersed in the Dewey schedules (for example, architecture of Chicago quite separate from geography of Chicago).

Classes Listed

The system is made up of seven tables and ten main classes, each of which is divided into ten secondary classes or subcategories, each of which contain ten subdivisions.

The tables are:

- Standard subdivision
- Areas
- Subdivision of individual literatures
- Subdivisions of individual languages
- Racial, ethnic, national groups
- Languages
- Persons

The classes are:

- *000*: Computer science, information and general works
- *100*: Philosophy and psychology
- *200*: Religion
- *300*: Social sciences
- *400*: Language
- *500:* Science (including mathematics)
- *600*: Technology and applied science
- *700*: Arts and recreation
- *800:* Literature
- *900*: History and geography

ADMINISTRATION AND PUBLICATION

While he lived, Melvil Dewey edited each edition himself: he was followed by other editors who had been very much influenced by him. The earlier editions were printed in the peculiar spelling that Dewey had devised: the number of volumes in each edition increased to two, then three and now four. The Online Computer Library Center (OCLC) of Dublin, Ohio, United States, acquired the trademark and copyrights associated with the DDC when it bought Forest Press in 1988. OCLC maintains the classification system and publishes new editions of the system.

The editorial staff responsible for updates is based partly at the Library of Congress and partly at OCLC. Their work is reviewed by the Decimal Classification Editorial Policy Committee (EPC), which is a ten-member international board that meets twice each year. The four-volume unabridged edition is published approximately every six years, the most recent edition (DDC 23) in mid 2011. The web edition is updated on an ongoing basis, with changes announced each month.

Linked to each full edition is the single volume abridged edition designed for libraries with 20,000 titles or fewer. Abridged 14 was published in 2004, Abridged 15 is due early 2012. The work of assigning a DDC number to each newly published book is performed by a division of the Library of Congress, whose recommended assignments are either accepted or rejected by the OCLC after review by an advisory board. to date all have been accepted.

In September 2003, the OCLC sued the Library Hotel for trademark infringement. The settlement was that the OCLC would allow the Library Hotel to use the system in its hotel and marketing. In exchange, the Hotel would acknowledge the Centre's ownership of the trademark and make a donation to a nonprofit organization promoting reading and literacy among children.

INFLUENCE

DDC's numbers formed the basis of the more expressive but complex Universal Decimal Classification (UDC), which combines the basic Dewey numbers with selected punctuation marks (comma, colon, parentheses, etc.). Adaptations of DDC for specific regions outside the English-speaking world include the Korean Decimal Classification, the New Classification Scheme for Chinese Libraries and the Nippon Decimal Classification (Japanese).

COMPARISON WITH LIBRARY OF CONGRESS CLASSIFICATION

Besides its frequent revision, DDC's main advantage over its chief American rival, the Library of Congress Classification system developed shortly afterward, is its simplicity. Thanks to the use of pure notation, a mnemonics system and a hierarchical decimal place system, it is generally easier to use.

DDC and UDC are more flexible than Library of Congress Classification because of greater use of facets (via auxiliary tables) while Library of Congress Classification is almost totally enumerative.

DDC's decimal system means that it is less hospitable to the addition of new subjects, as opposed to Library of Congress Classification, which has 21 classes at the top level. DDC notations can be much longer compared to other classification systems.

Another disadvantage of DDC is that it was developed in the 19th century essentially by one man and was built on a top-down approach to classify all human knowledge, which makes it difficult to adapt to changing fields of knowledge. The Library of Congress Classification system was developed based mainly on the idea of literary warrant. classes were added (by individual experts in each area) only when needed for works owned by the Library of Congress.

As a result, while the Library of Congress Classification system was able to incorporate changes and additions of new branches of knowledge, particularly in the fields of engineering and computer science (the greater hospitability of the Library of Congress Classification was also a factor), DDC has been criticized for being inadequate in covering those areas.

It is asserted that, as a result, most major academic libraries in the US do not use the DDC because the classification of works in those areas is not specific enough, although there are other reasons that may truly be more weighty, such as the much lower expense of using a unique "pre-packaged" catalogue number instead of having highly skilled staff members engaging in the time-consuming development of catalogue numbers.

The Library of Congress Classification system is not without problems. For example, it is highly US-centric because of the nature of the system, and it has been translated into far fewer languages than DDC and UDC.

DICKINSON CLASSIFICATION

The Dickinson classification is a library classification scheme used to catalogue and classify musical compositions. It was developed by George Sherman Dickinson (1886-1964), and is used by many music libraries, primarily those at University at Buffalo, Vassar, and Columbia Universities.

FACETED CLASSIFICATION

A faceted classification system allows the assignment of an object to multiple characteristics (attributes), enabling the classification to be ordered in multiple ways, rather than in a single, predetermined, taxonomic order. A facet comprises "clearly defined, mutually exclusive, and collectively exhaustive aspects, properties or characteristics of a class or specific subject". For example, a collection of books might be classified using an author facet, a subject facet, a date facet, etc.

Faceted classification is used in faceted search systems that enable a user to navigate information along multiple paths corresponding to different orderings of the facets. This contrasts with traditional taxonomies in which the hierarchy of categories is fixed and unchanging. The colon classification developed by S. R. Ranganathan is an example of faceted classification applied to the physical world, specifically for the purpose of organizing library materials. In the colon classification system, a book is assigned a set of values from independent facets.

It differs from traditional library classification schemas like the Dewey Decimal System and Library of Congress classification system, in which each document has a unique assignment in a single, hierarchically organized classification system. Faceted classification systems are also distinct from folksonomies or other tagging systems that do not break out the tags into independent facets.

FREINET CLASSIFICATION

The Freinet classification ("To organise everything") is used in the libraries of some elementary schools, and was invented by Célestin Freinet to facilitate the easy finding of documents, and the use of the "Bibliothèque de Travail". The principles are simple: Everything is split into 12 major divisions. 12 subdivisions along the principles of the Dewey decimal system are then divided into 10, and then 10 again.

Because of its logical classifications based on school work, this classification is seen by some educators to be more natural and more logical to students than official classifications based on organizational criteria. The last revision took place in 1984. It is still used, in addition to keywords, in IT and some data information organization systems.

THE 12 DIVISIONS

- 0. Reference:
  - 00 General
  - 01 English Dictionaries
  - 02 Dictionaries in foreign languages
  - 03 Bilingual, trilingual... dictionaries
  - 04 Other Dictionaries (proper names, places...)
  - 05 Encyclopedias
  - 06 Repertory, bibliographies
  - 07 Reference works (textbooks)
- 1. Natural Environment:
  - 11 Land (geology)
  - 12 Relief
  - 13 Freshwater
  - 14 The oceans and seas
  - 15 The climates and vegetation
  - 16 Heaven (astronomy)
  - 17 Nature and Life (ecology)

- 2. Plants:
  - 21 Study of the plant
  - 22 The flowering plants
  - 23 The plants without flowers or seeds
  - 24 The microscopic beings
- 3. Animals:
  - 30 General study of the body (in humans and animals)
  - 31 The health of humans
  - 32 Mammals (except humans)
  - 33 Birds
  - 34 Reptiles and amphibians
  - 35 Fish
  - 36 Insects (articulated)
  - 37 Other articulated
  - 38 Shellfish
  - 39 Other animals
- 4. Other sciences:
  - 41 Mathematics
  - 42 Physical Sciences
  - 43 Chemistry
  - 44 Technology
- 5. Food and Agriculture:
  - 51 Working the earth
  - 52 Cultures
  - 53 Livestock
  - 54 Forestry
  - 55 Fishing
  - 56 Hunting
  - 57 Food industry
  - 58 Foods
  - 59 Drinks
- 6. Labour and Industry:
  - 60 General
  - 61 Sources of energy and engines
  - 62 Mining and quarrying
  - 63 Metals
  - 64 Chemical Industry
  - 65 Textile and clothing industry
  - 66 Building industry, housing and furniture
  - 67 Other Industries

- 7. The city and stock exchanges:
  - 71 The city, the municipality
  - 72 Trade
  - 73 Road Transport
  - 74 Rail transport
  - 75 Inland waterway transport
  - 76 Maritime Transport
  - 77 Air transportation and space
  - 78 Post, Telecommunications and IT
  - 79 Travel and Tourism
- 8. Society:
  - 81 People
  - 82 Contracts (environmental and social issues)
  - 83 Administrative organization of society
  - 84 Organisation of social policy
  - 85 Reports from nations
- 9. Culture and Recreation:
  - 91 Education and instructions
  - 92 Languages
  - 93 Literature and Philosophy
  - 94 Religions
  - 95 Arts and Entertainment
  - 96 Sports and Games
- G. Geography:
  - G0 The study of geography
  - G1 General Geography
  - G2 Geography locally and regionally
  - G3 Our country
  - G4 Europe
  - G5 Asia
  - G6 Africa
  - G7 America
  - G8 Oceania
  - G9 The Polar World
- H. History:
  - H1 Prehistory
  - H2 The East, Greece
  - H3 Rome and the early Middle Ages (from "700 to 987)
  - H4 Middle Ages (from 987 to 1492)
  - H5 Absolute monarchy (1492 to 1789)

- H6 Struggles for Democracy (1789 to 1848)
- H7 Organization of the Republic (1848 to 1914)
- H8 Contemporary history (1914–present)

FRSAD

Functional Requirements for Subject Authority Data (FRSAD), previously known as Functional Requirements for Subject Authority Records, or FRSAR is a conceptual entity-relationship model currently being developed by a workgroup International Federation of Library Associations and Institutions (IFLA). It is a continuation of the work done on the FRBR model, further explaining how the Group 3 entities, that consists of "entities that serve as subjects of intellectual or artistic endeavour" can be related and controlled within the biblio-graphic universe. The model is meant to ease global sharing and use of subject authority data. The final draft of the report is to be presented in the spring of 2009 at the 75th IFLA General Conference and Council in Milan.

THE CONCEPTUAL MODEL

- *Work:* Work is a "distinct intellectual or artistic creation.
- *Thema:* Is anything that can be the subject of a work. This is the abstract idea of the aboutness of a given work. Thema is independent of language and disciplines.
- *Nomen:* Any alphanumeric, sound, visual, or any other symbol, sign or combination of symbols by which a thema is known, referred to or addressed. A nomen can be any expression of a thema. Ideally there will exist an authority file with every possible subject/thema. This means that it should be possible to exchange subject authority data between systems. If a user looks up a specific subject in a catalogue and wants to look in other places, he or she should not have to worry about translating the query, since the system would be able to recognize the underlying thema and automatically translate it into the relevant nomen. One way to understand this is to think about how a subject can be described in different ways. For example, if one looks at a work about the city Stockholm, the capital of Sweden, there are many ways to describe Stockholm. First, one must distinguish between the city Stockholm and the many other meanings of the word. for example, Stockholm is also the name of other cities, a record label, and a syndrome. When the thema is established in an authority file, it is possible to translate across systems. The nomen for Stockholm could be anything from "Stockholm", "Stockholm (City)", "Tukholma"-the Finnish spelling of Stockholm-or a range of Zip-codes, or the longitude and latitude, or a picture of the city, or a sound. FRSAR, if implemented, enables users to perform specific and precise subject searching across multiple systems.

RELATIONSHIPS

Works and themas have a Many-to-many (data model) relationship, meaning that any work can have more than one subject, and any subject can be expressed in one or more works. The same is true for the relationship between thema and nomen. A thema can be expressed in many different ways and a nomen can express many different themas, all depending on the given system. Besides these relationships, the workgroup has so far identified several other thema-thema and nomen-nomen relationships. Two nomens can, for example, be said to have an equivalence relationship, if they both are appellations of the same thema.

USER TASKS

The workgroup conducted two user studies in 2006 and 2007, and based on the results of these studies, four subject authority data user tasks were defined:

- *Find:* To find an entity (thema or nomen) or set of entities corresponding to stated criteria
- *Identify:* To identify an entity (thema or nomen) based on certain attributes/characteristics
- *Select:* To select an entity (thema or nomen)
- *Explore:* To explore any relationships between entities (thema or nomen), correlations to other subject vocabularies and structure of a subject domain

FUNCTIONAL REQUIREMENTS FOR BIBLIOGRAPHIC RECORDS (FRBR)

Functional Requirements for Bibliographic Records (FRBR), sometimes pronounced is a conceptual entity-relationship model developed by the International Federation of Library Asso-ciations and Institutions (IFLA) that relates user tasks of retrieval and access in online library catalogues and bibliographic databases from a user's perspective. It represents a more holistic approach to retrieval and access as the relationships between the entities provide links to navigate through the hierarchy of relationships. The model is significant because it is separate from specific cataloguing standards such as AACR2 or International Standard Bibliographic Description (ISBD).

FRBR ENTITIES

FRBR comprises groups of entities:

- Group 1 entities are work, expression, manifestation, and item (WEMI). They represent the products of intellectual or artistic endeavour.
- Group 2 entities are person and corporate body, responsible for the custodianship of Group 1's intellectual or artistic endeavour.

- Group 3 entities are subjects of Group 1 or Group 2's intellectual endeavour, and include concepts, objects, events, places.

Group 1 entities are the foundation of the FRBR model:

- *Work* is a "distinct intellectual or artistic creation." For example, Beethoven's Ninth Symphony apart from all ways of expressing it is a work. When we say, "Beethoven's Ninth is magnificent!" we generally are referring to the work.
- *Expression* is "the specific intellectual or artistic form that a work takes each time it is 'realised.'" An expression of Beethoven's Ninth might be the musical score he writes down.
- *Manifestation* is "the physical embodiment of an expression of a work. As an entity, manifestation represents all the physical objects that bear the same characteristics, in respect to both intellectual content and physical form." The recording the London Philharmonic made of the Ninth in 1996 is a manifestation. When we say, "The recording of the London Philharmonic's 1996 performance captured the essence of the Ninth," we are generally referring to a manifestation.
- *Item* is "a single exemplar of a manifestation. The entity defined as item is a concrete entity." Each of the 1996 pressings of that 1996 recording is an item. When we say, "Both copies of the London Philharmonic's 1996 performance of the Ninth are checked out of my local library," we are generally referring to items.

RELATIONSHIPS

FRBR is built upon relationships between and among entities. "Relationships serve as the vehicle for depicting the link between one entity and another, and thus as the means of assisting the user to 'navigate' the universe that is represented in a bibliography, catalogue, or bibliographic database." Examples of relationship types include, but are not limited to:

Equivalence Relationships

Equivalence relationships exist between exact copies of the same manifestation of a work or between an original item and reproductions of it, so long as the intellectual content and authorship are preserved. Examples include reproductions such as copies, issues, facsimiles and reprints, photocopies, and microfilms.

Derivative Relationships

Derivative relationships exist between a bibliographic work and a modification based on the work.

Examples include:

- Editions, versions, translations, summaries, abstracts, and digests

- Adaptations that become new works but are based on old works
- Genre changes
- New works based on the style or thematic content of the work

Descriptive Relationships

Descriptive relationships exist between a bibliographic entity and a description, criticism, evaluation, or review of that entity, such as between a work and a book review describing it. Descriptive relationships also includes annotated editions, casebooks, commentaries, and critiques of an existing work.

ICONCLASS

Iconclass is a specialized library classification designed for art and iconography. It was originally conceived by Henri van de Waal, and was further developed by a group of scholars after his death.

The Iconclass system is probably the largest classification system for cultural content. Initially designed for historical imagery, it is now also used to create subject access to texts and to classify a wide range of images, including modern photo-graphy. At the moment it contains over 28,000 unique concepts (classification types) and has an entry vocabulary of 14,000 keywords. It can be consulted with the help of the freely available Iconclass 2100 browser.

Iconclass was developed in the Netherlands as a standard classification for recording collections, with the idea of assembling huge databases that will allow the retrieval of images featuring particular details, subjects or other common factors. For example, the Iconclass code "71H7131" is for the subject of "Bathsheba (alone) with David's letter", whereas "71" is the whole "Old Testament" and "71H" the "story of David".

A number of collections of different types have been classified using Iconclass, notably many types of old master print, the collections of the Gemäldegalerie, Berlin and the German Marburger Index. These are available, usually on-line or on DVD. The system can also be used outside pure art history, for example on sites like Flickr. The content of Iconclass is currently maintained by the Rijksbureau voor Kunsthistorische Documentatie (Netherlands Institute for Art History). The online Iconclass browser is developed by the Henri van de Waal Foundation.

INTERNATIONAL STANDARD BIBLIOGRAPHIC DESCRIPTION

The International Standard Bibliographic Description (ISBD) is a set of rules produced by the International Federation of Library Associations and Institutions (IFLA) to create a bibliographic description in a standard, human-readable form, especially for use in a bibliography or a library catalogue. A consolidated edition of the ISBD was published in 2007 and revised in 2011, superseding earlier separate ISBDs for monographs, older monographic publications, cartographic materials, serials and other continuing resources, electronic resources, non-book materials, and printed music. IFLA's ISBD Review Group is responsible for maintaining the ISBD. One of the original purposes of the ISBD was to provide a standard form of bibliographic description that could be used to exchange records internationally. This would support IFLA's programme of universal bibliographic control.

INVENTORY

Libraries need methods, such as inventories, to determine whether their collections are in good shape, or whether some preservation or conservation activities are necessary. How do libraries identify which particular items sitting on their shelves that may not have crossed the circulation desk in a number of years need special attention?

ROLE OF INVENTORY IN THE MISSION OF LIBRARIES

Libraries have thousands of books. large academic libraries may have millions of books. therein lies our problem. Doing an annual (or less frequent) physical inventory with the laying on of hands on each individual item may not be financially feasible, employees required may not have extra time to devote to such an inventory, and there are no financial rewards for the Library for completing an inventory—essentially we are out looking for our problem books and missing items when we conduct an inventory.

The solutions to solving the problems that are discovered (books in need of repurchase, rebinding, repair, or digitization) are expensive and labour intensive. Inventories may not take place for decades, if ever, at large academic institutions because of these restraints.

Although collecting new materials is viewed as a central mission of the library, maintaining the condition of library collections, which includes less satisfactory activities such as weeding, book repair, shifting and counting what libraries think they have on their shelves, are also a vital part of the library's mission to provide access to current patrons, as well as those people who will use the library at some point in the future.

Adelphi University Libraries in 2004 completed a complete physical inventory of its collections (465,629 volumes) as part of its strategic planning process utilizing the Association of College and Research Libraries Standards for Libraries in Higher Education. Examining item by item with a barcode scanner and a laptop, the objective is to adjust bibliographic and item records in theirs and OCLC's WorldCat databases.

Complete inventory or stocktaking is often a regular part of the school library media specialist's job at K-12 institutions, where inventory may be a legal requirement that shows that the libraries are accountable for the money they have spent throughout the year. Checking for lost books and materials can be similarly compared to auditing. We are trying to guarantee that our collections as listed in our OPACs and Finding Aids do not lack integrity.

School libraries use the inventory to assess the collection (numbers, age and ratio:student) against benchmarks of accrediting institutions, and also to examine each resource and determine its future in the collection based on age, relevance, currency and condition—which may include repair, replacement, disposal or cleaning to ensure that attractive, up-to-date resources are available for patrons. Inventory can also identify anomalies in the catalogue and provide an opportunity to correct catalogue records and labeling of items. This is also a time when shelves can be rearranged to minimize overcrowding to prevent damage.

SAMPLING

Sampling is a compromise measure, which can be an important management tool. Random sampling of library collections can give a quick and clear assessment measure of a collection—whether the books are present, and whether those books present are in good physical condition.

In 1982, the California State University libraries, suggested inventory procedures to insure that the 19 campus collections were secure and intact. They recognized that a complete regular inventory was too expensive, and decided that the best method of assessing book loss would be to use sampling. Every three years, a sample was to be taken of an identified number of items in each Library of Congress letter classification. If loss rates were more than 1% for two years in a row, this would indicate that a full inventory was needed.

A random sampling of the collection serves as an indicator for the rest of the collection. If all the items are accounted for in a random sampling, then it can be assumed that rest of the collections' records is just as reliable. However, a complete inventory provides the institution with the knowledge that the entire collection can be accounted for. the random sampling is used to check the consistency of the collections' records.

MANAGEMENT OF SAMPLING SURVEYS

Once librarians are laying hands on individual books in their sample, what do they look for? They should check the cover of the book for discoloration, peeling, damage. Then they should open the book and look at the pages of the text—are they yellowing, brittle? An archival marking pen may be used to determine whether a book is acidic. How is the binding? Are the pages intact? This data can be recorded in a spreadsheet for use of later analysis of the entire sample.

Include the item's call number, place of publication, place of production, publication date, measurements (spine height, cover width, depth of back to front cover, the amount of shelving space surrounding the item, horizontally and vertically). describe the case style, leaf attachment and binding condition, text attachment, acidity, paper strength, and text contrast. list the damaged pages and describe the enclosure type and condition. record any additional notes that will be useful for future reference and analysis.

Costs for sampling 384 random items at the University of Illinois at Urbana-Champaign in 1987 were less than $5000. The UIUC Library employed eleven graduate students from the school of library and information science, who received training and supervision. Each surveyor collected forty samples, 90% of the surveys were completed on the first day in 5.5 survey hours.

ANALYSIS OF RESULTS

Information from samples can easily be recorded in Excel or some other spreadsheet programme, where simple analysis can be performed. For preservation purposes, librarians want to know the condition of their collections: what percentage of the books are acidic? What percentage of the collection is damaged? Does more damage take place on cramped shelves? Does the library need to be concerned with books printed in Eastern Europe? Etc. After identifying the issues of primary concern in the collection, preservation measures should be considered.

What needs to happen as soon as possible to preserve the collection? What choices can be delayed for some time? Does the library have a preservation plan in its collection management policy? Is there a budget for maintaining the collections? What can be extrapolated from the data about what might happen to the collection in ten to twenty years?

Using the results of the library's collection assessment, budgetary requests can be substantiated by data. The library needs an increase in budget to care for aging collections, or the library needs an increase in funding to add new materials for our students to meet deficiencies and weaknesses. This strategy was employed by the Joyner Library at East Carolina University after an inventory and shelf-analysis project in 2005.

OTHER USES OF SAMPLING IN LIBRARY COLLECTION MANAGEMENT

Sampling can also be used to calculate optimum intervals for shelf reading. Average misplacement of books on a shelf in a university library is 5.6%. Sixty-five per cent of the books were located on the correct shelf, but not in the right order. Cooper and Wolthausen developed equations indicating that the optimal shelf-reading interval is a function of the number of books in a part, the likelihood that a book in one part will migrate to another, checking and users costs, and the error rate of the shelf reader.

LIBRARY OF CONGRESS CLASSIFICATION

The Library of Congress Classification (LCC) is a system of library classification developed by the Library of Congress. It is used by most research and academic libraries in the U.S. and several other countries. for example, Australia and Taiwan, R.O.C. It is not to be confused with the Library of Congress Subject Headings or Library of Congress Control Number. Most public libraries and small academic libraries continue to use the Dewey Decimal Classification (DDC).

The classification was originally developed by Herbert Putnam in 1897, just before he assumed the librarianship of Congress. With advice from Charles Ammi Cutter, it was influenced by his Cutter Expansive Classification and by the DDC, and was designed specifically for the purposes and collection of the Library of Congress.

The new system replaced a fixed location system developed by Thomas Jefferson. By the time Putnam departed from his post in 1939, all the classes except K (Law) and parts of B (Philosophy and Religion) were well developed. It has been criticized as lacking a sound theoretical basis. many of the classification decisions were driven by the practical needs of that library, rather than epistemological considerations.

Although it divides subjects into broad categories, it is essentially enumerative in nature. It provides a guide to the books actually in the library, not a classification of the world. The National Library of Medicine classification system (NLM) uses the classification scheme's unused letters *W* and *QS–QZ*. Some libraries use NLM in conjunction with LCC, eschewing LCC's R (Medicine). Others prefer to use the LCC scheme's *QP–QR* schedules and include Medicine *R*.

LIBRARY OF CONGRESS CONTROL NUMBER

The Library of Congress Control Number or LCCN is a serially based system of numbering cataloguing records in the Library of Congress in the United States. It has nothing to do with the contents of any book, and should not be confused with Library of Congress Classification.

The LCCN numbering system has been in use since 1898, at which time the acronym LCCN originally stood for Library of Congress Card Number. It has been variously called the Library of Congress Catalogue Card Number. The Library of Congress prepared cards of bibliographic information for their library catalogue and would sell duplicate sets of the cards to other libraries for use in their catalogs. This is known as centralized cataloguing. Each set of cards was given a serial number to help identify it.

Although most of the bibliographic information is now electronically created, stored and shared with other libraries, there is still a need to identify each unique record, and the LCCN continues to perform that function.

Librarians all over the world use this unique identifier in the process of cataloguing most books which have been published in the United States. It helps them reach the correct cataloguing data (known as a cataloguing record), which the Library of Congress and third parties make available on the Web and through other media. In February 2008, the Library of Congress created the LCCN Permalink service, providing a stable URL for all Library of Congress Control Numbers.

FORMAT

In its most elementary form the number includes a year and a serial number. The year has two digits for 1898 to 2000, and four digits beginning in 2001. The three ambiguous years are distinguished by the size of the serial number. There are also some peculiarities in numbers beginning with a "7" because of an unsuccessful experiment applied between 1969 and 1972. Serial numbers are six digits long and should include leading zeros. The hyphen that is often seen separating the year and serial number is optional. More recently, the Library of Congress has instructed publishers not to include a hyphen.

MARC STANDARDS

MARC (MAchine-Readable Cataloguing), is an international standard digital format for the description of bibliographic items developed by the Library of Congress during the 1960s to facilitate the creation and dissemination of computerized cataloguing from library to library within the same country and between countries. By 1971, the MARC format had become the national standard for dissemination of bibliographic data and by 1973, an international standard. There are several versions of MARC in use in the world, the most predominant being MARC 21, created in 1999 as a result of the harmonization of U.S. and Canadian MARC formats, and UNIMARC, widely used in Europe. The MARC 21 family of standards now includes formats for authority records, holdings records, classification schedules, and community information, in addition to formats for the bibliographic record.

MARC RECORD STRUCTURE AND FIELD DESIGNATIONS

The MARC standards define three aspects of a MARC record: the record structure, the field designations within each record, and the actual content of the record itself.

Record Structure

ISO 2709

MARC records are typically stored and transmitted as binary files, usually with several MARC records concatenated together into a single file. MARC uses the ISO 2709 standard to define the structure of each record. This includes a marker to indicate where each record begins and ends, as well as a set of characters at the beginning of each record that provide a directory for locating the fields and subfields within the record.

MARC-XML

In 2002, the Library of Congress developed the MARC-XML schema as an alternative record structure, allowing MARC records to be represented in XML. Libraries typically expose their records as MARC-XML via a web service, often following the SRU or OAI-PMH standards.

Field Designations

Each field in a MARC records provides information about the item the record is describing. Since it was first developed at a time when computing power was low, and space precious, MARC uses a simple three-digit numeric code (from 001-999) to identify each field in the record. The bibliographic standard, for example, defines 100 as the primary author of a work, 245 as the title, 260 is used for publisher information, and so on.

Fields above 008 are further divided into subfields using a single letter or number designation. The 260, for example, is further divided into subfield 'a' for the place of publication, 'b' for the name of the publisher, and 'c' for the date of publication.

Content

MARC is a metadata transmission standard, not a content standard. Other than a handful of fixed fields defined by the MARC standards themselves, the actual content a cataloger will place in each MARC field is usually governed and defined by standards outside of MARC.

The Anglo-American Cataloguing Rules, for example, define how the physical characteristics of books and other item should be cataloged. The Library of Congress Subject Headings (LCSH) provides a list of authorized subject terms to describe the main content of the item. Other cataloguing rules, subject thesauri, and classification schedules can also be used.

MARC 21 allows the use of two character sets, either MARC-8 or Unicode encoded as UTF-8. MARC-8 is based on ISO 2022 and allows the use of Hebrew, Cyrillic, Arabic, Greek, and East Asian scripts. MARC 21 in UTF-8 format allows all the languages supported by Unicode.

MARC 21

MARC 21 is a result of the combination of the United States and Canadian MARC formats (USMARC and CAN/MARC). MARC21 is based on the ANSI standard Z39.2, which allows users of different software products to communicate with each other and to exchange data. MARC 21 was designed to redefine the original MARC record format for the 21st century and to make it more accessible to the international community. MARC 21 has formats for the following five types of data: Bibliographic Format, Authority Format, Holdings Format, Community Format, and Classification Data Format. Currently MARC 21 has been implemented successfully by The British Library, the European Institutions and the major library institutions in the United States, and Canada. MARC 21 allows the use of two character sets, either MARC-8 or Unicode encoded as UTF-8. MARC-8 is based on ISO 2022 and allows the use of Hebrew, Cyrillic, Arabic, Greek, and East Asian scripts. MARC 21 in UTF-8 format allows all the languages supported by Unicode.

MARCXML

MARC XML is an XML schema based on the fairly common MARC21 standards. MARCXML was developed by the US Library of Congress and adopted by it and others as a means of easy sharing of, and networked access to, bibliographic information.

Being easy to parse by various systems allows it to be used as an aggregation format, as it is in software packages such as MetaLib, though that package merges it into a wider DTD specification.

The MARC XML primary design goals included:

- Simplicity of the schema
- Flexibility and extensibility
- Lossless and reversible conversion from MARC
- Data presentation through XML stylesheets
- MARC records updates and data conversions through XML transformations
- Existence of validation tools

FUTURE

The future of the MARC formats is a matter of some debate among libraries. On the one hand, the storage formats are quite complex and are based on outdated technology. On the other, there is no alternative bibliographic format with an equivalent degree of granularity. The billions of MARC records in tens of thousands of individual libraries (including over 50,000,000 belonging to the OCLC consortium alone) create inertia.

VIRTUAL INTERNATIONAL AUTHORITY FILE

The Virtual International Authority File (VIAF) is an international authority file. It is a joint project of several national libraries and operated by the Online Computer Library Center (OCLC). The project was initiated by the German National Library and the American Library of Congress.

The aim is to link the national authority files (such as the German Name Authority File) to a single virtual authority file. In this file, identical records from the different data sets are linked together. A VIAF record: receives a standard data number. contains the primary, "see", and "see also" records from the original records. and refers to the original authority records. The data are made available online and are available for research and data exchange/sharing. Data set updating uses the Open Archives Initiative protocol.

UNIVERSAL DECIMAL CLASSIFICATION

The Universal Decimal Classification (UDC) is a bibliographic and library classification developed by the Belgian bibliographers Paul Otlet and Henri La Fontaine at the end of the 19th century. The UDC provides a systematic arrangement of all branches of human knowledge organized as a coherent system in which knowledge fields are related and inter-linked.

Originally based on the Dewey Decimal Classification, the UDC was developed as a new analytico-synthetic classification system with a significantly larger vocabulary and syntax that enables very detailed content indexing and information retrieval in large collections.

In its first edition in 1905, the UDC already included many features that were revolutionary in the context of knowledge classifications: tables of generally applicable (aspect-free) concepts-called common auxiliary tables. a series of special auxiliary tables with specific but re-usable attributes in a particular field of knowledge. An expressive notational system with connecting symbols and syntax rules to enable coordination of subjects and the creation of a documentation language proper. Although originally designed as an indexing and retrieval system, due to its logical structure and scalability, UDC has become one of the most widely used knowledge organization systems in libraries, where it is used for either shelf arrangement, content indexing or both.

UDC codes can describe any type of document or object to any desired level of detail. These can include textual documents and other media such as films, video and sound recordings, illustrations, maps as well as realia such as museum objects.

Since the first edition in French "Manuel du Répertoire bibliographique universel" (1905), UDC has been translated and published in various editions in 40 languages. UDC Summary, an abridged Web version of the scheme is available in over 45 languages. The classification has been modified and extended over the years to cope with increasing output in all areas of human knowledge, and is still under continuous review to take account of new developments.

THE APPLICATION OF THE UDC

The UDC is used in around 150,000 libraries in 130 countries and in many bibliographical services which require detailed content indexing. In a number of countries it is the main classification system for information exchange and is used in all type of libraries: public, school, academic and special libraries.

The UDC is also used in national bibliographies of around 30 countries. Examples of large databases indexed by UDC include: NEBIS (The Network of Libraries and Information Centers in Switzerland)-2.6 million records, COBIB.SI (Slovenian National Union Catalogue)-3.5 million records.

Hungarian National Union Catalogue (MOKKA)-2.9 million records. VINITI RAS database (All-Russian Scientific and Technical Information Institute of Russian Academy of Science) with 28 million records. Meteorological and Geoastrophysical Abstracts (MGA) with 600 journal titles. PORBASE (Portuguese National Bibliography) with 1.5 million records etc. The UDC has traditionally been used for the indexing of scientific articles which was an important source of information of scientific output in the period predating electronic publishing. Collections of research articles in many countries covering decades of scientific output contain UDC codes.

Examples of journal articles indexed by UDC:

- *UDC Code 663.12:57.06 in the Article "Yeast Systematics:* From Phenotype to Genotype" in the journal Food Technology and Biotechnology (ISSN: 1330-9862)
- UDC code 37.037:796.56, provided in the article "The game method as means of interface of technical-tactical and psychological preparation in sports orienteering" in the Russian journal "Pedagogico-psychological and medico-biological problems of the physical culture and sport" (ISSN 2070-4798).
- UDC code 621.715:621.924:539.3 in the article Residual Stress in Shot-Peened Sheets of AIMg4.5Mn Alloy-in the journal Materials and technology (ISSN 1580-2949).

The design of UDC lends itself to machine readability, and the system has been used both with early automatic mechanical sorting devices, and modern library OPACs. From 1993, a standard version of UDC is maintained and is distributed in a database format: UDC Master Reference File (UDC MRF) which is updated and released annually. The 2010 version of the MRF contains over 69,000 classes. In the past full printed editions used to have around 220,000 subdivisions.

UDC STRUCTURE AND CONTENT

Basic Features and Syntax

The UDC is an anlytico-synthetic and/or faceted classification. It allows an unlimited combination of attributes of a subject and relationships between subjects to be expressed. UDC codes from different tables can be combined to present various aspects of document content and form, *e.g.* 94(410)"19"(075) History *(main subject)* of United Kingdom *(place)* in 20th century *(time)*, a textbook *(document form)*.

Or: 37:2 Relationship between Education and Religion. Complex UDC expressions can be accurately parsed into constituent elements. The UDC is also a disciplinary classification covering the entire universe of knowledge.

This type of classification can also be described as *aspect* or *perspective*, which means that concepts are subsumed and placed under the field in which they are studied. Thus, the same concept can appear in different fields of knowledge. This particular feature is usually implemented in UDC by re-using the same concept in various combinations with the main subject, *e.g.* a code for language in common auxiliaries of language is used to derive numbers for ethnic grouping, individual languages in linguistics and individual literatures. Or, a code from the auxiliaries of place, *e.g. (410) United Kingdom,* uniquely representing the concept of United Kingdom can be used to express *911(410) Regional geography of United Kingdom* and *94(410) History of United Kingdom.*

Organization of Classes

Concepts are organized in two kinds of tables in UDC:

- Common auxiliary tables (including certain auxiliary signs). These tables contain facets of concepts representing, general recurrent characteristics, appli-cable over a range of subjects throughout the main tables, including notions such as place, language of the text and physical form of the document, which may occur in almost any subject. UDC numbers from these tables, called common auxiliaries are simply added at the end of the number for the subject taken from the main tables. There are over 15,000 of common auxiliaries in UDC.
- The main tables or main schedules containing the various disciplines and branches of knowledge, arranged in 9 main classes, numbered from 0 to 9 (with class 4 being vacant). At the beginning of each class there are also series of special auxiliaries, which express aspects that are recurrent within this specific class. Main tables in UDC contain more than 60,000 subdivisions.

Main Classes

- 0 Science and Knowledge. Organization. Computer Science. Information. Documentation. Librarianship. Institutions. Publications
- 1 Philosophy. Psychology
- 2 Religion. Theology
- 3 Social Sciences
- 4 *vacant*
- 5 Mathematics. Natural Sciences
- 6 Applied Sciences. Medicine, Technology
- 7 The Arts. Recreation. Entertainment. Sport
- 8 Language, Linguistics, Literature
- 9 Geography, Biography, History

The vacant class 4 is the result of a planned schedule expansion. This class was freed by moving linguistics into class 8 in 1960s to make space for future developments in the rapidly expanding fields of knowledge. primarily natural sciences and technology.

Common Auxiliary Tables

Common auxiliaries are aspect-free concepts that can be used in combination with any other UDC code from the main classes or with other common auxiliaries. They have unique notational representations that makes them stand out in complex expressions.

Common auxiliary numbers always begin with a certain symbol known as a facet indicator, *e.g.* = (equal sign) always introduces concepts representing the language of a document. (0...) numbers enclosed in parentheses starting with zero always represent a concept designating document form.

Thus (075) Textbook and =111 English can be combined to express, *e.g.*(075)=111 Textbooks in English, and when combined with numbers from the main UDC tables they can be used as follows: 2(075)=111 Religion textbooks in English, 51(075)=111 Mathematics textbooks in English etc.

- =... Common auxiliaries of language.
- (0...) Common auxiliaries of form.
- (1/9) Common auxiliaries of place.
- (=...) Common auxiliaries of human ancestry, ethnic grouping and nationality.
- "..." Common auxiliaries of time.
- -0... Common auxiliaries of general characteristics: Properties, Materials, Relations/Processes and Persons.
- -02 Common auxiliaries of properties.
- -03 Common auxiliaries of materials.
- -04 Common auxiliaries of relations, processes and operations.
- -05 Common auxilaries of persons and personal characteristics.

UNION CATALOGUE

A union catalogue is a combined library catalogue describing the collections of a number of libraries. Union catalogs have been created in a range of media, including book format, microform, cards and more recently, networked electronic databases. Print union catalogs are typically arranged by title, author or subject (often employing a controlled vocabulary). electronic versions typically support keyword and Boolean queries.

Union catalogs are useful to librarians, as they assist in locating and requesting materials from other libraries through interlibrary loan service. They also allow researchers to search through collections to which they would not otherwise have access, such as manuscript collections. The largest print union catalogue ever published is the American *National Union Catalogue Pre-*

1956 Imprints (NUC), completed in 1981. This achievement has since been superseded by the creation of union catalogs in the form of giant electronic databases, of which the largest is OCLC's WorldCat. Another example is Copac provided by Research Libraries UK. A third example is Amicus, provided by Library and Archives Canada.

UNIFORM TITLE

A uniform title in library cataloguing is a title assigned to a work which either has no title or has appeared under more than one title. It is part of authority control. The phrases *conventional title* and *standard title* are sometimes used. the forthcoming Resource Description and Access uses *preferred title*. and the 2009 Statement of International Cataloguing Principles deprecates it in favour of *authorized access point*.

There are many instances in which a uniform title can be used. Anonymous works such as sacred texts and folk tales may lack an obvious title: for instance, the Bible, *Epic of Gilgamesh*, *Beowulf* or the *Chanson de Roland*. Works of art and music may contain no text that can be used for reference. A uniform title allows all of the works to fall under one title and will reference all of the items to which the uniform title applies.

For example, if a library had 10 copies of *Crime and Punishment* but each copy was in a different language, an online library catalogue can display all of the copies of the book together under the chosen uniform title.

The library could also list any copies of *Crime and Punishment* in other mediums, such as film adaptations or abridged editions, under the same uniform title. This can help a library patron when searching the online catalogue find all of the versions of *Crime and Punishment* at once instead of searching for each foreign title or film individually. Uniform titles are particularly useful when cataloguing music, where pieces of music are often known by multiple valid titles and those titles are known in multiple languages, or when an individual work has been adapted as a contrafactum. The Library of Congress provides an example of how books of the New Testament are referred to in the Anglo-American Cataloguing Rules:

- Bible. N.T. Acts
- Bible. N.T. Colossians
- Bible. N.T. Corinthians, 1st
- Bible. N.T. Corinthians, 2nd
- Bible. N.T. Ephesians.

The complementary situation occurs with a single work that exists with more than one title, especially when translated into another language, excerpted or collected with other works. In this case, the name of the language or a phrase such as 'Selections' is added to distinguish works with the same uniform title. The MARC 21 standard uses fields 240, 243, 630, 730 and 830 for uniform titles.

SUBJECT ACCESS

Subject access refers to the methods and systems by which books, journals, and other documents are accessed in a given bibliographic database (*e.g.* a library classification system). The single records in a bibliographic file is structured in fields and each field can be searchable and combined with other fields.

Such searchable data from fields of records are termed access points. Some of these access points contain information such as author name, number of pages, language of publication, name of publisher etc. These are in library jargon termed "descriptive data". Other kinds of access points contains information such as title words, classification codes, indexing terms etc. They are termed subject access points.. However, a subject access point is defined as any access point useful for subject searching. There is no precise border between descriptive access points and subject access points. In theory any access point may hypothetically be used for subject searching.

PUBLIC INFORMATION NETWORK FOR ELECTRONIC SERVICES

The Public Information Network for Electronic Services (or PINES) is the statewide library consortium and its online library catalogue of the Georgia Public Library Service. By February 2010, the catalogue consisted of books from 282 library facilities in over 140 counties across the state of Georgia with a total item count of around 10 million, all of which are searchable by anyone with a PINES library card which can be obtained free of charge from any PINES-participating library.

The PINES system effectively turns most of the state of Georgia into one huge library. PINES cardholders are able to request that a copy of a specific book which is only available at a library out of town be shipped to their local library for them to check out-free of charge-all through the online catalogue.

In addition, PINES users can check out a book from one PINES-participating library and turn it into any other PINES-participating library without penalty. Another feature of the PINES network is that it allows members to place holds on items that they would like to check out from the library. PINES developed the open-source software, called Evergreen, which it and other library consortia use to manage their online catalogs.

OPEN CATALOGUE

Open catalogue is an open content catalogue or free content catalogue, *i.e.*, a structured database with information about products or other stored items in a standardized format. A catalogue implies categorization or classification of the items involved, and database normalization to increase the usability of the catalogue for searching and finding, and comparing items within the same category on their main attributes.

The term is first used by Prof. Dr. Martijn Hoogeveen of the Open University (Netherlands) for the Open ICEcat project, which resulted in an open catalogue for product information, often used by merchants as input for their mail-order catalogue. A DTD for the Open Catalogue Exchange Format is developed by Sergey Shvets and Dimitry Mitko.

NUCMC

NUCMC is the abbreviation for the National Union Catalogue of Manuscript Collections. It is a national-level programme based at the Library of Congress that seeks to promote free access to the documentary heritage of the United States. It does this by providing cataloguing for archives and historical societies around the country that do not have access to national online databases.

The programme started in 1959 and published bound volumes of cataloguing records until 1993. As of 1986, the cataloguing records were input into RLIN, the Research Libraries Information Network, an international online database. As of September 2007, all cataloguing records in RLIN have been migrated into the OCLC database (WorldCat), since RLIN was merged into OCLC. All cataloguing since that time has been input into OCLC. It is not related to the NUC Pre-1956 volumes.

NIPPON DECIMAL CLASSIFICATION

The Nippon Decimal Classification (NDC, also called the Nippon Decimal System) is a system of library classification developed for mainly Chinese and Japanese language books maintained by the Japan Library Association since 1956. It is based on the Dewey Decimal System. The system is based upon using each successive digit to divide into nine divisions with the digit zero used for those not belonging to any of the divisions.

NEWGENLIB

NewGenLib is an integrated library management system developed by Verus Solutions Pvt Ltd. Domain expertise is provided by Kesavan Institute of Information and Knowledge Management in Hyderabad, India. NewGenLib version 1.0 was released in March 2005. On 9 January 2008, NewGenLib was declared Open Source Software under GNU GPL Licence by Verus Solutions.

Currently NewGenLib 3.0.3 U2 is the latest version running. It is estimated that 2,500 libraries across 58 countries are using NewGenLib as their Primary integrated library management system.

FEATURES

The software modules are:

- Acquisitions

- Cataloguing
- Serials management
- Circulation
- Administration
- OPAC-Support for VuFind is also available
- MIS Reports
- End-of-day process (daily scheduler)

The system allows the creation of open access (OA) institutional repositories compliant with OAI-PMH. It is web-based software and has a multi-tier architecture using Java (a Swing-based librarian's GUI) and JBoss (J2EE-based application server). The default backend database is the open source PostgreSQL. NewGenLib is compliant with MARC 21 format, has a MARC editor, and allows seamless bibliographic and authority data import into cataloguing templates. Form letter templates are configurable using OpenOffice 2.0 as ODT and htm. SMTP mail servers can be configured for e-mails that can be sent from functional modules. NewGenLib servers are SRU/W compliant supporting MARC-21 and MODS 3.0 metadata formats. CQL (level 1) with both Bath and Dublin Core Profiles are supported. NewGenLib is Unicode 3.0 compliant and is RFID ready.

NewGenLib can be installed on Linux and Windows operating systems. It is an internationalized application (I18N) because it is Unicode 3.0 compliant, has an Arabic version available, is asily extensible to support other languages, and may use data entry, storage, retrieval in any (Unicode 3.0) language.

TYPES OF LIBRARIES

NewGenLib can be used for any type of library. In fact it is used by all types of libraries. This is because NGL is targeted towards public libraries.

The type of libraries in which NewGenLib can be used are:

- University libraries
- College/School libraries
- Public libraries
- Libraries in Research Institutes
- Church libraries
- Libraries in Offices/Corporates

COMMUNITY

Librarians and Library managers using NewGenLib Open Source for their libraries are part of this social network. Social networks are created on basis of geography so that the members of the social network can leverage a maximum benefit.

TECHNOLOGIES USED

- Java SE

- Apache Tomcat server
- Spring framework
- Hibernate and Solr
- JDOM for XML messaging
- Java Servlets, JavaServer Pages and Apache Struts
- Java Mail
- OpenOffice for form letters
- Jasper reports

Index